Barack Obama
in Hawai'i and Indonesia

Barack Obama in Hawai'i and Indonesia

THE MAKING OF A GLOBAL PRESIDENT

Dinesh Sharma

PRAEGER

AN IMPRINT OF ABC-CLIO, LLC
Santa Barbara, California • Denver, Colorado • Oxford, England

Library of Congress Cataloging-in-Publication Data
Sharma, Dinesh, 1955–
 Barack Obama in Hawai'i and Indonesia : the making of a global president/ Dinesh Sharma.
     p. cm.
 Includes bibliographical references and index.
 ISBN 978-0-313-38533-9 (hbk. : alk. paper) — ISBN 978-0-313-38534-6 (ebook)
 1. Obama, Barack—Childhood and youth. 2. Obama, Barack—Psychology.
 3. Presidents—United States—Biography. 4. Hawai'i—Biography.
 5. Indonesia—Biography. I. Title.
 E908.S52 2011
 973.932092–dc23
 [B]   2011028175

ISBN: 978-0-313-38533-9
EISBN: 978-0-313-38534-6

15   14   13   12   11   1   2   3   4   5

This book is also available on the World Wide Web as an eBook.
Visit www.abc-clio.com for details.

Praeger
An Imprint of ABC-CLIO, LLC

ABC-CLIO, LLC
130 Cremona Drive, P.O. Box 1911
Santa Barbara, California 93116-1911

This book is printed on acid-free paper ∞

Manufactured in the United States of America

Hope is both the earliest and the most indispensable virtue inherent in the state of being alive. If life is to be sustained hope must remain, even where confidence is wounded, trust impaired.

— *Erik H. Erikson*

To my Father,
who made a career at the U.S.
Corps of Engineers after migrating to America
and
To my Mother,
who has always been my biggest fan

Contents

Acknowledgments

In writing this book, I had the support of the Center for International and Cross-Cultural Research at St. Francis College, Brooklyn Heights, New York. Dr. Uwe Gielen in the Psychology Department, a cross-cultural psychologist and an expert on Kohlberg's moral development theory across cultures, spent a significant amount of time reviewing several early proposals for this book and a final draft of the manuscript. It would have been difficult to finish this book without his help.

In Jakarta, Professor Sarlito Sarwono, an expert on radicalization and counterterrorism at the University of Indonesia, provided invaluable support for the research reported in this book. He provided many of the contacts needed to complete the research and an assistant, Riani Astriyana, who spoke fluent English and Indonesian Bhasha. My research in Jakarta, a city I visited for the first time while searching for Obama's global roots, went off rather smoothly primarily because of Dr. Sarwono's invisible hand guiding the project and Riani Astriyana's on-the-spot cross-translations from Indonesian Bhasha to English and vice versa.

In Hawai'i, I was guided by Professor Alice Dewey in the Anthropology Department at the University of Hawai'i, who was Barack Obama's mother's mentor and colleague for many years. She provided valuable information about Obama as well as about his mother's life and career as an economic anthropologist and development aid expert, giving me access to a network of individuals in Indonesia who had known Ann Dunham for more than 30 years.

In Washington, D.C., I was helped by Neil Abercrombie and his office in the U.S. Congress. He provided valuable information about the island of Hawai'i, the Punahou School, and firsthand knowledge about the Dunham and the Obama families.

At the Punahou School, a paradise of learning, I want to thank Carlyn Tani for providing access to the school's premises and to several teachers who had taught Barack Obama. Punahou provided valuable information about their curriculum, history, and philosophy and how the school may have contributed to the shaping of a global president.

Other colleagues who provided advice included Dr. Sudhir Kakar, of Institut Européen d'Administration des Affaires (INSEAD), a well-known psychoanalyst, who provided some key insights about Obama's lifelong dreams. Also, Dr. Karan Singh, a former ambassador to the United States, a member of India's parliament, and a political scientist, provided insights about Obama's policies and how they may be perceived in the Asian hemisphere. Dr. Ashis Nandy, a renowned political psychologist at the Center for the Study of Developing Societies, provided insights about Obama's political rhetoric and persona, alerting me to the truism that politics is all about compromise and the art of the possible, not about achieving some vaguely wished-for and overly optimistic utopian ideal.

I must also thank Maya Soetoro-Ng, an educator and an activist in her own right, who is also Barack Obama's half-sister. She agreed to be one of my key sources early in the process. Whenever I had doubts or questions I was able to reach out to her. She responded promptly to my requests, within the limits of what was sanctioned by the White House. The depth and breadth of the book has been enhanced by her insights, openness, and intelligence.

I owe a debt of gratitude to several former teachers, especially Roderick Pugh at Loyola University, Chicago, who first pulled me aside and got me interested in clinical psychology in an undergraduate class. As one of the first African American PhD students to study with Carl Rogers at the University of Chicago, Pugh was a consummate scientist practitioner, who kept a private practice on Michigan Avenue, taught at the north shore campus of Loyola University, and lived in Hyde Park, Illinois. I am also thankful to Dan McAdams, who taught me personality psychology with a focus on the study of lives across the life span. He was a protégé of David McClelland at Harvard University and has a real passion for teaching. It was during McAdams' lectures that the psychological theories of Freud, Jung, Murray, and Erikson came alive for me. Finally, I have studied anthropology with Bob LeVine, a psychological anthropologist who still carries on the culture and personality tradition of interdisciplinary research started by Mead, Benedict and Sapir, and Whiting, which aspires to be truly global in its reach.

The acquisition editor, Robert Hutchinson, formerly with Praeger Publishers, showed a keen interest in this book. I am very appreciative of his understanding of current affairs, politics, and presidential history. Although most of the Obama biographers have focused on his political persona, Robert Hutchinson believed it was important to look at the complete Barack Obama, the person and the politician, the individual within the collective, or the man behind the larger-than-life image.

For editorial support, I was aided by Valentina Tursini at Praeger Publishers and Elizabeth Madden-Zibman, a professional editor, an adjunct faculty member at Rutgers University, and one of my trusted neighbors. Their editorial input enhanced the final product immensely.

I also want to thank several online and print publications, especially *Asia Times Online*, that have published my book reviews, essays, and editorials on Barack Obama and various other subjects: *Middle East Times*, *Middle East Online*, *Far Eastern Economic Review*, *Wall Street Journal Online*, *Wonkette.com*, *OpEdNews.com*, *Media Monitor Networks*, *District Chronicles*, *Fredricksburg.com*, *Free Lance Star*, *Health Affairs*, *Biotech Law Review*, *International Psychology Bulletin*, and other scientific journals.

Finally, I must thank my wife and two children for their enthusiastic support of this book. They have lived with the vicissitudes of the book-writing process, while I was busy traveling, researching, and writing; without their inspiration it would have been difficult to finish this project. The twinkle in my children's eyes reminds me that in America it is indeed possible that, as Adlai Stevenson said in a speech in 1952, any boy or girl can one day become president.

Prologue

Barack Obama is a sign of the changing times, a product of globalization spurred by American power, free-market capitalism, and a unique form of multiculturalism. I didn't realize how true or valid this statement really was until I started to research the childhood and adolescence of Barack Obama, the 44th president of the United States. As the historian Douglas Brinkley has said, "Obama came of age, really, after the Cold War, with the Internet being the transformative engine of society, and he now takes his multicultural heritage and the geographical diversity of his upbringing to the world" (Raasch 2009). Writing this book gave me an opportunity to learn about the changing nature of American society, politics, and culture.

Despite the risks and trepidation involved in writing a book about a current president, I feel a sense of cautious optimism about the American experiment, what Ronald Reagan called a unique "rendezvous with destiny" begun in the first half of the 20th century (AEI 2009), which is now a global phenomenon touching the lives of virtually every citizen on the planet. In chronicling the early years of Barack Obama, I hope to share some incredible stories, pivotal events, and important insights at the intersection of biography and history, culture and globalization, and race and politics. As we look over the horizon, Barack Obama's globe-trotting and diverse formative years in Hawai'i and Indonesia, the central focus of this book, signal the beginning of an interconnected and global world, where America's emerging role in shaping the 21st century is still evolving. Obama's biography, at least for the near future, has become intertwined with this nation's destiny. Given, as Shakespeare said, "what's past is prologue," a quotation also engraved at the National Archives Building in Washington, D.C., we might be able to glean some insights about our collective future by peering into Obama's early years.

When I first learned of Barack Hussein Obama, it was a revelation to me that a candidate with a name derived from Swahili and Arabic, an African American identity, and a biracial mulatto complexion could be elected the president of the United States. At a dinner meeting in New York City, attended by well-connected financial consultants and lawyers, I met one of Obama's classmates from Harvard Law School. This was well in advance of the 2007 primaries, and Obama's Harvard classmate planned to work for his campaign. According to many pollsters, Obama was at the bottom of the Democratic heap of candidates at the time, but Obama's friend had great confidence in him. "He will be the Democratic candidate in the next election," she said firmly. We wanted to know more about the source of her confidence. "He is a one-in-a-million candidate," she exclaimed, further mystifying most of us in the room. She seemed to be already looking beyond the primaries, while most of us were trying to figure out who Obama was. She said, "If Obama takes Iowa in the primaries, the rest of strategy will fall into place."

I distinctly remember that several people at the dinner party dropped their forks and knives in disbelief, demanding to know why the top contender, Hillary Clinton, was ruled out. "She is not necessarily the best democratic candidate in this election cycle. Her negatives are high!" Obama's classmate explained with poise and certainty. When I probed the various potential pitfalls surrounding Obama, such as his young age, ethnicity, and experience level, the future campaign expert suggested that we needed to think positively: "Anything can happen once the race starts," she said plainly. "We're not thinking about any negative scenarios." She was really drinking the Kool-Aid, I thought to myself, as I scooped up some more guacamole and gulped iced tea.

Having spent many years in the Midwest and on the East Coast of the United States, I was willing to entertain the thought that the American people were ready to elect a new candidate like Barack Obama, but I still needed to be convinced with hard evidence. As the primaries began, and we all saw the results from Iowa and the Northeast states, I, along with millions of other Americans, began to sense that something momentous and paradigmatic was taking place. I joined the army of bloggers and news junkies who were beginning to study the issues a bit more seriously.

In the months that followed I wrote several opinion pieces about the election. Some were picked up by local papers, some by online magazines, and a few by traditional print media. I became a citizen journalist overnight, something very easily done these days online, and began receiving interesting feedback from many readers, which gave me the encouragement to keep moving forward. This is when I began thinking about writing this book on Obama's diverse background.

In today's political climate, Obama's victory speech in Grant Park, Chicago, may seem like a long time ago. However, at the beginning of

2009, the two events in the popular culture that stood out in my mind were the Obama inaugural and the Hollywood/Bollywood crossover film *Slumdog Millionaire*. Both formed a flashbulb memory compressed by the passage of time, filtered through the clutter of the 24/7 news cycle and the grind of my day job in business consulting. Both events were also meaningfully connected in the popular culture, as many editorial writers noted.

There was a synergy between the improbable Obama win and the rags-to-riches story that went on to win the Best Picture Oscar: both stories are about outsiders who come from the fringes of society yet manage to beat all of the odds to win the big prize. Barack Obama as a Kenyan American from Hawai'i, via Indonesia and Chicago, took on the mantle of the first African American president and the first global president of the United States. The key protagonist in *Slumdog Millionaire* is a young man named Jamal, a Muslim minority orphan from one of the poorest slums in Mumbai, in a predominantly Hindu, India. The analogies are clear. Jamal not only managed to become a contestant on the popular game show *Who Wants to Be a Millionaire* but also, to the dismay of the game-show host and the local police authorities, was able to answer all of the questions correctly to take home the coveted prize. Obama came from behind to win the primary and the 2008 election.

Both narratives are also about the power of globalization. Obama's win represented the triumph of the American brand of multiculturalism at home and abroad, building on the hard-fought victories of the civil rights movement and the emerging post-racial world. *Slumdog Millionaire* represented the rise of an Asian economy, namely India's, following on the heels of economic successess of Japan, Korea, and China. It is about the flush of new capital pouring into the big cities like Mumbai and how it is changing the lives of slum dwellers. The movie extolled the virtues of free-market capitalism over and above the 2,000-year-old Hindu work ethic encapsulated in the Bhagavad Gita, which states that one should perform one's duties (dharma) as selfless action (karma) and not be motivated by the fruits of one's labor or profits, and captured the attention of audiences worldwide.

However, because we are living in an age of instant karma, we want everything faster, quicker, and cheaper, and even the highest ideals and spiritual values tend to veer toward a material end. Thus, both Barack Obama and *Slumdog Millionaire* benefited from a wave of the populism that often surfaces in hard economic times. Notwithstanding the hard-boiled film-making of Danny Boyle, the English/Irish director well known for making tough films about the downtrodden, the story of the orphan slum dwellers touched American hearts because the global economy had been in a downward spiral. Thus, a brutal yet beautiful film made us realize how blessed we are as Americans and how good we really have it as a society.

Observing the populist elation at the Obama victory, Frank Rich wrote in the *New York Times*, "We'll soon remember that the country is in a deep ditch, and that we turned to the black guy not only because we hoped he would lift us up but because he looked like the strongest leader to dig us out" (2008).

Populism can easily turn into rage against its chosen heroes, however. The actors from *Slumdog Millionaire* learned this when they returned home from the Oscar ceremonies to be greeted by angry mobs of slum dwellers, who were rightly upset at being depicted as a colony of a subhuman species. Recently, the Obama administration has also not been spared the populist outrage at the perceived lack of connection between the American people and bank and auto-industry bailouts, AIG bonuses, and anemic job growth. The midterm election results have clearly borne this out as the anger at the hard economic times has led to the ouster of many incumbents.

In an article written after the general election, Pico Iyer observed, "Our new president smiles less than did his predecessor, and many of us feel better for it. On a recent episode of the Japanese version of 'Who Wants to Be a Millionaire,' one question noted that the ringing word Barack Obama kept out of his inauguration address was not 'freedom'—or 'peace'—but 'dream'" (Iyer 2009).

Iyer observed that Obama spoke of hope and opportunity and the youthfulness of America, something the planet craves, but those who have read Obama's autobiography know that he comes from an older and more qualified place. His memoir is about the shock of discovering who his father really was and his hybrid racial identity. Throughout the book he describes how he was unsettled and haunted by his father's real image and by the oppression and poverty he witnessed in Jakarta. "His tone in recent months has been prudently sober, refusing to talk too easily of happy endings or quick victories," said Iyer. This may be the best development of the new century, an American president who is willing to wake America up from its bad dream. "What's being outsourced now are American dreams and Hollywood endings," suggested Iyer. After all, in the Oscar race *Slumdog Millionaire* eclipsed homegrown movies about a murdered San Francisco revolutionary, a dark knight, and a prematurely old little boy.

Americans as a people prefer openness, transparency, and change, but they want it instantly. However, while a segment of the American population who voted for Obama may have understood that they must adapt to the rapidly changing world, their systems of governance, economy, and infrastructure have not fully caught up with the massive structural changes swept in by the forces of globalization. And major segments of the American population are still wrestling with the idea of the change Obama promised. They believe the change is neither necessary nor welcome. They "want their country back," to quote a well-known phrase heard at the opposing Tea Party rallies.

America thrives on the principle of creative destruction (Schumpeter 1975; Foster and Kaplan 2001). Thus, technology diffusion may be an apt metaphor for the change we are witnessing in American society now (Rogers 1995). Many of the forces of change we are grappling with are driven by technological globalization, in many cases invented by American companies, start-ups, and venture firms. Indeed, many of Barack Obama's key changes are proposals for adopting new technologies in our lives, whether it is in the realm of health care, energy, or education.

The enduring lesson here is that change is hard, especially the turn-of-the-century type of change. The cycles of technology adoption offer an insight that may be useful. Like any adoption of a new, cutting-edge technology, invariably the early adopters grab onto the change right away, while the majority is slow to catch up. The truly laggard segments of the population, who don't want to adapt to the changing times, often have to be dragged along kicking and screaming.

Obama's political rise is significant because he is the first African American president to win a U.S. presidential election. In addition, there is a host of social, cultural, and developmental or psychological reasons why his rise to the presidency is also significant. The cultural context where he grew up is important for a multitude of reasons that relate to the challenges America faces today. The developmental or psychological factors in Obama's life narrative are noteworthy because they explain his underlying motivations.

Primarily because of the combination of these reasons—political, cultural, and developmental or psychological—I decided to write a book about Obama's early upbringing focusing on the disciplines I know best—psychology, anthropology, cultural studies, marketing, and marketing science. I began to understand Obama's life and rise from this unique vantage point, and this book is a culmination of my research.

This book has a unique advantage, because as an immigrant, I have both an outsider and insider perspective on American society and culture. I can easily relate to Obama's diverse background. As a psychologist and as a marketing and health care consultant who has worked in different cultural settings, I tend to view the American situation from within and without. Academically, the study of lives across cultures is a type of research I was trained to conduct during my graduate studies. I decided to bring that sensibility to this topic, which is not something usually done in political writing, because given Obama's unique childhood and upbringing this seemed to be an appealing topic and a crucial new perspective through which to view a world leader.

To my knowledge, this is the first cultural biography of the 44th president of the United States that attempts to unearth the enculturation and socialization of an individual with attention to the key developmental milestones in the life narrative. A cultural biography analyzes the multiplex and multilayered cultural context. Although the idea of a cultural biography is not new, I have applied it in uniquely different ways to meet the purpose of this book, which is to explore the connections between Obama's early years and his global worldview. In writing this book I am relying on many years of academic research, which has examined the lives of everyday people in different cultures across the life cycle.

A number of books have already been published on Barack Obama, including his two volumes of autobiography. Readers might rightly ask, "Why do we need another book on Obama?" Well, the most cogent answer to this question is that almost all of the books released thus far have been focused on his political life or on his rise as the first African American president. The first wave of books were about the 2008 election (Wolffe 2009), followed by another wave of books chronicling Obama's first and second years in the White House (Alter 2010). One of the most comprehensive political biographies presented Obama within the framework of race relations and African American history, a highly admirable goal except that approach pays very little attention to Obama's global roots and international persona (Remnick 2010). Alongside the well-balanced, positive biographies has been a steady stream of partisan, slash-and-burn biographies, trying to make the case against Barack Obama as a socialist, as a Manchurian candidate, and recently as an anticolonial administrator (Freddoso 2008; Klein and Elliott 2010). Thus, biographies from an empathic psychological or cultural perspective—that try to explain

Obama's rise—have been sorely missing from the debate. Certainly, there have been no biographies exploring the linkage between Obama's early upbringing and socialization in the diverse social and cultural contexts where he came of age and his global political outlook. Yet, this type of social and cultural analysis is essential for a complete understanding of Barack Obama's character and his agenda for America in the 21st century.

Because a cultural environment and psychological development are typically interwoven in a person's life, we cannot isolate the role of culture in a test tube or in a magic pill; thus, we take the impact of culture for granted. Like the air we breathe, social and cultural influences are all around us yet invisible; we are socialized to view, think, and feel in a particular way because of the place and time in which we are born and come of age. The opportunities and constraints in our environment interact in complex ways with our innate talents and skills, which shape and determine our life course. These options and limitations often push us along a specific cultural pathway. Our minds are shaped in very specific ways by the early influences that are present in our everyday environment, which in turn guide our journey through life.

The importance of the cultural context is something psychological and social research has recently acknowledged as important for human and psychological development. Evidence from around the world has helped to correct the often seen middle-class and Eurocentric bias in most of psychological and cultural theories, which are often built on evidence from experiments and interviews with undergraduates and from laboratory studies. I have written about the issue of context in social and emotional development in my earlier works. The application of cultural theories to the study of lives across cultures has become a lively topic of discussion and research. I hope to contribute to this debate by drawing on various fields of knowledge—cross-cultural studies of human development, personality and clinical psychology, cultural and psychological anthropology and professional experience in marketing science, opinion polling, and market research. However, my main interest in this book is to outline some of the important cultural underpinnings of the life of the 44th president of the United States, Barack Obama, at a critical point in the life of this nation and the world.

This book moves chronologically and thematically from Obama's birth in Hawai'i to his identity resolution in Chicago, relying on a widely accepted, classical framework for understanding an individual life cycle

(Erikson 1963; Levinson 1984; Sheehy 1996). Retrospectively, the child-hood and adolescence of a presidential leader are important, for they might reveal the developing gestalt of his early personality structure, the key role of his parents and early environment in shaping his path, and any signs of a political ambition that might break through his budding mind. Here I show how the early conditions in the family environment reveal the spark that began the journey, the emblematic event that might foretell his rise, and the set of conditions that might have shaped the rough edges of the growing individual in a determinative way.

In the opening chapter, I describe the context for many of the challenges America is facing today. I have framed the debate within the language and cultural tropes that Obama has himself employed, that is, the idea of a large-scale transformational change. Thus, the chapter is called, "Transformation of the American Mind," where several social trends that are driving the post-9/11 America are examined, whether it is demographic changes at home, the perceived threat of radical Islam, or the rising Asian economies. I suggest that Barack Obama represents a paradigm shift because of these mounting domestic and international challenges.

Next, I delve into many of the "Origin Stories" surrounding Barack Obama and his family of birth, which form the second chapter. The focus here is on Obama's infancy and early childhood as a developmental stage. I examine his parents' marriage, his father's stay in Hawai'i, and his extended family in Hawai'i, Indonesia, and Kenya. I reveal new details about the Obama and Dunham family based on interviews conducted on the Hawai'ian Islands, Jakarta, and the mainland United States, all trying to show that the family who raised him, although highly unusual and unique, put him on a path toward great success founded on the American values from the heartland.

In the third chapter, I take a closer look at the "Women Who Shaped Obama," which includes foremost his mother, Ann Dunham; his grand-mother, Madelyn Dunham; and his wife, Michelle Obama. This chapter covers Obama's preschool years in Hawai'i. Given that his biological father was absent throughout his childhood, the women who raised Obama had a direct hand in shaping his destiny. Based on original research, I argue that the Dunham women gave Obama a head start in life, both intellectu-ally, socially, and emotionally, which Michelle Obama fully recognized and helped to shape into presidential timber.

TABLE I
Obama's Pathway through Developmental Milestones

Stage	Erikson's Basic Conflict	Developmental Needs and Tasks	Obama's Milestones
Infancy (birth to 18 months)	Trust vs. Mistrust	Feeding, Caring, Affection	1961—Born and raised in Hawai'i, in a biracial family, Kenyan father and American mother
Early Childhood (2 to 3 years)	Autonomy vs. Shame and Doubt	Toilet Training, Physical Skills, Independence Training	1964—Parents divorce, raised by single mother and grandparents
Preschool (3 to 5 years)	Initiative vs. Guilt	Exploration, Control over Environment, Purposeful Activity	1966—Mother remarries, Barack moves to Indonesia with his mother from age 4–10 years 1967–71—Lives with stepfather in Indonesia
School Age (6 to 11 years)	Industry vs. Inferiority	Schooling, Academic Skills, Competence Learning	1967—Early schooling in Indonesia 1970—Half-sister Maya is born 1971—Moves back to Hawai'i to live with his grandparents, attends Punahou School 1975—Attends Punahou Academy
Adolescence (12 to 18 years)	Identity vs. Role Confusion	Social Relationships, Developing a Sense of Self and Early Identity Formation	1975—Joins the basketball team 1979—Graduates from high school 1979—Refuses to go back to Indonesia with his mother, attends Occidental College in Los Angeles
Young Adulthood	Intimacy vs. Isolation	Relationships, Love and Care for	1981—Transfers from Occidental College to Columbia University 1982—Father dies in a car accident

(Continued)

TABLE I (*Continued*)
Obama's Pathway through Developmental Milestones

Stage	Erikson's Basic Conflict	Developmental Needs and Tasks	Obama's Milestones
(19 to 40 years)		Significant Others	1983—Graduates from Columbia University
			1985—Moves to Chicago as community organizer
			1987—Attends Harvard Law School
			1992—Marries Michelle Robinson
			1995—Mother dies of cancer
			1995—First book, *Dreams from my Father*, released
Middle Adulthood (40 to 65 years)	Generativity vs. Stagnation	Work and Parenthood, Taking Care of Next Generation	1996—Elected to the Illinois State Senate
			1998—Re-elected to Illinois State Senate
			1999—First daughter born, named Malia
			2000—Challenges Bobby Rush and loses
			2001—Second daughter born, named Natasha
			2002—Gave speech against Iraq War
			2002—Re-elected to Illinois State Senate
			2004—Delivers the speech at DNC convention in Boston
			2004—Elected to the U.S. Senate, defeats Alan Keyes
			2006—Second book, *Audacity of Hope*, is released
			2007—Announced run for the presidency
			2008—Delivers the speech on race in Philadelphia
			2008—Wins the Democratic primary
			2008—Wins the presidential election

As a result of his mother's second marriage to an Indonesian man, when Obama was six years old he moved to Jakarta, commencing his home-to-school developmental transition. This transition formed the basis of his "Global Schooling in Jakarta," which is the subject of the fourth chapter in the book. The early formative experiences in Jakarta shaped Obama indelibly, providing a global perspective on the U.S. foreign policy in the Pacific and Southeast Asia. Here, Obama literally lived on the Muslim street; he had many secular and Islamic friends and classmates and was exposed to extreme poverty for the first time in his life. Based on extensive interviews and field research, I suggest that in the dusty streets and back alleys of Jakarta, the young Obama grasped the raw nature of political power in the making of a fledgling democracy. He saw firsthand the impact of the hard and soft arms of America's adventures in international diplomacy and nation building.

Interestingly, Obama's time in Indonesia was the only stretch of time during his childhood when he lived in a traditional nuclear family; he had a live-in stepfather, who was for a brief period in the Indonesian military. At this age a child's mind is highly imaginative and, according to Jean Piaget's cognitive phase of concrete operational thinking, tinged with a moral intuition and a magical sensibility. During this time Obama penned an essay expressing his wish to be president "because he wanted everyone to be happy." As a boy of nine and ten years old, he used to imitate the Indonesian president Suharto on television speaking to the Indonesian masses. Now, 40 years later, there is a statue celebrating Obama's boyhood at the Besuki School, near Menteng Park and a short walk from the U.S. Consulate in Jakarta, encouraging young children to "dream big."

At the age of 10 years, Obama returned to Hawai'i to enroll in an elite preparatory school, the Punahou School, the largest private school west of the Mississippi River. This marked Obama's adolescent years and the beginning of a search for an identity. A counterpoint to his life in Jakarta, Hawai'i was like a paradise, representing a new spring or *Ka Punahou*; this chapter of his life is thus appropriately titled "A New Spring in Hawai'i." It is here that Barack Obama learned the leadership skills that he is now well known for: to be a team player on the basketball court, to remain calm under pressure during debates, to think on his feet when confronted, to use his language skills in persuasion, and to motivate a large audience into action.

On the basis of direct interviews with several of his high school teachers and mentors, I demonstrate that the Punahou School sheltered Obama from the negative stereotypes of an African American identity on the mainland, even though he may have felt a bit alienated as a black man in Hawai'i. In the multicultural context of the Punahou School, which is a microcosm of Hawai'i, Obama learned the skills to walk into different cultural worlds with ease and to relate to people from all walks of life, something his mother had perfected as an anthropologist. The Punahou School also prides itself on offering Christian-based moral education, including mandatory chapel attendance every week, and fostering an engagement in community service projects. These experiences also planted many seeds in Obama's growing mind for a career in public service, which fully blossomed when he took a job in Chicago as a community organizer.

After graduation from the Punahou School, Obama, like many Hawai'ians, went to the mainland for college, first to Los Angeles and then to New York City. This journey across the United States from the West Coast to the East Coast turned into a journey of self-discovery as he was actively engaged in establishing a "Hybrid Identity on the Mainland," the sixth chapter in the book. This is the start of Obama's young adulthood, and it forms a fascinating rite of passage in the annals of presidential history. At Occidental College in Los Angeles, Obama discovered his true political voice while speaking against apartheid at a student rally, but the small liberal arts college was not big enough for his emerging and expansive dreams. He soon transferred to Columbia University in New York and started to test his true values in the financial capital of the world. While in New York City, Obama learned that his long-absent father, Barack Obama Senior, who had abandoned him at the age of two years, had died in a car accident. This loss only quickened and intensified his search for an identity. Thus, his time in New York City, often spent in isolation and reflection, is considered the lost years of his youth. Ironically, it was when he truly found himself. When Obama left New York City after graduation, he fully took on the name of his father, and Barry Obama began his conversion to Barack Hussein Obama. He committed himself to a public-service career because he found solace and comfort in improving the lives of those who lived in the African American communities on Chicago's South Side.

Next, I examine Obama's campaign imagery, his father's mythic image, and his mother's unfinished dreams. In interpreting the meaning of this rich symbolic content, both at the individual and the collective level, I find some consistent and common threads that link Obama's deeply private self and his public self. First, Obama is a reformer and a changemaker of global proportions. Second, he is driven by the heroic impulse to make the world a better place. Third, as a true reformer, Obama has lived out his family drama, neurosis, and complexes on the public stage by releasing an autobiography at a fairly young age. Though it has had different permutations and various twists and turns, Obama's life and work are a continuation of the kind of economic development work his mother undertook in Southeast Asia and what his father was trying to do on behalf of his African nation. His parents' guiding images, although somewhat tragic and cut short by early demise, served as a template for his identity resolution and his life's purpose and mission. I argue that, in response to his parents' improbable and failed marriage, Obama has built a larger-than-life narrative that bridges generations, races, and continents, in part driven by his mythic dreams, which he has unearthed from time to time. Thus, an analysis of "Obama's Mythic Dreams" forms the seventh chapter of this book.

In the eighth chapter, titled "The Obama World," I look for answers to the research questions posed in the opening of the book by exploring what we have learned by peering into Obama's childhood and adolescence in the preceding chapters. Why is Obama's upbringing in Hawai'i and Indonesia relevant for America at this turning point in history? Is there indeed a connection between the personal and the political, between the life of a politician and the life of a nation, and between psychology and history? I find that there is a remarkable degree of confluence between Obama's biography and the challenges America faces today as we look out on the horizon and see a rapidly globalizing world. Americans may have chosen a truly global president for the current challenging global times, where America has been engaged in two long wars in Islamic nations and has been confronted with economic challenges from anemic growth and the rising Asian economies. Will America retain its premier status as the leader of the free world? Will other rapidly growing economies try to take its place? Is there a nascent multipolar world already in formation, where America will have to play the role of a manager, a coach, and a team player? These are the central questions that the Obama world is wrestling with, all the while trying to revive and renew the American dream for the next generation.

In the last chapter of the book, I suggest that even if the midterm election returns are an indicator that Obama will be a one-term president, not a paradigm changer with linear coattails, he will nonetheless be a significant marker for future generations; he would still leave a legacy for the next generation, which is the central psychological concern for people as they reach middle adulthood and old age. Clearly, "the paranoid style of American politics" (Hofstadter 1996) has focused on Obama's public image, where he is often falsely portrayed as "the other"—the foreigner, the Muslim, the socialist. But as a progressive politician, he has unleashed several progressive tools and technologies that over time can deliver the change he has promised. His push for green energy technologies and the renewed science, technology, engineering, and math policy in education are ideal examples of the changes that Americans need to reimagine the American dream for the next generation.

1

Transformation of the American Mind

The dogmas of the quiet past are inadequate to the stormy present.... We must disenthrall ourselves, and then we shall save our country. Fellow citizens, we cannot escape history.

Abraham Lincoln (1862)

No one is more arresting than the person who breaks through his confining environment, seizes opportunities, overcomes all obstacles, and changes how the rest of us perceive, think, and act.

James MacGregor Burns (2004)

We have witnessed remarkable social transformations as we move into the new century. Globalization is rapidly changing emerging economies in Brazil, Russia, India, and China and driving the global flows of capital, markets, and labor. In the United States, the culture wars of the 1990s have receded as newer global concerns have emerged. The debate about America's changing cultural landscape has been overtaken by concerns about the contractions in the global economy, the financial meltdown, and the shrinking middle class. America's role in the emerging multipolar world hangs in the balance while the looming threat of Islamic fundamentalism has taken center stage in the American psyche. Many people are asking, is the American dream still alive?

As a rebuttal to Alan Bloom's *The Closing of the American Mind* (Bloom 1987), which bemoaned the loss of Western classics in American education, a well-known American historian, Lawrence Levine, argued that Americans risk losing sight of the cycles of history if they remain closed to the rest of the world. In *The Opening of the American Mind* (Levine 1997), Levine, writing about the crisis in higher education, stated that we cannot adopt a Paleolithic cave-dweller's mentality about cultural change. Modeled after *The Flintstones*, the cartoon show where modern humans live like cave dwellers in prehistoric times, anything that upsets the Paleolithic cave-dweller's mentality is seen as inherently dangerous.

Conversely, we must not be held back by a jeremiad view of history, pretending that the great nations and people do not confront massive setbacks or that somehow the American experience is not subject to the warp and woof of history and is immune to major transformations. We must be free to ask whether American exceptionalism can withstand the challenges of the 21st century.

Those issuing jeremiads tend to view American history as sui generis; American civilization seems independent of great social transformations. A country borne of a bloody revolution and an even bloodier civil war is somehow totally divorced from its complex origins and radical beginnings. Many historians and social observers are now questioning this assumption and its underlying implications. Is America, the accidental empire, subject to the same forces of history as other empires, such as the British and Roman empires?

America has been riding high since the end of the Cold War, adopting a cowboy-like swagger and an attitude of invincibility. Peter Beinart, a political scientist, in his recent book, *The Icarus Syndrome*, calls into question American hubris, which has led to misadventures in Iraq and Afghanistan. He claims that this hubris has guided American foreign policy for the past 100 years (Beinart 2010).

Americans have tended to operate with a denial of historical transformation, on the one hand, and an invention of a stable past, on the other. Levine (1997) reminds us that, like Abraham Lincoln, we must confront the judgment and dynamic of history; we must not try to hide from it. During the Civil War, Americans needed to confront several issues at the heart of the war, such as race, freedom, union, and the nature of the economy. Levine states, "The only way out of these issues was through them and the only way through them was to confront them with clarity and knowledge. Americans had to understand what was happening to them in the context of what had been happening" (Levine 1997, 240).

Similarly, the forces of globalization from without and the multicultural shift within are now the twin engines driving America forward; Americans cannot escape these major transformations. Samuel Huntington, whom Fareed Zakaria has described as the most "prescient and principled" political scientist of the past half-century, may have correctly identified the source of America's identity crisis (Zakaria 2009). In a book written shortly after 9/11, *Who We Are*, Huntington said, that Americans are confronting major social and demographic changes at home and transnational changes abroad (Huntington 2004).

According to many historians, social scientists, and business executives, the inherent diversity, complexity, and dynamism at the heart of American experience is a unifying and transforming force; it does not have to be a disuniting maelstrom as we move further into the new century. Americans have been responsible for spreading globalization; now that an increasing number of people are joining the liberal march toward human progress, human rights, and capital markets, Americans cannot simply run for the hills or retreat for the fear of the massive changes globalization might bring in the economic and geopolitical balance of power.

Thomas Friedman, a *New York Times* editorial writer, has been repeating this warning when it comes to America's economic, technological, and energy policy (Friedman 2010). American companies have helped to flatten the world with their high-speed PCs and fast-moving mobile devices, allowing new entrants in the global marketplace. These emerging economies are leading us out of the global recession. Likewise, Americans may have been the first to build modern solar panels, but now they have fallen behind Germany, Japan, and Spain in clean energy technologies. Friedman has argued convincingly that we cannot continue to pursue the same energy policies and believe crude oil will continue to flow cheaply, like beer at the local tavern.

Social and political paradigms shift generationally, at least in the way Thomas Kuhn, the brilliant historian of science, conceptualized them in the *Structure of Scientific Revolutions* (Kuhn 1963). Kuhn thought that progress in scientific enterprise moves according to large, stable worldviews. All stable worldviews rest on the importance of a culturally constructed cosmology until that cosmology is gradually subsumed by another construction and yet another and so on. Newtonian physics gave way to Einstein's theory of relativity, which gave way to string theory, and so on; this is the Tao of physics. It may also be the Tao of politics to the extent that political movements tend to swing back and forth across two or three different worldviews—conservative, liberal, and independent—while advancing the political discourse on major issues of the day. Thus, in politics the same process may operate, though perhaps with less structured regularity and messiness.

Samuel Huntington claimed that a huge paradigm shift was underway after the end of the Cold War, where global conflicts would be driven by cultural and economic differences in the world's major civilizations rather than political ideology. In *The Clash of Civilizations*, he posited a new world order where tensions will run high between radical Islam and the West and between the emerging economy of China and the economies in the Western world. During the Cold War, conflict mostly occurred between the capitalist West and the communist Eastern Bloc, but it is now most likely to occur between the world's major civilizations. The theory gained wide popularity as China began to rise as an economic powerhouse and especially after the 9/11 attacks in which a jihad was declared on American, civilization (Huntington 1998).

In U.S. politics, some of the recent changes have been monumental. Barack Hussein Obama, the 44th president of the United States, represents a significant cultural shift in domestic politics and America's international relations. It is a remarkable social and cultural change, at once generational, technological, and global in nature, that has been in the works since the civil rights era or perhaps longer. A paradigm shift of this magnitude is preceded by and leads to a significant change in perceptions, values, and beliefs and in the patterns of behavior within a social organization or a social system (Kuhn 1962).

Obama is the first African American president, but he is also the first truly global president. Born and raised in Hawai'i, his early socialization took place in the most culturally diverse state, the state that was the last to join the Union. In addition, he spent a significant part of his childhood in Asia, specifically, the nation of Indonesia, in which the majority of the population is Muslim. This archipelago in the Pacific region also happens to be the largest Islamic democracy on the planet. Of course, as George Will has pointed out, other presidents have had credentials in Asian diplomacy, such as Nixon, who opened the doors to China; Taft, who governed the Philippines; or George Bush Sr., who was ambassador to China (Will 2009). However, Obama is the first president who was born and raised in the Pacific region.

Though we may take the diversity of Obama's background for granted, the rare constellation of geopolitical, cultural, familial, and personality factors have clearly affected his worldview and electability, especially in the post-9/11 multipolar world. The countervailing forces of multiculturalism and the challenges of economic globalization, mixed with the rise of Islamic fundamentalism, have played a significant role in Obama's election. If we were to test a predictive model explaining Obama's win, these variables would have to be part of a multifactorial equation. We might discover that we have chosen a leader whose biography and political experiences resonate with the changing times. We might also discover that his biography has indeed become our destiny as a nation.

The first 18 years of Obama's life, from birth until he entered college, were spent essentially on two groups of islands—Hawai'i and Indonesia. He spent 14 years in Hawai'i, from 1961 to 1967 and 1971 to 1979, and 4 years in Indonesia, from 1967 to 1971. These formative years are an integral part of his life story and shaped his deep personality structure. Yet, these early years remain unexplored and have not been seen as central to his political persona, which has been shaped mainly on the mainland and on Chicago's South Side.

Is Obama's unique perspective on the world an outgrowth of his life in Hawai'i and Indonesia, an upbringing that formed the foundation of his hybrid cultural identity? In Hawai'i, Obama lived in a multiethnic and multicultural society that was economically developed, and in Indonesia he was exposed to a multireligious secular society in the early stages of economic development with very high levels of poverty. As he has reported himself, "I was raised as an Indonesian child and a Hawai'ian child and as a black child and as a white child. . . . And so what I benefited from is a multiplicity of cultures that all fed me" (Mendell 2007, 32).

In this book, based on original fieldwork conducted in Indonesia, Hawai'i, and mainland United States, we will explore how Obama's early upbringing shaped his views of civil society, secular Islam, and globalization. The early shaping of his personality, interestingly, also prepared Obama for the challenges confronting American society at the onset of the 21st century. This is where culture meets personality, where history picks its changemakers, and where destiny or luck favors the well prepared. Today, most social scientists believe childhood is socially and culturally constructed and has a strong impact on an individual's later development, even though an adult personality is not simply a bundled product of childhood complexes, strengths, and weaknesses (Erikson 1963; Kakar 1981; Sharma and Fischer 1989). We will closely examine Obama's family relations, early schooling and education, and the social and cultural milieu where young Barack Obama spent a significant part of his childhood, including the critical home-to-school developmental transition, which influenced his trailblazing journey.

Even among presidential historians there seems to be a growing consensus on the impact of early parenting on the shaping of a future president (Gullan 2001; Wead 2005). The lasting impact of a strong mother or a father on the personality of a would-be president is almost universal. Presidents Washington, Madison, McKinley, Wilson, Roosevelt, and Nixon all had strong and domineering mothers. The developmental impact of the early loss of a significant other or the lasting effect of parental bereavement seems to drive some people to aspire for the highest office in the land. Washington lost his father at the age of 11 years, Jefferson at 14, Monroe at 16, Harrison at 18, Andrew Johnson at 3, and Garfield at 1; Bill Clinton's father passed away shortly before his birth. Yet, other aspirants to the office seem to have possessed an overarching paternalistic figure, whose idealized image guided a future president to his ultimate destiny. Presidents Arthur, Cleveland, and Wilson had strong fathers who were preachers, and Harrison, Tyler, and Pierce had fathers who had been governors of major states. Finally, presidents John Quincy Adams and George W. Bush had fathers who had been presidents themselves. However, these consistent trends do not take away from the specific contextual variations or the peculiarities of a life narrative.

As we look at Obama's life story and unearth the psychological and cultural truths about his early upbringing, we can begin to understand his rise to power in the post-9/11 world, with the looming specters of Osama bin Laden and Saddam Hussein. In accepting the truism that all politics is personal, this book will present the first cultural biography of the 44th president of the United States by examining Obama's enculturation or cultural socialization; however, this is not a psychobiography in the traditional psychoanalytic genre, even though it relies heavily on psychological concepts. We will delve into Obama's history within the context of the most recent events and some distant or symbolic events, while trying to understand his global significance.

His life offers a window on American society at the start of the 21st century. We will track Obama's trajectory through the prism of American society and culture. We will follow his path as he moves from the Hawai'ian Islands to Jakarta, Indonesia, and back, and then follow him as he moves to the mainland to take on bigger challenges. According to passages in a man's life, Obama is at the midpoint of his life cycle (Erikson 1963; Levinson 1986). Some might argue that it is premature to take a measure of his life at such a young age. However, this book attempts to look at his life at the pinnacle of his power. By leaning over his shoulder and reviewing the Cliff Notes of his life story, we can gain insights into the man's remarkable ascent and the generative legacy he might leave behind for future generations. This book takes an interdisciplinary approach to the study of lives, reflecting my multidisciplinary social science training. It relies on already published sources of information, including journalistic reports and biographical materials, and interviews conducted with Obama's family, friends, teachers, associates, and supporters.

I have tried to avoid reductionism from all sides. Although psychological thinking is pervasive in this book, I don't try to psychoanalyze the president through the lens of current psychological theories or try to put Obama on the couch. This book relies on Erik Erikson's (1963) approach to the study of biography and society during turbulent times and other theories of analytical or depth psychological thinkers. The book has an eclectic theoretical approach, but cultural theories and social science ideas also permeate it as we try to understand the Obama phenomenon and his larger-than-life persona in popular culture. To understand Obama's current appeal, we must rely on marketing and opinion research for predicting social trends, even though such crystal-ball gazing may always vary with the changing moods and attitudes of the country. Finally, we must recognize that Obama, not unlike other transformational figures, may represent something de novo, a unique personality among public figures gracing political life.

Can we fully understand Obama's cultural and political significance? Is Barack Obama, along with his coterie of followers, operating in a zone that is beyond our weltanschauung or our socially constructed theories? Our realistic, naive, and sometimes outdated theories may be lagging, struggling to keep up with the world as it races ahead from one crisis to the next: 9/11, the Iraq War, and the global banking crash and liquidity crisis. Hence, this book attempts to contribute to the literature on the Obama presidency by moving ahead of the curve, by looking at the details of his life, by identifying general patterns, and by projecting into the future.

As part of my training, professional work, and travel, I have conducted behavioral, social science, and marketing research in different parts of the United States and different parts of the world. This professional experience has informed my understanding of Obama's cultural identity. What intrigued me about Barack Obama originally was his cultural narrative, that is, his ability to weave different parts of his self, his early experience, and his family life into a cohesive story. Although his credentials are gold-plated American, that is, Harvard-trained lawyer, Illinois state senator, U.S. senator, and now president of the United States, the bricks and mortar of his biography are inherently more diverse, ethnic in origin, international, and path breaking.

My interest was in the details of his cultural biography, particularly in the different points of tensions, the mélange of diverse, biracial, multicultural upbringing—his childhood in Hawai'i and Indonesia, his midwestern family roots through his grandparents from Kansas, and his marriage to an African American woman from Chicago, Illinois. How he has managed to come to terms with the naturally occurring tensions stemming from different parts of his background is truly unique. Like the patchwork of red states and blue states, Obama has created an overarching narrative truth. In an uncanny confluence of social and cultural forces, the Obama election has brought biography and history to a significant tipping point, offering an object lesson to the first global or the millennial generation on how to construct a seamless cultural identity in rapidly changing times and in so doing how to reshape the future of this country. His life represents the triumph of the American brand of multiculturalism and a melding of different histories of immigration. His election has also sent out a resounding yet firm message to the world declaring America's stake in the 21st century; to paraphrase Mark Twain, the reports of America's decline may be greatly exaggerated.

Making of a Transformational Leader

Obama has ushered in a new era of transformational leadership. In the process he has become somewhat of a transnational cult hero glorified from the streets of Jakarta to the streets of Johannesburg. There are strong parallels between the mythological hero and the prototype of a transformational leader; both try to bring about paradigmatic change among their people. Obama has fixed his sights high, admitting that he does not want to be just an ordinary president but rather a transformational president; this is a key theme in this book as we trace Obama's ontogenesis or evolution as a national and global leader, a person with a vision and mass appeal.

His success depends on his innate charisma, which has generated enthusiasm among diverse segments of the American society and the world. Obama has been compared to every charismatic leader under the sun, leaving little doubt that he has the ability to inspire, uplift, and motivate. During the campaign his followers waited for hours on end to hear him speak, crowded huge concert halls and sports arenas to get a glimpse of their new progressive avatar, and drove long distances to simply be in his presence. Such scenes were reminiscent of the peace rallies and flower-power concerts of the 1960s; some have even imagined Obama to be sort of a messiah-like figure or a great soul (Sharma 2008a).

Is Obama driven to preside over great social and cultural change? Although this may be the key to his underlying motivation, his long-standing critics, who say he is vapid, not charismatic, and lacking any core beliefs or substance, have thus far been proven wrong. As Maureen Dowd, the *New York Times* editorial writer, has commented, "For some of Obama's critics, it's a breathtaking bit of fungible principles, as though Gandhi suddenly donned a Dolce & Gabbana, or Dolce & Mahatma, loincloth" (Dowd 2008b). His smooth and unflappable presentations throughout the campaign befuddled his right-wing critics. Many of these critics could not fathom how a rookie senator could take on not only his own party machine but also a well-entrenched opposition.

Clearly, after eight years of the Bush administration, the American people were fatigued and hungry for a change. They were searching for an inspirational leader who could serve up some "hearty chicken soup for the soul." How did Obama acquire the gift of oratory, near-perfect pitch, and the ability to channel his voice to the underlying needs and complexes of the American people? This book will explore Obama's leadership style and its broad-based appeal.

Ideas about transformational leadership are inevitably traced back to the writings of Max Weber, a German sociologist writing before World War I (Weber and Eisenstadt 1968). He identified three types of leadership styles: traditional, bureaucratic, and transformational. Obama clearly fits the profile of a transformational or charismatic leader, whose authority rests on "power legitimized on the basis of a leader's exceptional personal qualities or the demonstration of extraordinary insight and accomplishment, which inspire loyalty and obedience from followers" (Kendall 2007, 432).

The presidential biographer and historian James Burns was the first to use the idea within the context of the American presidency (Burns 1978). Borrowing from Weber's sociology and Kohlberg's stages of moral development, he argued that a transformational leader tries to move a society to a higher level of moral reasoning and to an improved state of social functioning. Although a transactional leader is simply driven by the bureaucracy that has elected him, a real transformational reformer is driven by a higher vision of society and attempts to transform the social and moral order in collaboration with his followers.

Management gurus also agree that transformations in organizations have generally not occurred in a top-down manner. Transformations are brought about by leaders who offer inspiring vision and values, outline clear goals, and then provide the context and opportunity for people to participate in the process of change. "That's why, in general, leaders of large corporations have moved away from top-down 'planned change,' and, instead, adopted a values-based, decentralized approach to organizational transformation" (O'Toole 2008).

The Obama agenda clearly envisions a different society in the next four to eight years. He has put forth bold ideas about the economy, education, energy, and health care, attempting to totally transform American society for the 21st century. The degree to which he succeeds may depend on the strength of his leadership, ability to persuade, intellectual prowess, inspirational motivation, and ability to be a change agent. His leadership style will be fully tested through the coming years. He has been able to uplift and inspire through his words and speeches, but the implementation of his plans may determine the long-range success of his vision.

Yet, his impact on the civil rights movement in this country has already been immense, as judged by the support he garnered and the emotional uplift he generated among the African American population. Many of the early leaders of the movement did not anticipate the Obama tsunami in the 2008 election, as the journalist Gwen Ifill has documented (2008). The previous generation of civil rights leaders, however, eventually had to accept Obama's impact as his quest in many ways represented the culmination of their long march and struggles. As a result, the dialogue within the civil rights community has now been transformed into a post–civil rights debate, handed over to the next generation of African American politicians.

The key to a transformational leader is the ability to unlock the hearts and minds of the people. This ability, while it may require emotional intelligence, is deeply rooted in a bedrock faith in the species. It requires a deep understanding of the historical circumstances, a symbiotic connection with the unmet needs and wants of a population, and a visionary perspective on the future. Finally, a truly transformational leader must possess a disciplined mind; a high level of cognitive capacity that is grounded in everyday realities; and a regimented, structured, and controlled self that is nevertheless spontaneous and forward looking.

Personality psychologist Howard Gardner, building on the work of David McClelland and others, studied biographies of transformational leaders like Mahatma Gandhi, Albert Einstein, and Nelson Mandela, and posited that a visionary or transformational leader would not be possible or even necessary in a country like the United States (Gardner 2004). With a stable political system and high levels of human development, the needs of the population just did not demand revolutionary change or systemic overhaul of the political order. The preconditions of a modern political system, driven by big money and big media, were not necessarily conducive for a leader with a transformational vision.

What is it about the current times that calls for revolutionary change or transformational leadership? Why has the American population responded to a call for a major political change? Are the current challenges of such high magnitude that a bureaucratic leader may not be up for the job? We will delve into these questions as we examine Obama's rise to the presidency.

American Multiculturalism

America is going through a significant demographic shift. In many ways, Obama's successful marketing of his biracial and multicultural biography mirrors the social and demographic changes already underway in this country. The Obama win may not have been possible without the ethnic voting blocks, which he gathered in large numbers from African American, Hispanic, and Asian voters (Todd 2008). Does the Obama election represent the full-fledged triumph of multiculturalism over and above the culture wars of the 1990s? I believe this is one of the clear outcomes of the historic 2008 election.

Again, Samuel Huntington (2004) predicted this correctly. He identified several important microtrends that are reshaping the fabric of American society. Loss of the Soviet empire as a traditional adversary led to allegiances to subcultural or subnational interest groups based on ethnicity and language. Liberal calls for a great multicultural revolution hit new heights.

The new immigration laws of the 1960s allowed persons from Latin America and Asia to come to this country in larger numbers. All of these trends have led to a major demographic change in the United States.

Huntington also believed the American identity will shift between various positions in the coming decades: a multicultural position with an ideological allegiance to a creed in the founding documents and principles; an exclusionist stance with a backlash from the white majority; a bifurcated alignment along Anglo and Hispanic lines; and a nativist or cultural move with a return to Protestant values, culture, and ethics. With the Obama election, we have already seen several of these positions playing out in the American electorate.

America's impressive human capital, a necessary precondition for fighting the challenges of globalization, was on display during the 2008 election. The Democratic delegates were 43 percent minority, 25 percent African American, and there were more women than men. This diversity was forward looking, an early sign of the demographic changes that will sweep this country by midcentury, according to the latest report from the U.S. Census Bureau (Sharma 2008b).

The idea of cultural pluralism has been espoused by a long line of Western thinkers, including James, Dewey, and Bourne, which has led to multiculturalism as a policy in several Western countries, such as Canada and Australia. In America, continuous immigration has been a cornerstone of the society and economy, which in an earlier era gave rise to the idea of the melting pot (Norgren and Nanda 2006). Though cultural assimilation formed the basis of the melting pot with previous waves of immigration, it no longer holds the same power over the American population (Jacoby 2004).

The immigration policies set forth in 1965 by the Johnson administration led to a major influx of new immigrants. Not only are we celebrating the first African American president but Obama is also the first multicultural head of state of any Western democracy. Even though Canada and Australia have spearheaded multiculturalism as an official policy of the state, it is America that has taken the lead in electing a multicultural leader to the highest office in the land.

However, multiculturalism has come under serious attack throughout Europe and in other parts of the world in the post-9/11 world (Oxford Analytica 2006). The criticism that multiculturalism, especially as portrayed by fanatical Muslim youth, is not consonant with Western secular values and freedoms is at the heart of this attack. Europe is pulling back on multiculturalism, considered a highbrow elitist idea constructed by armchair liberal thinkers, and is suggesting that cultural policies related to bilingualism and education in the schools and workplace keep immigrants from embracing Western democratic ideals and values.

In a rapidly globalizing world, does multiculturalism offer distinct advantages that the world cannot do without? Historian Ronald Takaki has argued that multiculturalism is inherent in America's DNA (Takaki 1993). Is the American brand of multiculturalism a distinct strength in business and geopolitics? Have Americans elected a diverse leader for diverse times precisely because the history of the American people is multicultural and diverse at the core, shaped by the indigenous Indian and African American populations?

Several years ago, I heard sociologist Nathan Glazer lecture at Harvard University about the virtues of multiculturalism (Glazer 1996). Almost a generation ago, as one of the younger members of the New York intellectuals, Glazer, with Daniel Patrick Moynihan, had coauthored the report *Beyond the Melting Pot*, which documented the melding of changing ethnic identities in New York City. Yet, during the Harvard lecture he argued that the evidence was indisputable that assimilation policies of the melting-pot era have not worked for the traditional minority groups.

John Ogbu, the Nigerian-born anthropologist at the University of California, Berkeley, based his life's work on the cultural theory that the achievement gap between voluntary and involuntary minorities compared with the majority population formed the basis of a caste-like system in American society (Ogbu 1978). Involuntary minorities are African Americans and American Indians, the traditional ethnic groups that by default do not have an alternative homeland. Voluntary minorities, on the other hand, consist of the new immigrants, such as Chinese Americans, Indian Americans, and other ethnic groups.

Involuntary minorities tend to perform poorly on achievement tests compared with the majority population. Because of their histories of self-perception, involuntary minorities interpret barriers to advancement as institutionalized discrimination. In some parts of the country, well-performing minority students may even carry the stigma of acting white. Voluntary minorities, on the other hand, view challenges in American society as opportunities.

Obama has confounded these cultural theories and stereotypes by transcending the race barriers many African Americans feel still exist in this society (Sharma 2008c). However, Obama also represents to some degree a growing number of African immigrants, about one million in major U.S. metro areas. Part and parcel of the demographic transition sweeping America, these new Africans are not descendants of slaves, even though they are often lumped with the African American population. Thus, the Obama tent consists of a broad spectrum of demographic segments.

According to Benjamin Akande, the dean of the Webster University School of Business, some of the notable personalities of the Obama generation include several prominent Africans in America: Kwame Anthony Appiah, Wole Soyinka, and Chinua Achebe in academia; Hakeem Olajuwon and Joseph Addai in sports; and Gbenga Akinnagbe and Akon in entertainment (Akande 2008). In many respects, these recent Africans are different from the African American population.

As an American of Kenyan descent, Obama's story validates Ogbu's theory that the caste-like pathologies that plague some segments of the American population and can be a social barrier are not evident among the new African immigrants. If race were not a real or perceived barrier, then Americans would already have narrowed the achievement gap and there would be more African Americans vying for the executive office. Now, with the help of a transformational leader like Obama, can America move Ogbu's involuntary minorities into the promised land and shore up its human capital? The achievement gap is only one of the challenges confronting us as we move into the 21st century.

Post-Osama World

Psychologists have abundantly documented the presence of flashbulb memories. Often related to historical events, these memories mark a significant turning point in our everyday lives, whether it is the Pearl Harbor attack, the first lunar landing, or the Kennedy assassination. These memories form such a powerful residue that when recalled they inevitably stir up related memories and situational context. Many who may not have witnessed the JFK assassination or a similar catastrophic event can remember where they were when the event took place or what they were doing at the time. These historic events carry such emotional and symbolic meaning that they are often considered catalysts for systemic social change. Very few people will dispute that the events of 9/11 were a significant turning point in American history. Our world has not been the same since.

On the morning of 9/11, I remember driving on a busy highway in New Jersey and listening to the radio when the news broke of the first plane striking the World Trade Center. Sportscaster Warner Wolf provided the first-person account on the Don Imus show from his apartment window overlooking the Twin Towers in lower Manhattan. I recall Imus expanded his program that day to cover the horrific events as they unfolded. Around ten o'clock in the morning, Wolf reported, "The tower is not there. It's gone. It's gone. It's collapsed. It's not there. It's disappeared. . . . I can't believe what I am seeing. I just can't believe it" (WABC Radio 2009).

I was stunned with disbelief. Don Imus reported, "It's the worst attack on this country since the Pearl Harbor attacks. . . . The news is that both towers of the World Trade Center have collapsed. The congressional leadership has been taken to a secure location. The country is clearly under a serious threat" (WABC Radio 2009). Our lives were changed forever and have not been the same again.

The events of 9/11 represented an attack on the U.S. financial nerve center and by extension an attack on the forces of globalization and progress. In the greater New York City area, all sense of normalcy and safety was fundamentally changed, and Americans became conditioned to looking over our shoulders, feeling a phobic sense of paranoia when boarding planes, getting painstakingly searched at airport check-ins, and always feeling on guard in public places.

The historian Eric Foner claims that we will continue to debate the significance of the events. Our world changed in many irreversible ways: "September 11 rudely placed certain issues on the historical agenda. Let me consider briefly three of them and their implications for how we think about the American past: the invocation of freedom as an all-purpose explanation for the attacks and a justification for the ensuing war on terrorism and invasion of Iraq; widespread acquiescence in significant infringements on civil liberties; and a sudden awareness of considerable distrust abroad of American actions and motives" (Foner 2004). Even as we pull out of Iraq, the impact of the events of 9/11 shifted toward Afghanistan, where American forces will remain involved until 2014, the new NATO deadline for withdrawal.

I have visited Ground Zero on many occasions and have seen the displays of human emotions plastered to the walls of the Trinity Episcopal

Church; the shards of memories and broken dreams serve as a stark reminder of the fragility of goodness. Trinity Church became a sanctuary on the day of the attacks and continues to be so on every anniversary of the attacks. The subway system under Ground Zero, which I have observed through the thick and hazy window of a moving subway car, used to be a massive crater under the former Twin Towers. As the last stop on the Path Train and the E line, Ground Zero is a reminder of a gaping wound on America's cultural subconscious. The event will continue to be a turning point in history, when on an ill-fated day the forces of evil for a flashbulb moment overtook the forces of progress and development.

Ground Zero's redesign offers a place for collective grief and mourning. Psychologically, grief and mourning can lead to transformation and renewal; thus, it may foster the birth of a new collective consciousness born of the sacrifice of people from all over the world, both the workers in the global economy and the countless innocent victims. Metaphorically, the ashes and the bellowing smoke of 9/11 touched all corners of the earth.

Some have called this a great human tragedy, a towering inferno for our times; others see these events as the seeds of a new beginning, a call for a renewal of the American agenda for the next century. Yet others view 9/11 as emblematic of the passing of the old American glory, the fading away of an empire, and the start of the post-American world. Even as I was putting the last touches on this book, the recent uproar about the plan to build an Islamic cultural center near Ground Zero opened up old wounds among the families of victims and the general population. It also brought to the forefront the underlying dynamic, the "paranoid style of American politics," operating in the American psyche (Hofstadter 1996). As the protests about the mosque began to spill over into hate speech and violence against Muslim cab drivers in New York City and against other mosques around the country, the perception that Obama is a Muslim who sympathizes with the Islamic agenda reared its ugly head again. Bipartisan polls by the Pew Research Foundation found that almost 30 percent of Republicans continue to believe Obama is a Muslim (Pew Research 2010a). Clearly, this perception seems to have become reality in the minds of millions of Americans, very much like the claim that Obama is a socialist out to take over or destroy the American economy.

A large percentage of Americans, mostly made of those who may not have voted for Obama in the first place, continue to believe he is the other, a foreigner who is taking the country in the wrong direction. Here, the issue of Obama's identity might go to the heart of the American identity. Disputes about his social and economic policies always seem to invoke the image of a socialist or Marxist law school professor lecturing us from the teleprompter and appearing somehow clueless about the basics of real capitalism and disrupting the American way of life, a common refrain from his opponents. As a *Newsweek* cover story pointed out, just two years after assuming office, the hopeful and ebullient Obama image seems to have transmogrified into the worst misperceptions and fears of the extreme right; he is now turned into the "terrorist-coddling, war mongering, Wall-Street-loving, socialistic, Godless, Muslim President" (Media Matters 2010). Although before and during the election it was only a fringe group that believed Obama is an extreme left-leaning politician, a larger number of people have now joined in the anti-Obama chorus.

In many ways, the events of 9/11 shook American identity to its core, and we are still living through the aftershocks. Not unlike the Pearl Harbor attacks or the JFK assassination, 9/11 will continue to shape successive generations of Americans. According to an intelligence expert, the 9/11 attacks

> ushered in a new age of American vulnerability and exposed the dark side of globalization. A radical Islamic group whose idealized conception of society is rooted in the seventh century turned the hallmarks of our 21st century networked world—the Internet, satellite phones, and commercial jets—into weapons. The increased proliferation of dangerous technologies and the existence of terrorist groups such as Al Qaeda that would not hesitate to use weapons of mass destruction raise the specter of potentially worse mass-casualty attack in the future. (Litwak 2002, 77)

On the ninth anniversary of the attacks I went down to Ground Zero to witness the progress on the reconstruction and to take part in the rallies a few blocks away. As I walked into crowded lower Manhattan with a professor and a colleague who teaches at a local college, I was impressed by the civil discourse taking place in a 10-block radius. The anti-mosque rally stretched many blocks and featured speeches by the families of 9/11 victims, representatives from local churches and synagogues, and firefighters and first responders. Two blocks away the pro-mosque rally had an equally strong presence of Muslim men and women in traditional Islamic garb and many other supporters. The discourse for the most part was rather peaceful, despite overblown rhetoric on both sides, but New York City like the rest of the nation seemed divided; almost 70 percent opposed the mosque because it is too close to what many consider hallowed ground (Pew Research 2010c).

Both sides carried diametrically opposed poster-board signs for the Obama presidency. The crowd against the mosque, led by the organizers like the blogger Pamela Geller, said Obama is a socialist and not the best leader for America. The pro-mosque crowd said Obama is one of them; they were carrying signs depicting Malcolm X and Muhammad Ali, claiming that Islam has been in America for 400 years. Is the rise of a president like Obama partly a reaction of the soul searching Americans have been engaged in since 9/11? Will Obama be able to help America negotiate its emerging yet shifting global identity vis-à-vis its allies and enemies, especially in the Islamic world? Is Obama really a sign of things to come in the 21st century?

Obama watched the events of 9/11 from downtown Chicago. As he reported in his biography, he was filled with horror and disbelief:

> The reports on my car radio were sketchy, and I assumed that there must have been an accident, a small prop plane perhaps veering off course. By the time I arrived at my meeting, the second plane had already hit, and we were told to evacuate the State of Illinois Building. Up and down the streets, people gathered, staring at the sky and at the Sears Tower. Later, in my law office, a group of us sat motionless as the nightmare images unfolded across the TV screen—a plane, dark as a shadow, vanishing into glass and steel; men and women clinging to the windowsills, then letting go; the shouts and sobs from below and finally the rolling clouds of dust blotting the sun. (Obama 2006, 291)

Did something stir in Obama's heart and mind that day? Americans had not been attacked at home in such a dramatic manner since the Pearl Harbor attacks, something Obama was very familiar with having grown up in Hawai'i near the U.S. naval bases. The sheer chaos and loss of life at Pearl Harbor have been imprinted on the minds of Hawai'ians for generations. "Now chaos had come to our doorstep. As a consequence, we would have to act differently, understand the world differently. We would have to answer the call of a nation" (Obama 2006, 345).

Almost immediately, Obama began to understand the specific purpose and timing of his run for the U.S. Senate:

> By the fall of 2002, I had already decided to run for the U.S. Senate and knew that possible war with Iraq would loom large in any campaign. When a group of Chicago activists asked if I would speak at a large antiwar rally planned for October, a number of my friends warned me against taking so public a position on such a volatile issue. Not only was the idea of an invasion increasingly popular, but on the merits I didn't consider the case against war to be cut-and-dried. . . . What I sensed, though, was that the threat Saddam posed was not imminent, the Administration's rationales for war were flimsy and ideologically driven, and the war in Afghanistan was far from complete. (Obama 2006, 347)

Obama had begun to position himself mentally for another political run, and deep in his heart perhaps he was preparing himself for the political run of his life, the run for the presidency.

Obama went ahead and gave the now well-known antiwar speech at the Federal Plaza in Chicago, which a few years later led to the antiwar platform for his presidential run. Thus, the events of 9/11 touched the core of Obama's identity as a would-be senator, a global citizen, and a progressive thinker. I argue that as an aspiring politician, who had spent his early years in Hawai'i and Indonesia and his college days in New York City, Obama knew that the events of 9/11 had pushed American history and world history to a cataclysmic point. Not unlike what happened with the Pearl Harbor attacks, civilization was witnessing the forces of extremism and progressivism in a clash of epic proportions. Obama was determined to play a role in the shaping of the events.

The candidate Obama had accurately diagnosed the problems stemming from 9/11: the overextension of the American military empire to the detriment of the domestic agenda. Obama may have also had Osama in his crosshairs for a long time given Osama was on the most-wanted terrorists list as the head of the worldwide network, Al Qaeda, the public enemy number one.

Notwithstanding the linguistic similarity of their Arabic names, separated by only one letter (i.e., Obama vs. Osama), which often created confusion in the minds of reporters and the general public, the Obama–Osama binary opposition formed the archetypal good and evil image in the minds of millions. In the American psyche, Obama's rise represented "the good" in opposition to "the evil" image of Osama, the face of global jihad. In Obama's mind, Osama bin Laden came to represent not just an evil genius but also a false prophet on the Muslim street, which America itself had been actively courting. As Obama said in a recent Mid-East speech: "Bin Laden was no martyr. He was a mass murderer who offered a message of hate—an insistence that Muslims had to take up arms against the West, and that violence against men, women and children was the only path to change. He rejected democracy and individual rights for Muslims in favor of violent extremism; his agenda focused on what he could destroy—not what he could build" (Obama 2011).

As it has been argued, President Bush went after Saddam Hussein with a personal vengeance because of the leftover baggage from his father's unfinished Gulf War (McAdams 2011; Renshon 2004). Obama threw himself into the race for the presidency to solve the big challenges posed by the events of 9/11 and to take down Osama's global network. Although the bluster of the war on terror has been turned down by several decibels, Obama has prosecuted the war with a quiet resolve, including the killing of Osama bin Laden. By killing Osama, Obama brought a painful chapter in recent American history to a remarkable close.

Yet, Osama may have managed to do the damage he intended by forcing America's hand in overextending its military reach for more than ten years. From a remote cave in Tora Bora and from his residential hideout in Abbottabad, Pakistan, Osama drained the United States' precious resources in lives and treasures. As Pepe Escobar of the *Asia Times* has suggested, it is not clear whether America can recover from the military misadventures after 9/11 and regain control of its slumping economy (Escobar 2011). Now that Osama bin Laden has been killed, will China emerge as the real winner of the war on terrorism?

The American Century Redux

What does the Obama presidency symbolize for America? Furthermore, what does it mean for the rest of the world? We can tackle these questions by moving into the future as we check the rearview mirror and look for the emerging gestalt of the post-Obama world or the shape of things during the Obama years. Can the Obama presidency restore some semblance of the American competitiveness that defined America during its heyday? Internally, can America close the achievement gap in education? Can America reestablish its cherished image as the moral arbiter of the world? Can America defeat the scourge of Islamist threat around the world?

How we answer these questions over the next four to five years will determine the Obama legacy, that is, the legacy of race relations in America, America's relations with foreign countries, and America's economic standing in the world. The Obama election may be a testament to the genius of the American experiment that the new immigrants can renew the nation's promise in successive generations. However, it remains to be seen whether America can retain its preeminent economic status as the rest of the world rapidly moves toward globalization, free markets, and capitalism.

Can the Obama presidency be the harbinger of the next American century? The 20th century, with all its fits and starts, may have prepared the way for total globalization. The 20th century, although it was dubbed the first American century (Brinkley 2010; Hachigian and Sutphen 2008), was hampered by several cataclysmic events, two world wars, and the long, drawn-out Cold War. These events clearly obstructed the spread of free markets, capitalism, and democratic institutions.

I heard development economist Jeffrey Sachs, in a tour-de-force lecture at Yale University, describe the spread of globalization within the context of world economic history (Sachs 1998). His main point, which now seems intuitively clear, was that for the latest wave of globalization to fully take hold we need strong legal and regulatory structures. This assertion echoes the prescription many financial experts have made in light of the boom-and-bust cycles of the 1990s and the recent banking and the liquidity crises. Sachs raised a question that we all need to think about: Can America foster a strong rule of law while it disseminates Western democratic values and free-market capitalism?

The market integration of capital flows attempted several times in the previous century did not fully take hold until the last two decades of the 20th century. As the Berlin Wall came tumbling down, the nonaligned, state-run economies of Brazil, Russia, India, and China, the so-called BRIC emerging markets, gradually came into their own. How will America compete globally with the rise of the BRIC economies (Hachigian and Sutphen 2008; Zakaria 2008)? In the meantime, the established economies in the European Union and Japan continue to compete with America in a post-9/11 world that has been flattened by the information technology revolution.

Economic anthropologist Keith Hart (2000) has suggested that if we take a long view of civilization and human cultures, the rise of "virtual capitalism" offers an unprecedented opportunity to level the economic field, equalize humanity, and digitally connect the entire globe. The nature of money, machines, and markets has been transformed right before our very eyes with the communication revolution, which has brought new entrants into the global economy. Considering the long span of human progress from nomadic hunter-gatherers to virtual nomads in the information age (Sharma 2004), his claim that we will not return to the old order of state-owned national economies seems fairly intuitive. Nevertheless, this transition may be easy to think about or imagine, but actually very difficult to implement. For example, consider the recent banking crisis emanating from a multitude of root causes in the housing and mortgage industry, which quickly spread to all of the major banks and nearly ground global banking and emerging markets to a halt. How are we to arrive at a unified, interconnected, and fair world? What role can an American president play in advancing this agenda?

A multifaceted change is occurring in the American psyche and the *conscience collective*, epitomized by the Obama election, consisting of a broader change in the constellation of attitudes, ideas, beliefs, and lifestyles. Market researcher John Zogby, who has kept his finger on the pulse of the American people, has suggested that the American dream is indeed in the midst of a significant realignment (Zogby 2008). Based on thousands of surveys conducted over the past few years, he has identified several trends that might bode well for the future of the American people and the larger world: a greater consumer interest in living within one's means, an openness to diversity in views and ways of life, a deeper search for spiritual meaning and comfort, and a greater demand for authenticity and transparency in public officials and institutions. The Obama campaign spoke to all of these issues during the elections.

The presidential historian H. W. Brands, in the history of the United States since World War II, notes that with the election of Barack Obama Americans reasserted their right to dream big dreams. According to Brands: "The historic nature of Obama's victory—the first African American president would be inaugurated just weeks before the two hundredth birthday of Abraham Lincoln, the emancipator of African American slaves—brought joyful tears to the eyes of his supporters and a moment of respectful reflection even to many of those who voted against him" (Brands: 2010, 380). Yet, the sobering reality descended the next morning: the recession-bound global economy was in a tailspin and on the foreign-policy front the picture looked rather bleak. At the start of his term, Obama's challenges seemed insurmountable, yet the country seemed to be ready for the dream of transformation Obama had promised.

Will President Obama be able to seize the historic moment and take advantage of the revolutionary mood in this country and around the world? Robert Kuttner bluntly asked whether Obama would follow the path of Jimmy Carter, a well-intentioned but one-term president, or the path of Bill Clinton, a centrist who governed by placating the opposition (Kuttner 2008). Kuttner has suggested that both of these outcomes are possible, although the latter seems more plausible than the former.

Alternatively, will Obama follow a road less traveled, charting a more arduous path for the 21st century, one that follows the road of earlier wartime presidents, such as Abraham Lincoln, Franklin Roosevelt, and Lyndon Johnson, all of whom presided over cataclysmic changes? Major social, cultural, and economic transitions call for a transformational leadership. Obama is clearly in an unprecedented position to make a difference not only in the lives of Americans but also in the lives of countless others around the world because he has answered a generational call. How far will he succeed in changing the world? We will be in a better position to answer this question after we delve into Obama's narrative truth. Surely, the change Obama has promised depends partly on how we extract the teachable lessons from his life and try to support or defer his overall dream.

Understanding Obama's Truth

This book is about Obama's narrative truth—his cultural upbringing, narrative psychology, and transformative leadership. We will examine Obama's cultural pathway through the life cycle and examine how he resolved the various developmental and psychosocial challenges he confronted. We will rely on a classic psychosocial framework for highlighting Obama's developmental transitions and the turning points where he suffered setbacks or encountered a developmental crisis (Erikson 1963;

Levinson 1984; Sheehy 1996). The resolution of each of these crises has set an underlying emotional tone in Obama's self and has shaped his thinking and behavior about how to resolve similar conflicts in the future.

We will also examine Obama's self-identifications, relationships, and long-term influences that have determined his core personality, while we delve into Obama's cultural narrative. If Obama's historic rise represents the full manifestation of multiculturalism at home and the quickening of globalization abroad, then the genius of the American people may have been forward looking, representing a quantum leap in consciousness. Americans have witnessed an increasingly diverse mass of humanity coming through their shores and borders. The American people also sense that the challenges they confront for the next century may be radically different than the challenges their parents and grandparents confronted. In the aftermath of the 9/11 attacks, Americans have felt under siege at home and abroad, especially in the Middle East, Afghanistan, and Iraq. In electing Barack Obama, Americans have made a choice; a clarion call has been sent out to the world that America is still one of the most egalitarian nations on the planet. Around the world, the tired, hungry masses yearning to be free were waiting to see which way the pendulum would swing in this election and with the Obama presidency.

We will focus on Obama's symbolic transformation from Barry to Barack and analyze his relationship with his biological father—or lack thereof—throughout his youth. His journey from a childhood and youth in Hawai'i and Indonesia, where he was known as Barry, to his time in Los Angeles, New York City, and Chicago, where he emerged as Barack, is a remarkable American story. It is a story of a multicultural youth moving from the margins to the center and from the ground floor to the highest office in the land; Obama grew up on the fringes of American society but found his place at Ivy League universities and in the corridors of power in the state legislature and the United States Senate.

What may have driven Obama through these years were the dreams of an ambitious African father, who abandoned him at the age of two years, yet whose image, voice, and message were kept alive and transmitted to the son by a progressive, liberal American mother, who herself lived at the outskirts of American society. Why has Obama emerged as a global symbol of the hopes and dreams of millions of people around the world? Does his life story represent the stuff of myths? Is he a man blessed with the ability to resurrect the American myth of the self-made individual for our times?

His images on T-shirts, magazine covers, and television screens throughout the world may be a harbinger as we look ahead to the evolving 21st century. The question many observers are asking, both domestically and internationally, is, will America be able to lead in the foreseeable future?

From the outset, the 2008 election was an improbable election for Obama to win. In examining it from different vantage points, we can understand how Obama's success was the result of a generational election in which the personal biography of the candidate had a significant influence on the outcome, another important reason why this psychological and cultural study is highly relevant. Based on the turnout of the voting blocs, it was also the watershed election demographically, where the ethnic constituencies, the women, and the younger voting blocs all contributed to turning the tide against the status quo.

The 2008 election may have changed the discourse on race relations, especially among African Americans. From Alex Haley's fictional Kunta Kinte to Barack Obama, we have come a long way in race relations in this country (Sharma 2008d). During the campaign, Obama repeatedly said it's in his DNA to unite this country. How far he succeeds in this goal will reshape the country's social and cultural fabric which, in the coming decades, will be increasingly diverse (Sharma 2008b).

Finally, we will look at Obama's marketing accoutrements—the Obama Web site, messaging, and campaign signs. His campaign built the largest online community, ushering in an Internet presidency. Conversely, President John F. Kennedy was referred to as the first television president. The way Obama built a grassroots online movement throughout the campaign, relying on his "intelligent mobs," reflects positively on his mission and his appeal to the diverse segments of American society (Rheingold 2002).

Psychologists, biographers, and historians have often noted that at significant turning points in history, a charismatic person may be chosen to lead a nation and an entire generation of people. But how or why a particular person may be called upon remains shrouded in mystery; our theories can estimate but cannot fully decipher and predict. What drives a particular person to emerge as a transformational leader is partly a combination of personal biography, societal and cultural needs, and the historical times. Thus, we may articulate the conditions that led Barack Obama to embody a paradigm shift at the turn of the 21st century, a once-in-a-lifetime cultural, generational, and technological shift. From this point forward we may measure social progress in terms of a pre-Obama and a post-Obama world (Sharma 2008c).

Paradigmatic change is shaped by people who are catalysts of the new social order, which in turn moves the masses to follow their lead. What Obama means to millions of aspiring youth around the world may be best encapsulated in his life story. Although it may be difficult to make pre-scriptive or policy statements based on an individual case history, Obama projects a uniquely structured narrative by virtue of his background. His life may offer teachable lessons for future generations.

As a cultural archetype of the new political leadership, Obama is already spearheading new African American leaders across the promise land. On the global stage, however, he may represent the best example of America's multicultural heritage, a symbol that is highly needed for the 21st century. The trend on this issue is clear as Obama has already significantly improved the U.S. image abroad. Can the change he has ini-tiated be fully realized in our times? Do we need to raise a million more Baracks to bridge the achievement gap among traditional ethnic minori-ties that has persisted for more than a generation despite the promises of affirmative action?

Parents naming their newborns "Barack" or "Obama" may be taking a step in the right direction, but following Obama's footsteps may not be easy, especially for parents with lesser means or for people living in far-off villages in Africa (Lee 2008). Yet, hope springs eternal, and many parents with babies born during and after the 2008 election are already preparing their children to be the next Barack Obama. For the Obama generation to fully realize its potential we may need a large cohort of the population to want to become significant change agents in their own lives. However, the challenge will still remain: How does one become a vital person while liv-ing a purposeful life in a world adrift amid larger geopolitical and market forces? As a powerful and original story for our times, I believe Barack Obama's life narrative offers a solution to this vexing problem for our global or transnational age.

2

Origin Stories

A cursory review of these variegated hero myths forcibly brings out a series of uniformly common features, with a typical groundwork, from which a standard saga, as it were, may be constructed.

Otto Rank (1914)

The adventure begins with the hero receiving a call to action, such as a threat to the peace of the community, or the hero simply falls into or blunders into it.

Joseph Campbell (1949)

A transformational journey has a redemptive narrative. Irrespective of culture and history, at the center of stories of deliverance, or what some call the hero's journey, lies a monomyth, an idea that has been distilled by mythologists and psychologists for more than a century (Campbell 1949; Jung 1956; Eliade 1954; Rank 1914). The structure of the heroic story consists of a gifted person, often born in obscurity, who must respond to the call of an adventure and who must fight an established order for the sake of our survival. The hero must ultimately emerge victorious, bring knowledge, wisdom, and fortune to his people, and find a way to liberate them from tyranny and self-ignorance. Such a gifted person is a change-maker or a "hero with a thousand faces" (Campbell 1949).

This is the stuff of great stories, from *Gilgamesh* to *Star Wars*, where real life sometimes imitates great art because the grandest of all narratives are the most compelling human stories. Barack Obama's story is particularly compelling as it has all of the qualities of a redemptive story for our times, one in which even children can intuitively grasp its structure, tone, and meaning.

Obama seems to have lifted the spirits of the world and inspired confidence in the slumping American ideals and values. As Obama said during his 2004 Democratic National Convention speech, "my story would not be possible in any other country." He has connected people from diverse backgrounds and evoked feelings of American Exceptionalism (Obama 2004b). After listening to Obama's speech, Bernard Henri-Levy, who was traveling in America following the footsteps of Alexis de Tocqueville, was impressed by Obama's ability to transcend traditional racial and political categories. Tocqueville's countryman wondered aloud, who is this "white black man who isn't even descended from a slave in the Deep South" (Henri-Levy 2007, 49), Was he a black Clinton, perhaps, who wants to be America's promise and not play on its white guilt? Was he heralding the beginning of the end for identity politics? We all watched historical events as citizens around the world, people of different political stripes, responded to the 2008 American election with great enthusiasm and anticipation.

A multinational survey of 22 countries, which was conducted by the BBC in advance of the political convention, indicated that most respondents believed Obama would improve world relations and be a better leader than Senator John McCain. The percentage of respondents favoring an Obama victory ranged from 9 percent in India to 82 percent in Kenya; overall, an average of 49 percent of respondents preferred Obama and 12 percent preferred McCain (BBC News 2008). The results were similar when *The Economist* polled residents in a large number of countries and found that people in all but four countries (Algeria, Cuba, Congo, and Iraq) supported the candidacy of Barack Obama over that of John McCain (*The Economist* 2008). A New York–based blogger while watching the inauguration on the giant TV monitors reported from Times Square:

The explosion of joy in Times Square was so big that I was deaf for a moment! There were so many tears that for a second I felt suffocated and drowned in that sea of joy! The happiness was so great that for a second I felt I had a lump in my throat! The air, so hot that in seconds I felt the heat of the human race! A heat that I had never felt before! In Times Square today I discovered that when there are big ideals and hope, there is only one race—the human race! There is no black or white, mulatto or Latinos, African or Asian, red, blue, poor, rich, Scandinavians, Australians, Pakistanis, Kenyans, Zambians, Dominicans, Costa Ricans, Japanese! The diversity of races, nationalities, social strata represented there reminded me of the biblical figure Noah's Ark! (Onofre 2008)

In Kenya, which is proud to be Obama's ancestral homeland, feelings were monumental:

> Back home in Kenya, President Mwai Kibaki was not just among the first to send a congratulatory message to the new President-elect, but he also declared Thursday November 6th 2008 a public holiday throughout Kenya. Almost everywhere around the country, Kenyans are in celebratory mood as people digest the fact that a man whom they share an ancestry has been elected to the helm of global political and economic power. (Onofre 2008)

In "Obama's Party in Bali," a play organized to celebrate Obama's inauguration, people handed out Indonesian masks of Obama, prayed for his late mother, and went on a pilgrimage to all of the Javanese villages where she had done her research fieldwork. One of the characters went into a trance-like state and started a traditional Balinese song and dance:

> I am a dancer. I am God's worshipper. I am the Wind's worshipper. Therefore, I believe in karma. What happened to me was a reflection of my karma. Since the '65 incident I have not danced. I defied my karma. But my karma called me in, calling me in, calling me in again to dance for Obama's victory. Dancing with due respect to humanity, dancing for the freedom of skin color that has been oppressed for ages. Dancing for my own wounds; dancing for the brassiere and the underpants that I did not wear in ages. (Hendrowinoto 2009, 1)

An outburst of such emotions was anticipated close to home. In Chicago's Grant Park tears flowed from well-known observers, including Oprah Winfrey, Jesse Jackson, and Spike Lee. These feelings were not unique to celebrities. Jabari Asim, author of *The N-Word* observed that his 77-year-old mother, who still "remembers Emmett Till, Medgar, Malcolm and Martin," had been transformed by the Obama moment:

> By the night of Obama's remarkable triumph, she had digested far more than his trademark phrases. Still, she was more than thrilled when, during his victory speech at Chicago's Grant Park, he once again proclaimed, "This is our moment." Obama's victory seemed "just too good to be true, overwhelmingly good," she told me. "There are no words to describe how I feel. 'Elated' is not good enough." (Asim 2009, 2)

A Heroic Journey

In myths, as in real life, the setting for a hero's journey is some far-off exotic place that indelibly shapes his destiny. In the aftermath of the Pearl Harbor attacks and the growing importance of the Asian-Pacific region, America's strategic and geopolitical goals were focused on the statehood of Hawai'i, the last state to join the Union. The East-West Center at the University of Hawai'i was an outgrowth of the United States' interest in fostering cultural exchange with the rising Asian economies. Then Senate majority leader Lyndon Johnson passed a bill in 1959 to establish a research center, where in 1960, Obama's father, Barack Obama Sr. was one of the first East African students.

A grant of $10 million from the Congress was given to the center the summer Ann arrived in Hawai'i. This institution would play a critical role in both her personal and professional life for nearly 25 years. "An advance team set off for Bangkok, Rangoon, Saigon, Calcutta, Dhaka, Kathmandu, Karachi, Colombo, and points beyond, touring twenty countries that might be encouraged to send students. . . . The center's emphasis would be the exchange of ideas, information, and beliefs through cooperative study, training, and research" (Scott 2011, 77). Ann would meet her future husbands at the center, receive a PhD, raise a family, and set off on her own field research through the sponsorship provided by this institution.

At the center's 50th anniversary, Lynda Johnson Robb, the daughter of the former president said, "The dream from which the Center grew, breathtaking in its ambitious reach was simple in concept—to bridge the historic gaps separating the two worlds" (East-West Center 2010). Likewise, the former governor of Hawai'i, George Ariyoshi, claimed, "The East-West Center has become even more important now; their mission is more important, and they have more work to do. As we set focus on the Asia Pacific region, the people who live in this area will have a better understanding and feel for Americans as well as vice versa due to the efforts of the Center" (East-West Center 2010).

Barack Obama Sr. came to the United States during the period of the "Airlift to America," which was the brainchild of the charismatic Kenyan Tom Mboya and a young American entrepreneur, William X. Scheinman (Shachtman 2009). However, the Obama family biographer claims, based on extensive research, that Obama Sr. was not part of the Mboya airlift: "There were 140 serious applications from East African students for places on Mboya's 1959 chartered aircraft but only 81 seats, and Obama did not make the final selection." Obama Sr. made his way through the support of other American donors (Firstbrook 2010, 206).

However, some of his moral and financial support may have come from African American leaders, including Jackie Robinson, Harry Belafonte, Sidney Poitier, and Martin Luther King Jr. The airlift consisted of nearly 800 East African young men and women who wanted to change Africa. The African airlift may even have affected the 1960 presidential race; vice president Richard Nixon pressured the State Department into funding the project because he did not want Senator John F. Kennedy's family foundation to reap the political benefits.

After being educated in one of the most diverse parts of the United States, Obama Sr. was eventually expected to return to Kenya to help build the fledgling Kenyan democracy. However, shortly after arriving at the East-West Center, Barack Obama Sr. met Ann Dunham in a Russian class. Ann Dunham was an intelligent yet shy young woman of 18 when she fell in love with the dark and handsome African student; his elegant English manners and eloquence of speech won her heart. She became pregnant with a child, who was born the following year in Hawai'i on August 4, 1961. They named him Barack Hussein Obama Jr. In the beautiful island setting, popular among honeymooners, the couple had barely consummated their marriage before going their separate ways.

Whether the marriage actually took place remains shrouded in mystery. Barack Obama stated in his autobiography that they married in 1960, but the divorce decree suggests that they eloped in 1961. Several biographers have claimed that they may not have been married at all. Obama himself has not been able to find a marriage certificate, wedding rings, wedding invitations, or a guest list (Obama 2004a).

Based on the available documentation, it appears that Obama's grandparents' apartment was just a couple of blocks away from Kapi'olani Medical Center, the hospital where Barack Obama was born. The "birthers," a group of conspiracy theorists, continue to cling to the notion that the president was not born on the Hawai'ian Islands but rather in a village in Kenya; hence, they claim that he may not be a natural-born citizen and thus ineligible to be president.

After yet another CNN/Opinion Research poll showing that an increasing number of Republicans continue to believe that the U.S. president Barack Obama was not born in Hawai'i (CNN/Opinion Research 2011), the White House released the long-awaited long form of his birth certificate, in hopes that it would put to rest the misinformation campaign that he is not a natural-born citizen.

Obama trumped real-estate magnate Donald Trump, who had recently been clamoring for a full disclosure of Obama's birth certificate, in what appeared to be an opening salvo of the 2012 national campaign. At the annual White House Correspondents' Dinner, Obama not only flaunted the long form repeatedly but also showed a clip of the young cub Simba, from Disney's *The Lion King*, to poke fun at those who believe he was born in Kenya.

Now that both the long and short forms of Obama's birth certificate have been released, the birthers have staked out another claim that the long-form certificate is a fake (Corsi 2011). "I think the birth certificate released by the White House is a fraudulent document," Corsi told *Media Matters* (Strupp 2011). Corsi has also decided to track down Obama's British and Indonesian citizenship status, based on the claim that his father and stepfather, respectively, were not U.S. citizens but rather citizens of their countries of origin. Thus, Obama's natural-born status at birth would have been affected because Kenya was an English colony, and his father was a Kenyan citizen; in other words, Obama at birth was a dual citizen of the United States and the United Kingdom. His citizenship would have been further altered if and when he was adopted by his stepfather. Obama may be a native-born citizen, not a natural-born citizen, Corsi claims. None of these claims has been proven in the court of law, but Corsi's new mantra is that Obama's dual citizenship makes him ineligible.

On the basis of the Hawaiʻian and Indonesian evidence presented throughout this book, I show that Corsi's claims are based on weak evidence and plainly unfounded. Birthers seem intent on challenging the fourteenth amendment in the 2012 election; they want to throw out the baby Obama borne of America's multicultural roots with Hawaiʻi's pacific bathwater.

As a fringe group, the birthers seem conspiratorial, while highlighting the anti-intellectualism in American politics (Hofstadter, 1966). Inflaming the debate about "tourist babies," the birthers have amplified yet another leitmotif central to the monomyth, the birth of the hero under unusual or difficult circumstances. While analyzing the hero myth, Otto Rank, the youngest student in Freud's inner circle, first noted the pattern in all hero myths: "[In] the prominent civilized nations—the Babylonians and Egyptians, the Hebrews and Hindus . . . the newborn hero is the young sun rising from the waters, first confronted by lowering clouds, but finally triumphing over all obstacles" (Rank 1914, 1).

Later, Mircea Eliade, Joseph Campbell, Carl Jung, Alfred Adler, and many others followed this line of inquiry and developed a complete psychological theory around the hero myth.

Barbara Nelson, a former teacher at the Punahou School, remembers Barack Obama's birth. On the night Obama was born, she had dinner with Dr. Rodney T. West, a physician from Kapi'olani Hospital (McAdam 2009). From the dinner conversation, she remembered Obama's father's unusual name, which seemed to have a lyrical quality. She also remembered that his father was the only African student in Hawai'i who was happy to have a mixed-race son. She also correctly recalled that Dr. West was not the attending physician. As confirmed by the long-form birth certificate, Dr. David A. Sinclair was the attending physician at his birth. Both Dr. West and Dr. Sinclair died several years ago, leaving room for birthers to speculate.

She would hear that name again 10 years later when Obama Sr. visited his son's fifth-grade classroom at the Punahou School, hosted by Mabel Hefty, who had spent a year in Kenya teaching English to schoolchildren. Nelson was a guest in Hefty's classroom. The conservative online publication *World Net Daily* (WND), which has been following up on the legal challenges to Obama's birth certificate, claims that Barbara Nelson's story does not provide any credibility to Obama's birth in Hawai'i as she was not present in the birthing room; she has secondhand knowledge obtained through a doctor who may not have been the attending physician. The WND and other such publications have been calling for full disclosure of all personal documents connected with Barack Obama. Absent this evidence, the WND and the birthers continue to question Obama's constitutional legitimacy as a president.

Although now significantly diffused, the birther issue became a focal point for many of Obama's supporters and detractors. Supporters demanded to see the evidence of the nativity scene with the three wise men and the star pointing in the right direction. The detractors want nothing less than to prove that Obama is not a natural-born American, not qualified to be president of the United States; the more serious implications of this theory would constitute a virtual coup-d'etat, something most Americans cannot even fathom.

However, the evidence from the certificate of live birth and the long form available in the public domain is clear—namely that Barack Obama was born in Hawai'i. It is also clear upon closer examination of the facts that Barack Obama Sr. was in Hawai'i from 1959 to 1962. If so, then why would his wife go to Kenya to give birth to his son? Why would Ann Dunham travel to Kenya to a remote village that she did not know and where by all accounts she was not welcome? Who would have funded such a trip? Why would the birth announcements declaring Obama's birth, independent of his parents' actions, appear within a couple of weeks in the local newspapers? On facts and plausibility, the conspiracy theory seems to fall short, even according to some WND writers, who have attested to the fact that there is no credible evidence supporting the counterclaim that Obama was born in Kenya (Klein and Elliott 2010).

Probably unaware that most Kenyan men practice a form of polygamy, Ann Dunham remained in the dark during her brief marriage to Obama Sr. that he was already married and had a Kenyan son, Obongo (Roy) Obama, and daughter, Auma Obama. As Peter Firstbrook (2010), the Obama family biographer in Kenya, has documented, "In Kenya, polygamy was (and still is) legal, and there is no limit to the number of wives a man can have. Muslims usually consider five wives to be maximum, but there are many instances where a Kenyan—Muslim or Christian—takes many more" (203).

As Ann Dunham's mentor and friend Alice Dewey explained to me, "She may have known that most African men are polygamists because she was studying anthropology but we can't be certain." When the news of their marriage, which took place on the island of Maui on February 2, 1961, reached the remote Kenyan village of Nyang'oma Kogelo, Ann Dunham was already two to three months pregnant. The Obama elders, especially Obama Sr.'s father, Hussein Onyango, refused to accept the marriage, for it did not follow the proper village customs, and most importantly, he did not want a white woman sullying the Obama blood (Obama 2004a).

A year later, June 2, 1962, Obama Sr. graduated from the University of Hawai'i and decided to move to Harvard University for a degree in economics. A copy of Barack Obama Sr.'s résumé from this period, which I have exclusively obtained during my research, does not even mention Ann Dunham and his newborn son, though it mentions that he has a wife and two children in Kenya; the omission of his newborn son is consistent with the recent finding that Obama Sr. may have entertained the idea of giving his son up for adoption (Jacobs, 2011). The résumé states that Obama Sr. is a Luo; fluent in his tribal language, Swahili, and in English; and 28 years old. It says he graduated from the University of Hawai'i with a BA in economics and gives his address as 1482 Alencastre Street, Honolulu, and a P.O. Box in Nairobi, Kenya.

When Obama Sr. arrived in America, his objective was to complete a PhD in economics from Harvard or Berkeley. He planned to return to Kenya and work for the government in economic development. He had already clerked for an Indian law firm in Nairobi, worked as a surveyor for a British engineering firm, and written three adult literacy books in his native tongue.

At the University of Hawai'i he had received the highest score in English on the entrance exam for foreign students. He then went on to complete four years of work in three years, earn a GPA of 3.6, and became a member of the Phi Beta Kappa honor society. As Neil Abercrombie, the governor of Hawai'i, told me in an in-depth interview, Obama Sr. was a driven man.

Yet Obama Sr. also made time for social activities; chaired the University's International Week in the summer of 1960; prepared and presented several papers on economics; and, as the first African student at the University, spoke at the Rotary, Kiwanis, and Elks clubs and at several local churches. His résumé stated that he was accepted to the PhD program in economics at Harvard, Yale, Michigan, and the University of California at Berkeley, but only Harvard offered him $1,500 toward financial assistance. His undergraduate studies had been sponsored by the Kirk family, the Laubach Literacy Fund, and the African-American Institute, and he received some financial support from the University of Hawai'i. However, because these sources of funding had now dried up, Obama Sr. decided to attend Harvard for the reputation and the financial assistance it offered, which meant he would have to leave his newly formed family behind.

With the hopes of a lasting marriage dashed, the Dunham household was not an island of peace and tranquility but a house divided. Alice Dewey claimed that when Obama Sr. failed to support the family after moving to Harvard, the marriage was essentially over, and Ann Dunham filed for divorce. This explanation, although understandable, may not fully align with the evidence, which suggests that Ann Dunham was already an undergraduate at the University of Washington shortly after giving birth to Barack (Corsi 2009). She had traveled thousands of miles to her old hometown of Seattle, Washington, far away from her husband, to continue her undergraduate studies. During this time several reports also suggest that Obama Sr. was seen at social gatherings without Ann Dunham and his newborn son. While at Harvard, Obama Sr. would marry another American woman, Ruth Nidesand, who would move to Kenya with him and bear him two more sons, Mark Ndesandjo Obama and David Ndesandjo Obama.

Many years later, while visiting her son at Columbia University in New York City, Ann Dunham revealed the details of their final breakup. After viewing her favorite film, *Black Orpheus*, she told her son that Obama Sr. had received a full scholarship, including all the expenses to move his family, to the New School of Social Research in New York City. Yet, Obama Sr. insisted on attending Harvard because he was "such a stubborn bastard, he had to go to Harvard. How can I refuse the best education? he told me. That's all he could think about, proving that he was the best" (Obama 2004a, 126). Ann Dunham may have also visited Barack Obama Sr. at Harvard, with the young Barack in tow, but she failed to save her marriage; she may also have learned that he had already found another romantic interest.

Barack Obama recounts that watching the classic film with his mother revealed her heart. Halfway through the film he was bored and wanted to leave, yet his mother was beaming with joy and amazement at the scenes of black and brown children playing on the screen on a green hill high above the San Paolo beach. "I suddenly realized that the depiction of childlike blacks I was now seeing on the screen, the reverse image of Conrad's dark savages, was what my mother had carried with her to Hawai'i all those years before, a reflection of the simple fantasies that had been forbidden to a white middle-class girl from Kansas, the promise of another life, warm, sensual, exotic, different" (Obama 2004a, 124).

Bronwen Solyom, a fellow graduate student at the University of Hawai'i and long-time friend, who shared Ann's interest in Indonesian art and archaeology, said that shortly before she died, Ann briefly mentioned Barack's book and commented on the *Black Orpheus* episode. Solyom's fleeting yet important recollection after many years is that, according to Ann, Barack's interpretation of the event was his own and that as it was his book, he had the right to tell the story as he understood it. Solyom had the impression that Ann felt it did not fully reflect her state of mind or subjective feelings and that she may have had a different response to the film.

When I asked Obama's Indonesian sibling, Maya, about the movie, she said the movie did not have the same significance for her; her brother has a better memory of it. Instead, she remembered that the musical score of the movie by the well-known Brazilian singer, Antonio Carlos Jobim, used to be one of her mother's favorite and she often danced to it.

In a recent interview, Obama admits that the "unreflective heart of her youth" that he glimpsed during the viewing of *Black Orpheus* may have shown the naively idealistic core of his mother's personality, something she may not have fully come to terms with herself. This is a trait she may have passed on to her children in varying degrees and permutations. They both admit that this was the most endearing part of her life and something they still cherish (Scott 2011, 231).

Obama's mother completed her studies in Hawai'i and later married Lolo Soetoro, a cultural exchange student sent to Hawai'i by the Indonesia government. Later she and her son would accompany him to Jakarta. After almost 13 years of marriage and another child, a daughter named Maya Soetoro—Barack's half-sister—Ann divorced Lolo and returned to Hawai'i, where she ultimately received a PhD in cultural anthropology. Thus, Obama's formative years were spent in two exotic locations—the islands of Hawai'i and Indonesia, both of which deeply shaped his character. Hawai'i and Indonesia are both melting pots of different kinds and have deeply rooted ethnic and cultural synergies. Hawai'i has the unique demographic distinction of not having a majority population with a political hold on the power structure. Indonesia is one of the most diverse Islamic societies on the planet.

Jerry Burris, a long-time resident of Hawai'i and a senior editor for the *Honolulu Advertiser*, told me during a jaunt to one of Barack's local hangouts, Rainbow Drive-In, that Barack was like everybody else in Hawai'i and part of the one big family or *ohana*. However, the islands did not have many African Americans, so Barack sought out writers like Frank Marshall Davis as friends and mentors. Driving around Waikiki near Davis' former home, I realized how Hawai'i molded the core of Barack Obama's personality, imbuing him with an externally cool temperament, and a tolerant and optimistic outlook on life, yet also a sense of alienation about his racial identity. Indonesia, on the other hand, coincided with his elementary school years and the home-to-school developmental transition, which gave Obama a global worldview afforded to only a few of his generation.

In every hero's journey there occurs an early setback from which the hero must recover. In Obama's case, as a consequence of his parents' divorce in 1964, young Barack Obama would grow up without a biological father from the age of two. As Barack tells in his autobiography, he met his father only once, when he was 10 years old; the meeting was brief, more of an intrusion on the Dunham family than a welcome surprise. Yet, throughout Barack's childhood his single working mother and his maternal grandparents fed him a staple of wonderful stories about his father's oratory and intellectual skills, projecting a larger-than-life image of his absent father. Thus, although Obama grew up without a live-in father, he may not have felt completely fatherless. In his heart and mind, his imaginary father, about whom he would construct elaborate origin stories, one day imagining him as African royalty or the next as a high-ranking government official, but he was a real flesh-and-blood African man.

Throughout his early years Obama was sheltered from his father's real image. In the remote recesses of his mind, his father's real image and his parents' brief and improbable marriage remain veiled in mystery to this day. Like the islands of memory, it only consists of shreds and patches of scattered images, thoughts, and feelings. Only the very brief and fleeting moments when he actually saw them together resurface to his everyday consciousness; they are like the glossy postcards from an island—where one cannot tell what is real or what is imagined.

As a young teenager, Obama seemed not to be cognizant that he did not have a live-in father or that his racial designation was different from that of his other family members. This double realization dawned on him only gradually during the years at the Punahou School and later while moving through the mainland from Los Angeles to New York and finally to Chicago. This realization eventually sent him on a journey to Africa in search of his real father. His interactions with writers like Frank Marshall Davis in Hawai'i added to his knowledge of the alienation of African Americans on the mainland.

Neil Abercrombie, who was a student at the University of Hawai'i with Barack Obama Sr., recalled their friendship very fondly. At a chance meeting with Barack in 2003 at Maya Soetoro's wedding, Abercrombie remembered the years gone by:

My mind flooded with thoughts of his African father and *haole*—Hawai'ian for Caucasian—mother from the mainland. I had met them at the University of Hawai'i in Honolulu, just after statehood in 1959. Barack's father was determined to be a part of the birth of a free Kenya, just as the civil rights movement his mother had championed was breaking through old boundaries in the United States, not the least of which was statehood for multicultural Hawai'i.

Now, here was their son speaking of a vision of hope in a changing world, the concept of community and family living in harmony, within our grasp if we would commit ourselves to it. I heard echoes of his parents' dreams of a renewed world in Barack's voice and words as he held the crowd with his vision. Not a speech, not ritual remarks, but a conversation unfolded, almost a series of intimate observations from a friend to an extended family. (Glauberman and Burris 2008, vi-vii)

Barack Obama Sr., according to many accounts, was a charismatic man who could hold the attention of a room full of people with his oratorical skills and inspiring ideas. James Patterson, a colleague of Obama's maternal grandmother, Madelyn Dunham, and whose parents hosted Obama Sr. for Thanksgiving dinners and Christmas holidays, described to me that his clipped British accent and dark complexion left many who met him simply awestruck. He was always a vocal member of the group and an active participant in the conversation, and with his pipe smoking he looked the part of a serious intellectual and an economist.

Abercrombie can still recall the long evenings spent over coffee and drinks at the Manoa campus, where students would gather in an informal group to engage in political discussions, never-ending debates, and philosophical ruminations. Both Obama Sr. and Ann Dunham were members of this group, and to many onlookers it was clear that the mixed-race couple was madly in love. Ann Dunham was drawn to his ideas, and he seemed enchanted with her youthful yet stoic beauty; they gravitated toward each other despite the push and pull of their different worldviews and despite the thousands of miles and the continents that separated their everyday social and cultural realities.

Trying to reconcile his parents' disparate worlds, Barack Obama would later write, "My father looked nothing like the people around me. That he was black as pitch, my mother white as milk, barely registered in my mind" (Obama 2004a, 10). His fair-skinned mother, who idolized his father, revealed to Barack that while he had inherited her eyebrows, his character and his brilliant mind had been inherited from his father. Similarly, his sister, Maya, who looked up to her big brother, concurred that Barack was the perfect combination of all his predecessors: his impulsive, iconoclastic, secular-humanist mother; his driven, charismatic, and tragic father; his pragmatic, businesslike maternal grandmother, who wrote the book on the escrow laws in the state of Hawai'i; and his grandfather, Stanley Dunham, a traveling salesman who was a bohemian at heart and yearned to be a poet.

From his father's side of the family, Obama inherited the soul of Africa, which allowed him direct but limited access to the African American history in the United States. From his mother's side of the family, Obama was offered the rest of the world, including a strong drive to change the world, to befriend strangers in different walks of life, and to value humanity in all kinds of people and places. The deeply layered Polynesian, multiracial, and multicultural context of Hawai'i pushed Obama along a path of a unique liberal-arts education, imbued with ethical values and a naturally occurring course of development. As his wife, Michelle, has commented, "You can't really understand Barack until you understand Hawai'i" (Glauberman and Burris 2008, 1); and I would echo this point with the claim that Indonesia also played a critical role in Obama's family life, early development, and in the shaping of his worldview.

Contextual Complexities

Obama's unique perspective on the world was an outgrowth of his life in Hawai'i and to a significant degree Indonesia, an upbringing that formed the basis of his hybrid cultural identity. He admitted to this when he described his socialization as an Indonesian child, a Hawai'ian child, a black child, and a white child; these multiple cultures shaped his early self and conditioned his preferences and dislikes (Mendell 2007). In Hawai'i, Barack Obama lived in a multiethnic and multicultural society that was economically developed, and in Indonesia he was exposed to a multireligious yet fairly secular society in the early stages of economic development but with high levels of poverty.

The coordinates of Obama's life in Hawai'i were defined by the five-block radius around Punahou Circle apartments, where his grandparents decided to settle to facilitate Barack Obama's education. Although the apartment, near the heart of Honolulu's commercial district, is an ordinary-looking structure made of concrete and glass, it is surrounded by a residential area that has many parks, playgrounds, and leafy green streets. From his 10th-floor apartment, Barack could see the path he would walk for the next eight years on his way to the Punahou School, the elite preparatory school where his grandfather got him admitted. When I visited the apartment building, I was impressed by the modest surroundings and its clean, open, and residential appeal.

Sara Lin has reported that in 1971, when Obama moved into this area, Honolulu had undergone a real estate boom. "Many of the clapboard plantation-style cottages had been bulldozed and replaced by concrete cinderblock walkups two and three stories high with open walkways, private lanais and louvered glass windows. By the late '60s, high-rise buildings were starting to muscle their way in" (Lin 2008). Barack Obama's grandparents moved into one of these buildings on Beretania Street and Punahou Street to be near the Punahou School and his grandmother's workplace.

His grandmother rented a one-bedroom apartment for nearly four decades, until her death two days before the national election. "Wellwishers left leis made of flowers, maile leaves and yarn and a strand of origami cranes in her building's lobby in remembrance" (Lin 2008). The apartment now has a colorful window display in the lobby to commemorate the childhood residence of the 44th president, but there are no descendants of the Dunham or the Obama family living at this location any longer.

On the islands of Hawai'i, a young person's emerging identity is defined by the high school he or she attends. Obama may not have known it at the time, but the Punahou School would turn out to be an immeasurable gift, especially for a growing boy who did not have a live-in father or a stable, traditional family structure. Punahou shaped Obama's emerging mind and provided a richly nuanced social and cultural influence in his early years. At Punahou, Obama melded into the background and seems to have fit into the Punahou family. His color did not seem to make a difference to anyone because everyone was of a different color and hue: "We're all different but it does not make a difference," Obama's homeroom teacher Eric Kusonoki told me during one of my visits to the school.

Obama may have been one of the few black children in the school, but this would not have been an obstacle because there were no overarching or long-standing stereotypes about blacks on the islands. In the setting of Punahou School, Obama would learn the fundamental lessons of life through community service, ethics, multiculturalism, and rough-and-tumble competition on the basketball field. These lessons he would carry with him to the mainland and to a public service career.

The elite prep school has a well-deserved reputation in Hawai'i as the toughest and the best school for young and growing minds. When I toured the campus and wanted to interview some of Obama's educators, I felt I was walking through a college campus. I could easily imagine how Obama, having been schooled in such a high-minded environment, wished for an Ivy League education at Columbia or Harvard; he had been groomed for it by his mother, his grandparents, and the social milieu at Punahou School.

The imposing physical structures—the large athletic fields and the well-paved driveways with guarded security posts where golf carts transported officials from one end of the campus to another—all conveyed a kind of stability and permanence. The sense of time and place seemed to stand still; it allowed for the fine tuning of the mental and ethical behavior so that young minds could reach their fullest potential. Smaller, more modest schools simply do not possess such a supportive and facilitating environment. Indeed, for more than 150 years the Punahou School has been the school that islanders have both admired and envied for its rich cultural history, deep financial resources, and well-connected network that affords access to the best jobs on the islands.

For many graduates, the Punahou School represented a ticket to a higher social and business standing. All of this was costly, however, and Obama's mother had to rely on her parents for some of the funding. It was the Dunham family's collective wish to send Barack Obama to a reputable and stable institution of learning, something not possible in Jakarta at the time on Ann Dunham's limited salary, that sent Barack on a return journey to Hawai'i. In this respect, the family that raised Obama put him on the path to success and set his sights even higher.

"In 1971, Barry's mother wisely sent him back to Hawai'i to live with his maternal grandparents," wrote Endy Bayuni, a chief editor of the *Jakarta Post*. However, his childhood in Jakarta added depth and dimensionality to his experience. He learned to live with and respect different cultural and religious traditions, and this may have prepared him for his return to the United States, where race continued to divide people (Bayuni 2009).

In Indonesia, Barack Obama spent less than two years in a government-run Islamic school and almost three years at a Catholic school as part of his elementary education. "In the Muslim school, the teacher wrote to tell my mother that I made faces during Koranic studies. My mother was not overly concerned. 'Be respectful,' she said" (Obama 2004a, 154). While discussing his experience in the Catholic school, underscoring his secular upbringing and outlook, he observed, "When it came time to pray, I would pretend to close my eyes then peek around the room. Nothing happened. No angels descended; just a parched old nun and thirty brown children, muttering words" (Obama 2004a, 154).

Biographers have been at odds over the amount of time Barack Obama spent at the Islamic school when he lived in Jakarta (Corsi 2008). Much of this speculation has been politically motivated, however, generating heated debates on both sides of the political aisle about whether he spent one year or two years there. It seems clear, however, from Obama's autobiography that he spent at least one full year in a secular public school that required Islamic religious instruction for part of the school day. During this period he may have learned to recite the daily Islamic prayer, which he has praised as one of the prettiest religious prayers (Kristoff 2007).

The more important question has not been fully addressed by biographers, but it never seems to fade away. Was Obama raised as a Muslim child in Indonesia? His stepfather was a Muslim, and in the school's registration documents Barack's name was listed as Barry Soetoro. A close friend from that period, Zulfan Adi, has said, "His mother often went to church, but Barry was a Muslim. I remember him wearing a sarong" (Watson 2007). A teacher named Israella Darmawan, who taught him in the first grade, has confirmed, "At that time, Barry was also praying in a Catholic way, but Barry was a Muslim. . . . He was registered as a Muslim because his father, Lolo Soetoro, was a Muslim" (Watson 2007).

Another classmate, Rony Amir, who was tracked down by reporters in Jakarta, has claimed that Barack used to spend time in the prayer room close to their house on Haji Ramli Street, in the Menteng Dalam area of Jakarta. He used to wear the sarong and because his body was chubby he was perceived as funny by his friends. He was darker and had a different type of hair, but in other ways he did not differ from the other children in Menteng Dalam. He liked football and playing marbles but the only thing that was different was that he was an American child with a darker skin (Siddiqui 2007; Pipes 2008).

Reporter Nadhifa Putri found a slightly different variation of the same story. She explained that Barack lived "his life in the middle of Muslims. . . . Barry had a funny face and his friends made fun of him by putting a sarong on him even though he didn't pray. . . . The emphasis here is that even though Barry was a Muslim and was in the mosque and was wearing Islamic clothes, that he was only 'playing' and not really 'praying'" (Putri 2008).

This is some of the evidence that is produced to argue that Obama might have been raised as a Muslim, but where is the conclusive evidence that would constitute his childhood conversion to Islam, something that would make him a true believer? At the time he was admitted to the St. Francis Assisi School his religious affiliation may have been specified as Muslim, but does that make him a believer and a true Muslim? The school administrators at the St. Francis Assisi School told me that they did not do any background checks on his religious affiliation or his legal adoption by his stepfather; they are not required by law to conduct such background checks. They took his stepfather's religion as prima facie evidence that Obama was a Muslim because his name and religion were in accordance with his stepfather's name. And there was no rule against a Muslim child attending the Catholic school.

His stepfather practiced a brand of Islam that Barack Obama has said "could make room for the remnants of more ancient animist and Hindu faiths," which is fairly common in Indonesia. "[Lolo] explained that a man took on the powers of whatever he ate: one day soon, he promised, he would bring home a piece of tiger meat for us to share" (Obama 2004aa, 37). Clearly, his stepfather was a liberal Muslim with a rather secular outlook. There seems to be no hard evidence to suggest that Obama ever converted to the Islamic faith. Neither is there any evidence to suggest he ever went through any religious ritual—a naming ceremony, a circumcision, or a rite of passage—not even a simple ceremony where he took on his stepfather's name. Furthermore, his half-sister, Maya, has confirmed for me that her brother was never legally adopted by her father during the years he lived with them.

What is undisputed, however, is that from the age of five to ten years, young Barack Obama's role model was Lolo Soetoro. Soetoro tried hard to fill the shoes of his stepson's absent Kenyan father. He instructed Barack Obama in the skills of boxing as a form of self-defense, taught him how to fend for himself, and showed him how to enjoy different kinds of carnivorous meals that included snake and tiger meat. Barack Obama was a good student and learned what it meant to be a strong man.

Lolo Soetoro explained to him that people take advantage of any sign of weakness in others, and this is the way weak nations are manipulated and abused by stronger nations. "The strong man takes the weak man's land and forces him to work in his fields. If the weak man's woman is pretty, the strong man will take her for his own. What kind of a man did Obama want to become?" asked Lolo.

At the time Barack had no answers, according to John Meacham, the presidential biographer and *Newsweek* reporter, "but in a way Obama's whole life has been a reply to the question Soetoro posed four decades and half a world away, in the dusty heat of Jakarta after the boxing lesson" (Meacham 2008). When asked about this event recently, Obama said he remembered it vividly and that his stepfather was a decent and hard-working man, who passed on some very helpful lessons to him. One of the things I learned from him was a stark and hardheaded view of how the world worked, Obama said (Meacham 2008).

During my trip to Jakarta, I walked through the backyard where Obama learned the skills of boxing. Now tucked behind a concrete wall and a fence, what remains of the backyard is a small piece of land, hemmed in by urban-style homes on all four sides, half-paved roads, and open sanitation lines. I walked to and from Obama's childhood home to the local mosque, Masjid-al-Mubarak, with his former classmate and friend Yunaldi Askiar. In the narrow side streets and back alleys, Obama would run with his friends and classmates to the grocer, to the local butcher shop, and to the mosque for Friday prayers accompanied by his stepfather.

Barack's home life in Indonesia was like a page from Kipling's *The Jungle Book*, and he was filled with vivid memories of encounters with wild animals and colorful characters. In Jakarta he was introduced to the giant Hanuman, the Hindu monkey god with supernatural powers. He also had a pet ape named Tata, whom Lolo had brought from Papua New Guinea. He lived with a jungle of animals in Lolo's backyard zoo, including "chickens and ducks, running every which way, a big yellow dog with a baleful howl, two birds of paradise, a white cockatoo, and finally two baby crocodiles, half-submerged in a fenced-off pond toward the edge of the compound" (Obama 2004a, 34).

On his recent trip to Jakarta in November 2010, Obama reflected on those enchanting days. He said Jakarta's landscape is now completely changed; the only landmark he recognized was a high-rise shopping mall, Serena. "I learned to love Indonesia while flying kites, running along paddy fields, catching dragonflies, and buying satay and baso from the street vendors. Most of all, I remember the people—the old men and women who welcomed us with smiles; the children who made a foreigner feel like a neighbor; and the teachers who helped me learn about the wider world," reminisced Obama (Obama 2010). Young Indonesians are now communicating on their cell phones and Blackberries and are connected with the rest of the world. Obama did remember his stepfather fondly as a strong military man and reminded his audience that his Indonesian half-sister, Maya, was born there (Nurbaiti 2010).

In his autobiography, Obama goes on to describe his Javanese stepfather in more detail. One day when Lolo wanted to buy a rooster from a street vendor and take it home for dinner, Ann objected to her son's witnessing the decapitation, but the stepfather insisted that Obama witness it. Reminiscent of the denouement of an Indonesian cockfight made famous by the anthropologist Clifford Geertz (1977), the street vendor proceeded to butcher the bird. As Obama described it:

> I watched the man set the bird down, pinning it gently under one knee and pulling its neck out across a narrow gutter. For a moment the bird struggled, beating its wings hard against the ground, a few feathers dancing up with the wind. Then it grew completely still. The man pulled the blade across the bird's neck in a single smooth motion. Blood shot out in a long, crimson ribbon. . . . Lolo rubbed his hand across my head and told me and my mother to go wash up before dinner. . . . Later, lying alone beneath a mosquito net canopy, I listened to the crickets chirp under the moonlight and remembered the last twitch of life that I'd witnessed a few hours before. (Obama 2004a, 51–52)

Cockfighting offers a unique window on Indonesian life. The bird that loses the fight symbolizes life and death and is slaughtered at the ring. The Indonesian male temperament is on full display at the cockfight, akin to Spanish men at bullfighting arenas. What is portrayed in both Obama's description and Geertz's description is the theme popularized by Hemingway's novels that life is worth fighting for when challenged. According to anthropologists, the popularity of the sports like Indonesian cockfighting reveals the male obsession with blood, masculinity, and power. Thus, the episode described here may have been a screen memory related to some of the oedipal lessons Barack Obama had learned from his stepfather.

In the flux of changing identities, Obama began to peel away the layers of his emerging social reality, much like one would remove a decorated Indonesian mask. Once when he accompanied his mother to the American embassy, where she was employed, Obama recalled working on his homework in the library and coming across an article in *Life* magazine that caught his attention. It was about a skin pigmentation treatment that altered the complexion of a dark elderly man. We know from psychological research that small children are aware of race and skin color at an early age, as early as three years old, and for Obama learning that such treatments existed may have been a stunning and devastating revelation (Ausdale 2002).

Although this story may also be a screen memory for deeper traumatic events occurring in Obama's life, it has been criticized by several biographers as apocryphal (Corsi 2008) and possibly borrowed from an event described in Franz Fanon's *Black Skin, White Masks* (1967) and possibly other African American literary sources. However, it does not change the narrative fact that Obama may have become aware of his budding racial identity for the first time in the highly diverse environment of Indonesia, while attending a mosque with his stepfather or playing in the streets of Jakarta with kids who did not look like him.

The other important fact that Obama seems to have grasped during this period was an appreciation of having a live-in father, not a remote father who lives in a distant land. As Obama spent increasingly more time with Lolo Soetoro, his social world began to expand; he was slipping away from his mother's cocoon and into the larger social milieu. Psychoanalyst Avner Falk (2010) claims that Obama's memories of racial awareness may hide a trauma generated from the birth of his sister, Maya Soeoro-Ng. Possibly, his awareness of racial identity may have masked yet even deeper anxieties related to the tension between his mother and stepfather or their disagreements about involvement with American oil businessmen, which has been well documented in Obama's autobiography.

These screen memories hearkened back to the same period when Americans were making inroads into the Indonesian economy and government, a source of deep tension for his mother's plans for her career. She resented the encroachment of American business in Indonesia and may have become an anthropologist and a development aid expert as a result. She may have deeply resented Lolo Soetoro's turning into a profiteering businessman overnight, which eventually contributed to their separation and divorce.

One night, Barack Obama returned home with a large gaping cut on his arm that he had received from playing on a mud slide that hurtled him into a barbed wire fence. His mother had a wake-up call that her son might be slipping away from her. Ann wanted to immediately take him to the hospital, but it was late at night and there was no public transportation available. Furthermore, Lolo did not wish to be disturbed from his sleep. Because she feared the wound might become infected, Ann decided not to delay going to the hospital and took Barack in an auto rickshaw.

When they arrived at the hospital, the doctors were busy playing cards and did not want to tend to the patient, though they eventually treated the badly wounded boy after much delay. It was partly due to this event that his mother returned Barack to the safety of his grandparents' home in Hawai'i, where he would be enrolled at the Punahou School; Obama was only 10 years old.

Having lived with the mass of humanity on the heavily trafficked streets of Jakarta, including hordes of children begging for money and food, Obama realized that although he had not enjoyed a Norman Rockwell childhood, he was nevertheless fortunate enough to have had an extended American family. In a 2004 interview, Obama revealed that his time in Indonesia made him value the blessings afforded to him as an American citizen. Furthermore, he acknowledged the powerful role of fate in the lives of children where one child can end up wealthy and another extremely poor (Mendell 2007).

American Extended Family

Young Barack's extended family included his grandparents from Kansas, Stanley and Madelyn Dunham, who had lived through the Great Depression and tended to be more politically conservative. They could afford to send him to the best private school in Hawai'i because his grandmother, Madelyn Dunham, had risen from the job of secretary to become vice president at the Bank of Hawai'i. Dennis Ching, who worked with her for more than 20 years, told me that in the late 1960s, when Madelyn became vice president, the management of the bank consisted of a small network of conservative, elite men, most of whom were white. For a woman such as Madelyn to succeed in a heavily male-dominated environment, she had to be very tough.

Obama's gritty pragmatism, which he acquired from his grandmother, has been pivotal to his success. He credits her for giving him the spine to take on big challenges. Before Obama became a United States senator from Illinois, Madelyn said in an interview (Mendell 2007) that her grandson might have pursued international law or possibly become a judge rather than enter the dirty business of politics. She was a self-made woman, who had big dreams for her grandson despite her own lack of formal education. We know from psychological research that children adopt life's enduring lessons from what their parents and grandparents actually do, and not from what they often preach (Baumrind 1966, 1967). Thus, although Obama inherited his mother's progressive vision and idealism, it was his hard-knuckled grandmother who gave him his steely spine.

Dennis Ching recalled Madelyn Dunham as a stern boss who wrote the book on escrow laws in the state of Hawai'i; "I used to be afraid of her," he said. But she showed her softer side at home with Stanley and at social gatherings; at these times, she was totally feminine. The Dunhams attended Ching's wedding, he recalled with a fond smile. Ching also remembered meeting Barack Obama on several occasions when Barack was around 10 or 11 years old; Barack would come to his grandmother's office and do his homework there. Once the 10-year-old tried to teach Ching how to do the escrow calculations his grandmother had taught him. "I didn't listen to him then, but I would listen to him now," said Ching jokingly. His grandfather used to pick Barack up from the bank and take him home and to other after-school activities. Ching has no recollection of ever meeting Obama's mother as she was either traveling or living in Indonesia.

In the midst of the 2008 presidential campaign, Obama flew nearly 5,000 miles, from Chicago to Honolulu, to visit his grandmother on her 86th birthday because he feared she might not live to see the election. His voyage was a reminder of his biracial heritage, the extended family who had raised him, and the long distance he had traveled in life. Madelyn Dunham was the rock, Obama's foundation, notwithstanding the cast of characters that floated in and out of his life—his Kenyan father who abandoned him, his anthropologist mother who was busy doing fieldwork, his stepfather who was his companion for four years, and his bohemian grandfather who was perpetually searching for a new venture.

Madelyn Dunham was the down-to-earth person, "from where I get my practical streak," said Obama. "She's the one who taught me about hard work, who put off buying a new car or a new dress so I could have a better life, and the one who poured everything she had into me" (Barnes 2008). But Toot, as Barack called her (short for *tutu*, the Hawai'ian word for grandparent), was a virtually unknown figure in her grandson's onstage political life. In a somewhat dramatic fashion, as she bid farewell to this world on November 3, 2008, her early vote might have been the most important vote cast on Obama's behalf. News of her death came one day before the election and one week after Obama interrupted his White House campaign to return to Hawai'i for a final good-bye. At her passing, Obama and his sister released a statement: "She was the cornerstone of our family, and a woman of extraordinary accomplishment, strength and humility. She was the person who encouraged and allowed us to take chances" (Usborn 2008).

Stanley Armor Dunham, a World War II veteran, was Barack's constant male companion from age 10 to 18, and on several occasions he reprimanded young Barack for experimenting with drugs during adolescence. "Gramps" as Obama referred to him, was a traveling salesman and a life insurance agent "who could sell the legs off a couch" (Pickler 2008). In his autobiography, Obama reported that his grandfather was a bohemian at heart and that "it was this desire of his to obliterate the past, this confidence in the possibility of remaking the world from whole cloth, that proved to be his most enduring patrimony" (Obama 2004a, 21).

Stanley's friend and colleague Rolf Nordahl, who worked with him at the Williamson Insurance Agency, recalled the day Stanley asked him, "Ever seen the movie, *Guess Who's Coming to Dinner*? Well, I lived it," he said. Stanley told Rolf the story of his daughter marrying Barack Obama Sr. and told him about his grandson, who was now living with him and his wife; the Dunhams sacrificed a lot because they saw in Barack an intelligence and curiosity that warranted a good education. "He's smart and he has a heart; Barry could be president one day," Stanley would boldly claim on several occasions on the fourth floor office of the insurance agency (Nordahl 2008, 130).

At a rally in Kansas, as at many rallies across the country, Obama informed a group of reporters that his grandfather was a "wild child" in his youth and that he had married his high school sweetheart from nearby Augusta, Kansas, despite the objections and consternation of both their families (Pickler 2008). Barack's grandfather went to college on the GI Bill after World War II; and his grandmother, who had stayed in Wichita during the war, worked on a bomber assembly line while raising their only daughter, Stanley Ann.

What is less well-known about Stanley Dunham is that at the center of his life was a trauma, a significant trauma that may have affected the course of his life. When Stanley Dunham was eight years old his mother committed suicide, and he was the one who found the body (Meacham 2008; Obama 2004a). His young mother, 26 years old at the time, "had written a letter saying she had taken poison because her husband no longer loved her, the newspaper reported" (Scott 2011, 22).

This event may have given the young man a restless temperament and the constant need to be on the move from one town to another. Shortly after losing his mother, Stanley's father abandoned the family, forcing Stanley and his brother Ralph to move in with their maternal grandparents, not unlike Barack Obama. The intergenerational pattern between the kind of restlessness Stanley Dunham displayed in his youth and the kind his daughter, Ann, would later make her professional lifestyle is rather striking.

The African side of Obama's family also included some fierce trailblazers. His paternal grandfather, Hussein Onyango Obama, had traveled the world while working as a cook on British naval ships. Onyango was known for his stern, authoritarian, and English manners; his children and grandchildren nicknamed him "Terror" (Obama 2004a). The grandfather was not only a cook but also a farmer, a medicine man, and a respected elder in the Luo tribe. He had fought in the Mau Mau rebellion for Kenya's independence and had been imprisoned for approximately two years.

Onyango was an animist by virtue of his birth into a Luo tribe, but he had converted to Christianity for a brief period and had taken the name Johnson. Somehow Christianity did not suit his temperament, so he then converted to Islam. He took the name Hussein and was circumcised according to custom. Onyango practiced polygamy, which is the most common form of marriage and kinship pattern in Kenya. He had been married at least four times, and one of his wives was a white woman whom he had met while serving on British naval ships in Burma.

Barack Obama's father, Obama Sr., was born the son of Onyango's second wife, Akumu, who left her husband for another man and moved to another village when Barack Obama's father was only nine years old. Thus, Barack Obama's father was raised by Granny Sarah, Onyango's third wife; this is the paternal grandmother Barack Obama has visited on his trips to Kenya. The early abandonment was a source of considerable pain and sorrow for Barack Obama Sr., which may have deeply shaped his personality from a young age. Thus, as a father he would more than once abandon his own children, including, most notably, the boy who would go on to become president of the United States. Again, the intergenerational pattern of early loss in his father's life was passed on to Barack Obama, and it affected his life and destiny.

Unlike his predecessors, the 44th president of the United States has a starkly different lineage and genealogy. At his inaugural ceremony,

President Obama was surrounded by the different branches of his family tree, a lineage that would have been unimaginable in the more than 200 years since the birth of this nation. In a rapidly changing world, where allegiances can be short-lived, it is refreshing to see a person with roots planted in different parts of the world.

As a reporter from the *New York Times* observed, the union of Barack and Michelle Obama truly brought together the colors of the American rainbow: "black and white and Asian, Christian, Muslim and Jewish. They speak English; Indonesian; French; Cantonese; German; Hebrew; African languages including Swahili, Luo and Igbo; and even a few phrases of Gullah, the Creole dialect of the South Carolina Lowcountry" (Kantor 2009a). The Obamas have not inherited any great wealth, do not boast lineage to any kings or queens, and only a generation ago were quite poor. Thus, as Americans celebrated the inauguration of the first African American president, the world had many reasons to join in celebrating the first global president. Not unlike the human family tree, the genealogical narrative of the Obama clan, with all its twists and turns, has multicultural roots and includes great migratory journeys, testing the limits of the human spirit.

Thus, Barack Obama's story is a quintessentially heroic saga of an American family, emerging from the depths of the American psyche or soul, the same cultural crucible that has given rise to American individualism and democracy. Above all, it extols the American virtue of upward social mobility, determination against all the odds, and "the refusal to follow the tracks put down by history, religion, or parentage." As Maya Soetoro-Ng described, "Our family is new in terms of the White House, but I don't think it's new in terms of the country. . . . I don't think the White House has always reflected the textures and flavors of this country" (Kantor 2009).

Yet, Obama's genealogical history from his mother's side of the family is every bit as American as that of some of the earlier presidents; as Obama used to jest during the campaign, he is a distant cousin of the previous vice president, Dick Cheney (Wade 2007). Obama's American ancestors can be traced back to earlier historical eras: they were abolitionists, they were Midwesterners who lived through the Great Depression, and a few of them even fought in the Revolutionary War. Obama's wife, Michelle, on the other hand, "is the descendant of slaves and the daughter of the Great Migration," the mass exodus of African Americans to the north in search of greater freedom and jobs during the first half of the 20th century (Kantor 2009a).

In this unique melding of culture, history, race, and ethnicity not seen in other developed or socially democratic societies, the Obama presidency symbolizes its global reach. If we realize that Obama is indeed half-Kenyan, "not the seed, but the flower of the civil rights movement" (Dowd 2008b), only a generation removed from his father, who landed in Hawai'i with a "funny sounding name" less than a half century earlier, we may be able to actualize the promise of the Obama generation.

3

Women Who Shaped Obama

A man who has been the indisputable favorite of his mother keeps for life the feeling of a conqueror, that confidence of his success that often induces real success.

Sigmund Freud (1957)

Not surprisingly, a number of presidents' mothers seem to have done everything right....In studying presidents, one trend is hard to ignore. Many had very strong relationships with their mothers ... they are almost without exceptions mama's boys.

Doug Wead (2005)

Shelby Steele, a senior fellow at Stanford University's Hoover Institute, has convincingly argued that Obama was caught between the two classic postures black men have typically adopted to make their way in American society: bargaining and challenging. Bargainers offer a bargain to white Americans that tacitly states, "I will not force America's history of racism upon you if my race is not held against me." Challengers use the reverse strategy; they hold whites responsible for inherent racism and demand that they propitiate their white guilt by supporting black causes and policies.

In *A Bound Man*, Steele maintained that Barack Obama's political persona has been constrained by these historically situated dynamics; thus, he cannot really find his true political voice. "Obama has the temperament, intelligence, and background—an interracial family, a sterling education—to guide America beyond the exhausted racial politics that now prevail. And yet he is a Promethean figure, a bound man" (Steele 2007, 1).

Because of these historical dynamics, Steele claimed that Obama would lose a national election against John McCain, which of course turned out to be wrong. However, several political commentators and legal scholars would at least partly agree with Steele's claim that Obama played the role of a nonchallenging bargainer as opposed to a threatening black man. These scholars also claim that Obama deftly deployed his feminine personality to win over not only the white American voters but especially the white women's vote.

Relying less on a stereotypical masculine or black male persona, Steele's challenging type, Obama took on the role of the gentler black man, the professor or the teacher, the Sidney Poitier–like image from the film *To Sir, with Love*. Frank Cooper, a professor at Suffolk Law School, has suggested the idea of the "bipolar black masculinity" to understand Barack Obama during the campaign, especially in his dealings with white female candidates. "The media tends to represent black men as either the completely threatening and race-affirming Bad Black Man or the completely comforting and assimilated Good Black Man. For Obama, this meant he had to avoid the stereotype of the angry black man," stated Cooper (2009, 633). He called Obama's performance "unisexual" for drawing on his feminine side, which has far-reaching implications for the dialogue on race and gender in America.

Ann McGinley, a professor of Law at the University of Nebraska, also agrees that Obama walked the tightrope of gender and race during the 2008 campaign, tactically deploying his "cool," empathic, and listening style as part of his feminized black identity routine. As a counterpoint, his female opponents, Hillary Clinton and Sarah Palin, had to appear to be macho and put on a hypermasculine performance to stay in the long, drawn-out campaign. Obama, on the other hand, simply could not risk appearing too hard, too masculine, or too black (McGinley 2009).

We know from psychology, specifically from men's psychology, that a man's feminine side is partly a composite image of the long-term interactions with the important women in his life. Barack Obama, of course, was raised by several strong women who sent him on his path-breaking journey. In myths, as in real life, the hero must integrate the powers of the great woman protagonists at the center of his life. The role of the great goddess in hero myths from a variety of cultures remains uncontested (Campbell 1949; Jung 1956; Neumann 1972).

Obama's life has been shaped principally by three strong women, namely his mother, grandmother, and wife. The voices and visions of these three women guide Obama's innermost self. Although Obama has had several important surrogate father-figures, his grandfather, his Indonesian stepfather, literary mentors like Frank Marshall Davis, and his pastor

Reverend Wright, they have never fully measured up to the ideal image of his biological father lodged in his heart and mind. Thus, the women in Obama's inner world have by far had the strongest influence on shaping his destiny. Because of these three women, all of whom originally came from the Midwest, Obama established his roots in the Midwest and displays the personality traits that he is now famous for—progressive idealism, pragmatism, and a steely determination.

Though Obama's autobiography, *Dreams from My Father*, is principally concerned with father loss, it is no coincidence that it is also a reflective meditation on race, Chicago, and Kenya; it shows Obama's personality before he became a politician (Obama 2004a). His later book, *The Audacity of Hope*, dedicated to the key women in his life, is an overtly political book focused on emotions like hope, faith, and trust as well as the fundamentals of the American dream, which he acquired in his family and communities in Hawai'i, Indonesia, and Chicago (Obama 2006).

A Humanist Mother

Ann Dunham, the most consistent influence during the first 10 years of Obama's life, has been described by many as a secular humanist, a feminist, and an anthropologist. She played all of these roles publicly. However, in her personal life with her family and friends she was a mother, wife, friend, and teacher. She believed in improving people's lives. The decisive force of her personality was a progressive impulse to bring about positive change in people's economic well-being and living standards by affecting their cultural worlds. She seemed particularly concerned with people in different, exotic, and far-off cultures and devoted her life to empowering those at the bottom strata of society.

One of the enduring legacies Barack Obama inherited from his mother was the progressive heart and soul of America. She influenced him greatly. "He learned from her that if you did the right things in the local cultures with everyday people that over time you could a make positive difference in people's lives," said Alice Dewey, Ann Dunham's mentor and colleague.

Kay Ikranagara, another close friend of Ann Dunham, who watched Barack Obama grow up in Jakarta, told me that because he has lived in many different cultures he is able to listen to and relate to people from diverse backgrounds. Ann Dunham is the only mother of a president who was an anthropologist, someone who worked for international development agencies most of her professional life and tried to enhance the cultural survival of local populations. I argue in this chapter that Ann Dunham was ahead of her times socially and intellectually; she was a progressive and pragmatic visionary who imparted to Barack Obama the values and the worldview needed for America to succeed in the 21st century. She may have also given him the impetus to become the first black president.

Alice Dewey said, "Ann Dunham was becoming well-known in her own right and getting recognized for her development work before she passed away. She worked till the very last days from her sick bed, calling and emailing Bank Rakyat Indonesia in Jakarta, to ensure her projects were on track." Almost a year before her death, Ann Dunham had prepared her organization to attend the United Nations' conference on women in Beijing, where Hillary Clinton—then first lady—was the keynote speaker (Moore 2009). Ann did not make it to the conference, however, as she was struggling with the last bouts of cancer.

Bronwen Solyom, the art historian at the University of Hawai'i, who also worked in Indonesia with Ann Dunham, told me in an interview that Ann did not have any particular theory of social capital and economic justice. She was really interested in people; she was a humanitarian. Although she wrote a thousand-page doctoral dissertation on economic anthropology, she was inspired by reformers like Mahatma Gandhi and Martin Luther King Jr., the proponents of nonviolent social change.

Ann Dunham's passion for working with the rural poor in Indonesia was founded on her belief in equality and the civil rights movement; her choices in life partners were also a reflection of this commitment. Barack Obama literally grew up in the field. When Ann Dunham traveled around the islands of Indonesia and to other cultures, both Barack and his sister, Maya, often accompanied her.

There is a well-known picture of Barack as a toddler in Ann Dunham's arms—he is sitting on the fence with his back turned toward her, smiling contentedly at the camera. Ann is holding Barack and admiring him, scaffolding his body with her strong arms, while he is boldly taking on the world, as every toddler is naturally inclined to do. The image conveys unconditional love, support, and affection, key to a mother-son bond. As Freud has famously said, a child who is his mother's favorite can conquer any task in life; Obama has certainly been a testament to this psychological dictum.

As young children we are all shaped by strong, godlike parental influences: the image and voice of a mother and the guiding touch of a father. At the root, most social actions stem from the underlying parental influences that are an amalgamation of biological, cultural, and political conditioning. In Obama's case, given the absence of a live-in father, the conditions of his early upbringing and self-development were shaped by his mother. At the center of Obama's self is a mother's voice—"the single constant in my life" (Obama 2004, xii). The importance of this developmental fact cannot be underestimated, and it has also been seen in the lives of other important presidents, such as Abraham Lincoln, whose stepmother was his ardent supporter, and Franklin Delano Roosevelt, whose mother was obsessively concerned about her son's welfare even after he was a grown man.

When Obama speaks about social justice, equality, and concern for the downtrodden, he instinctively echoes his mother's progressive voice. Ann Dunham grew into a woman of significant intellectual strength and vision, a romantic at heart but levelheaded. She also had a way of involving herself in complicated life situations, but then managing to work her way out. Driven by unique strengths and blind spots, Dunham was the embodiment of what the French accept as the *celebration de la difference.* She embodied these unique qualities and traits due in part to her early socialization and often marched to the beat of a different drummer.

Ann, born in Kansas in 1942, was the only child of a couple who lived through the Great Depression. She was named Stanley Ann Dunham after her father, Stanley Armour Dunham, who had wanted a son; this may have created some lasting confusion about her sex and identity. Ann may have been driven to rebel against her father's directives at the disappointing realization that in his eyes she was the "second sex" (de Beauvoir 1989).

The preoccupation with son preference prevalent in underdeveloped and developing economies is a holdover from an agrarian mode of adaptation, where boys are highly valued as human labor. In Ann Dunham's case, her father's preoccupation with having a son may have been due to the lingering aftereffect of World War II, where a whole generation of young men and boys had died. As a veteran of the war, Stanley may have deeply wished for a son, but to give his daughter his masculine name may suggest other issues perhaps related to a narcissistic personality stemming from an early trauma, that is, the suicidal death of his mother at a young age.

However, Ann Dunham's drive to rebel and break free from her domineering father may have significantly shaped her path; and this motivation may have been much more forceful in the 1960s than we can imagine today in the post-1970s liberal feminist era (Collins 2009). Her biographer documents a telling episode that captures this underlying psychological drive. In the fall of 1959, Ann was only 17 years old when she took off on a late-night escapade in a Cadillac with her high school friend, Bill Byers. They decided to keep driving south because school was awful and there was no point in going home. Ann and Byers, who recounted the event 50 years later, ended up in San Francisco and had to be hauled back by the local juvenile authorities. "There is a temptation to see in the midnight road trip a foreshadowing of events yet to come in Stanley Ann's life. It certainly suggests a willingness to take a risk, an aptitude that flows, like a leitmotif, through the history of the Dunhams and the Paynes" (Scott 2011, 70).

Despite her midwestern Kansas roots, Ann felt at home in exotic far-off cultures like Hawai'i and Indonesia, where she spent most of her adult life. Though naturally shy, bordering on being innocent and nerdy, as described by her daughter, Maya (Ripley 2008), Ann took big risks with her life, and only some paid off before her untimely death at age 52 from ovarian and cervical cancer.

Amanda Ripley, a reporter from *Time* magazine described Ann Dunham as a bundle of contradictions: "Each of us lives a life of contradictory truths. We are not one thing or another. Barack Obama's mother was at least a dozen things. S. Ann Soetoro [Stanley Ann Dunham Obama-Soetoro] was a teen mother who later got a Ph.D. in anthropology; a white woman from the Midwest who was more comfortable in Indonesia; a natural-born mother obsessed with her work; a romantic pragmatist, if such a thing is possible" (Ripley 2008).

In no small measure because of Ann we can see some of the same traits in Barack Obama as well: he is cerebral and aloof, yet pragmatic with an idealistic streak. He is a self-made man of many parts, with multiple selves all competing with each other—part African and part American, part Hawai'ian and part Midwesterner, lawyer, writer, teacher, and community organizer—yet an all-American politician, held together and pushed upward by his faith in the universal ideals of freedom and democracy.

A closer look at young Barack's upbringing indicates that his late mother, who went on to live the life of a social activist and an academic, had a big hand in shaping the budding personality of this president. Although he may have inherited his Kenyan father's oratory skills and eloquence, it was his mother who gave him the gift of language and tutored him in English for four hours each morning before sending him off to school. In these early experiences of love and care, Obama learned the rhythm and discipline of daily life. At times when he did not want to wake up and study, she would nudge him repeatedly, reminding him, "This is not easy for me either, buster" (Obama 2004a, 48).

Interestingly, the person who shaped Obama's early self and sent him on his path-breaking journey is the one we know very little about. Amanda Ripley says this is "because being African in America is still seen as being simply black and color is still a preoccupation above almost all else" (Ripley 2008). There is not enough room in the story about his mother's struggle due in part to Obama's own reticence and his ambivalence in talking about his mother.

President Obama has openly admitted that he has not defined the coordinates of his life based on his mother's nomadic lifestyle. Whereas Ann was known for taking her children around the world to live in foreign lands, Barack Obama has sought stability. This is perhaps most clearly reflected in his choice of a life partner and soul mate. Michelle Obama is a woman who, in all appearances, may have had very little in common with her late mother-in-law.

Maya has concurred, "I would say Michelle is much more like our grandmother" (Scott 2011, 296). When Ann met Michelle for the first time during a Christmas vacation, she wrote to her friend Julia Suryakusuma in Jakarta: "She is intelligent, very tall (6'1"), not beautiful but quite attractive . . . a little provincial and not as international as Barry" (Scott 2011, 297). However, in Obama's inner world the soon-to-be wife provided what had been lacking in his upbringing.

"We've created stability for our kids in a way that my mom did not do for us," Obama has said. "My choosing to put down roots in Chicago, and to marry a woman who is very rooted in one place indicates a probable desire for stability that perhaps I was missing," disclosed Obama (Ripley 2008). Clearly, Obama's maternal image is somewhat split between a stable woman, his wife, and a somewhat peripatetic woman, his mother.

Ann was aware that by settling in Chicago, her son was charting his own path. "She felt a little wistful or sad that Barack had essentially moved to Chicago and chosen to take on a really strongly identified black identity" (Scott 2011, 298). The black identity had not been part of his life in Hawai'i while growing up. Ann may have felt that by settling in Chicago and marrying a woman remarkably different from her that he was making "a professional choice" (Scott 2011, 298). "It would be too strong to say she felt rejection . . . that he was distancing himself from her" but clearly this process of separation individuation may have begun a long time back when Ann was away for years in Indonesia.

Conversely, Barack Obama's soaring rhetoric mirrors his mother's humble attempts to change the world one village at a time. When traveling from one town to another in trying to raise hope and inspiration about social and economic changes that grip this country, Barack Obama is doing what his mother practiced in underdeveloped and developing economies. She worked on microfinancing for poor villagers in Southeast Asia and believed in economic development and democracy for underserved populations around the world.

Like his mother, who studied different cultures the way other people look at gems through a magnifying lens, Obama can inspire a crowd of thousands of people by giving hope, meaning, and purpose, something he learned at his mother's knee. Although many of his detractors continue to complain that he lacks real-world experience, he was raised by someone who was thoroughly tested in life. In this sense, President Obama is on the same path as his mother and feels at home on the global stage.

It is difficult to carve up a person's life into neat compartments, but Ann Dunham seemingly raced through at least four major life transitions in the span of her 52 years. According to Gail Sheehy, author of *New Passages*, Ann Dunham's transitions may have been too rocky and stressful, however. Sheehy reminds us that, based on the latest scientific evidence, a "woman who reaches age fifty today—and remains free of cancer and heart disease—can expect to see her ninety-second birthday" (Sheehy 1996). This was not to be Ann Dunham's fate; she passed away prematurely in 1995, almost five months after Barack Obama released his autobiography.

Each phase of Ann Dunham's adulthood was filled with romance and marriage, which eventually led to divorce and new academic pursuits that included foreign travel and fieldwork. Through every transition, she left her two children in her parents' care. She spent her early years in Kansas, where her father had a furniture business, but moved with her family to Texas, California, and Washington before they finally put down roots in Hawai'i. As Alice Dewey suggested to me, Ann Dunham may not have felt completely at home in Hawai'i either given that she finally settled and worked in Jakarta. Hawai'i was her parents' home and Barack's childhood home, but not necessarily Ann Dunham's.

In high school, Ann Dunham was "a strong-willed, unconventional member of the Mercer Island High School graduating class of 1960," according to a report in the *Chicago Tribune* (Jones 2007). She was concerned with cutting-edge issues of her times and "wasn't part of the matched-sweater-set crowd," observed one of her classmates. She was thinking about different cultures, philosophies, and worldviews as a young teenager, according to her mother (Mendell 2007). She was what Carol Gilligan, a feminist psychologist, has called a member of the adolescence resistance, one of the "I know" girls who dared to speak "in a different voice" and was not afraid to challenge the patriarchal social order (Gilligan 1993).

Ann did not espouse any religious affiliation or traditional faith and claimed to be an atheist. Armed with strong convictions, she often defended her views, according to Maxine Box, who was Dunham's best friend in high school (Jones 2007). She seemed very analytically minded, always challenging, comparing, and arguing. She seemed to be concerned with things that most of her peers were simply not preoccupied with, such as different cultures and how to change the world.

The developmental impact of these traits in a teenage mother indelibly shaped Obama's mind. His mother socialized him with a contrarian worldview, a rejection of organized religion, and a questioning nature. Due partly to her own challenging nature, Ann Dunham provided a somewhat itinerant and tempestuous family environment for Obama's early upbringing. As he has admitted on many occasions, he felt constantly uprooted and adrift as a child with his mother's itinerant personality and lifestyle.

The log-cabin version of Ann Dunham's formative years as the white woman from Kansas who married a black man from Kenya overlooks the impact of her impressionable high school years. During the presidential campaign, when Obama visited the Seattle area he revealed that his mother had attended Mercer Island High near Seattle, Washington, before moving to Hawai'i and stayed at Mercer Island long enough to graduate. This was more than a quick educational adventure. Ann Dunham spent 8th grade through high school graduation on the 5-mile-long island; it is a "South America-shaped stretch of Douglas firs and cedars, just across from Seattle in Lake Washington" (Jones 2007).

Interviews with Dunham family friends from Kansas and interviews with Ann's former classmates and teachers have revealed a portrait of Barack Obama's young mother "as a self-assured, iconoclastic young teen seemingly hell-bent to resist Eisenhower-era conformity" (Jones 2007). With the name Stanley Ann, she had every right to be tomboyish; she was prone to quiet dissension and often rolled her eyes when she disagreed with something or someone. She was concerned about her weight, did not like the appearance of her pudgy nose, and often ranted about her domineering father. "Her sarcasm could be withering and, while she enjoyed arguing, she did not like to draw attention to herself. The bite of her wit was leavened by a good sense of humor" (Jones 2007).

Although her peers regularly babysat for the kids in the neighborhood, Ann Dunham was not interested in such mundane activities. She didn't do much dating, nor did she feel that marriage and having children was important. "It wasn't a put-down, it wasn't hurtful. That's just who she was," said Box (Jones 2007). Ann could barely tolerate her masculine-sounding name, and over the course of her life she changed her last name five times. A friend, Elaine Johnson, who used to wait with her for the school bus, remembered the episode when Dunham introduced herself one morning and then quickly followed up with an explanation: "I know, it's a boy's name and no, I don't like it. I mean, would you like to be called Stanley?" Johnson recalled her complaint. "But my dad wanted a boy and he got me. And the name 'Stanley' made him feel better, I guess" (Jones 2007). Susan Blake, another classmate and a former city councilwoman from Mercer Island, who recalled changing little Barack's diapers on several occasions, said of her friend: "Hers was a mind in full tilt" (Jones 2007).

Alice Dewey told me that Ann eventually got over the pain of having a masculine-sounding name and the confusion that stemmed from it; eventually, she began to derive some pleasure from it. She dropped the name "Stanley" when she arrived in Hawai'i and started to use "Ann" as her formal name. Dewey, who advised Ann Dunham on her final name change after her divorce from her second husband, remembered that Ann was a bit confused about what to do about her Javanese last name. Dewey recalled, "I just said to her, just drop the 'oe' and put in the 'u.' That is how she arrived at the modern pronunciation of the Javanese last name, 'Sutoro.'"

With the passage of time, the often disparate qualities of Madelyn, Stanley, and Ann Dunham have been fused, smoothed over, and polished in the political persona of their grandson and son, Barack Obama, but the traces of the family resemblance remain. Obama's voice and tenor emerged closer to his biological father's and lower than his excitable grandfather's. The overt skepticism of his mother and grandmother was channeled into an evidence-based, scientific approach to life. Ann Dunham's aversion to seeking attention and the constant nomadic drive were domesticated. The president who wants to bridge America's racial, religious, and cultural divides has embraced diversity like his mother, yet he has abandoned his mother's rejection of organized religion, calling his Christian faith "a vessel for my beliefs" (Mansfield 2008, 24).

Apparently, Obama inherited his grandfather's sales skills, attracting enough big money and support to reshape the race for the presidency. Although he credits his grandmother for bankrolling his early education, in a recent interview, Obama identified his mother as the dominant figure in his formative years. Thus, she reigned supreme in his inner world; like Athena, the Greek goddess of knowledge, Ann was the fountain of wisdom about world cultures, philosophies, and literature. Obama has said that the values his mother taught him "continue to be my touchstone when it comes to how I go about the world of politics" (Gammell 2009). These values are partly traceable to the get-rich-quick oil fields east of Wichita, Kansas. Mack Gilkeson, a friend of Madelyn and Stanley and a retired engineering professor who grew up in El Dorado, Texas, has watched the Dunham's now-famous grandson run for the highest office in the world. "If I were to squint my eyes and look at Barack," he said, "I'd almost see his grandparents" (Jones 2007).

The Dunhams as a family were constantly on the move from one end of the country to the other. They moved from El Dorado to Seattle for a bigger opportunity, when Stanley secured a more lucrative sales job with a newly opened furniture store. At the time, Seattle was not the hub of technological innovation that it is now. The family settled on Mercer Island, now an affluent haven to corporate executives; in the 1950s it was just an isolated, "rural, idyllic place," said Elaine Johnson. She recalled the safe, quiet, politically conservative, all-white suburbs, where high school children would have sleepovers along the water.

However, the turbulent undercurrents would erupt by the decade's end. The chairman of the Mercer Island school board, John Stenhouse, had already been commissioned to appear before the House Un-American Activities Committee for his membership in the Communist Party. Several teachers at Mercer High School were also rabble-rousing the students into questioning traditional authority. The duo of Val Foubert and Jim Wichterman had created the "anarchy alley," which was a source of parental consternation (Jones 2007). Their lectures regularly inspired students to confront cultural norms and challenge traditional authority. Foubert, who taught literature, relied on challenging English texts, such as *Atlas Shrugged*, *The Organization Man*, *The Hidden Persuaders*, and *1984*.

Wichterman, on the other hand, taught philosophies of Sartre and Kirkegaard, which encouraged musings on the existence of God. The hallway between Foubert and Wichterman's classrooms was known for heated discussions and became home to a group of anarchist students. The provocative high school lessons were having a direct effect on the students outside the classroom. "I had them read 'The Communist Manifesto,' and the parents went nuts," said Wichterman (Jones 2007). Conservative parents did not like their children to discuss sex and religion, and often the mothers would march into the principal's office to complain.

Many of Ann Dunham's friends began challenging their parents about religion and politics. For some of the parents this was deeply upsetting, and Foubert and Wichterman were almost fired. Although the Dunhams stayed away from the uproar, Ann was one of the students directly influenced by the group of anarchists, caught halfway between the generational change. For their part, Madelyn and Stanley joined the Sunday services at the East Shore Unitarian Church in nearby Bellevue. According to the *Chicago Tribune*, "In the 1950s, this was sometimes known as 'the little Red church on the hill,'" in reference to the effects of McCarthyism (Jones 2007). The kind of rational skepticism that Stanley embraced and passed on to his daughter was welcomed at this church.

For Ann Dunham, the teachings of Foubert and Wichterman provided the intellectual arsenal that fueled her excitement about life beyond the walls of her little high school; she was ready to grow up and embrace the larger world. Her high school classmates were tuned into the larger social reality; they were living between two markedly different generations. The Beat poets had waned in their influence but the 1960s era of protests had not yet materialized. Dunham's classmates believed "they were on the cusp of societal change, the distant early warning of the '60s struggles over civil rights, women's rights and war" (Jones 2007).

Ann Dunham seemed to be ahead of her cohort and always up on the current events. If an event was upsetting the order of things or something "was going wrong with the world, she was the first to know," said Chip Wall, a former classmate. Wall remembered her fondly as "a fellow 0traveler. . . . We were liberals before we knew what liberals were." Another classmate, Jill Burton-Dascher, said Ann Dunham was a little bit "off-center" but ahead of her times both intellectually and socially (Jones 2007).

Ann Dunham's father seemed to be full of good cheer and often tried hard to welcome her classmates to their house, but he often embarrassed her because he tried too hard, said Maxine Box. The father and daughter were often seen arguing in front of her friends, and her mother would play the role of the mediator. Another friend, Susan Blake, said Ann's father was known for his provocative stories and jokes, always trying to get a reaction out of people. Every time her father opened his mouth, Ann Dunham would roll her eyes in disagreement.

When it came time for graduation, Ann's classmates scribbled the usual best wishes to their friends in the year book; they remembered the fun times they had shared. Dunham wrote a somber message to Maxine Box: "Remember me when you are old and gray. Love & Luck, Stanley." Suddenly, after Ann Dunham's high school graduation, her father had found a job in Hawai'i with a new furniture store. "He just couldn't settle," Box recalled (Jones 2007).

Ann Dunham didn't want to go to Hawai'i, recalled Box, but looked forward to it because she did not have a choice. The move to Hawai'i was just the opening surprise for her friends. Shortly after she started classes at the University of Hawai'i, Box recalled she received a letter "saying that her friend had fallen in love with a grad student. He was black, from Kenya and named Obama" (Jones 2007). The Dunhams weren't pleased, but parental objections didn't matter. For Stanley Ann, her newfound love interest seemed to be part and parcel of her contrarian worldview, a natural extension of her philosophical ruminations in Seattle and the radical classes she took with teachers Wichterman and Foubert. She felt she was coming of age and making her own decisions, however reckless they may have been at the time. Her new circle of friends now included older graduate students from the University of Hawai'i, who spent their free time drinking and debating politics and world affairs. The distinguished-looking, confident, and opinionated Obama Sr. spoke with an eloquence and depth of voice so deep it "sounded like James Earl Jones may have been a tenor," recalled Neil Abercrombie, the governor of Hawai'i who was part of this group.

When the news of Ann Dunham's new love and marriage reached Mercer Island, it completely floored her former classmates. Her close friends could not imagine her life changing so quickly. In high school, Ann hadn't cared for marriage and motherhood, and she was so independent minded that the whole thing seemed like a page out of a romance novel.

Abercrombie has admitted that privately he feared the relationship between Ann Dunham and Obama Sr. would not last. Obama Sr.'s ambition was too strong; he was self-focused and had come to America to complete a mission. After Obama Sr. was accepted to study at Harvard, recalled Abercrombie, Ann Dunham simply disappeared from the University of Hawai'i student gatherings. Abercrombie remembered that he rarely saw her after that point. Like the Greek goddess Persephone, who disappeared to the underworld at the start of the fall, Ann Dunham may have descended into another world altogether and completely left Hawai'i. In time, she returned to complete her undergraduate studies at the University of Hawai'i, but then she departed for another distant shore in the Pacific when she met another cultural exchange student, Lolo Soetoro, who eventually moved the family to Jakarta, Indonesia.

Abercrombie believes Obama Sr. loved Ann Dunham, but the constraints of family life were not something he had planned for. He expected great things of himself and was not about to let his family life get in the way, said Abercrombie. A few years later, when Abercrombie and another friend from Hawai'i looked up Obama Sr. during a backpacking trip to Kenya, they found a bitter man. According to the former Congressman, Obama Sr. believed he had been denied opportunities to influence the running of his country and had taken to drinking; he did not even ask after his ex-wife or his son.

Obama biographer David Mendell has described Ann Dunham as an academically precocious student with a passion for reading. She was offered early admission to the University of Chicago, but her father would not permit her to attend because he thought she was too young. Madelyn Dunham described her daughter as having "very advanced ideas [and was reading the work of] heavy philosophers by the time she was sixteen" (Mendell 2007, 25).

In the revised edition of his memoir, Obama reflected on the passing of his mother. "I think sometimes that had I known she would not survive her illness, I might have written a different book—less a meditation on the absent parent, more a celebration of the one who was the single constant in my life. . . . I know she was the kindest, most generous spirit I have ever known, and that what is best in me I owe to her" (Obama 2004a, xii).

An eternal optimist, she was driven to seek happiness in faraway places in the world. She was a New Deal, Peace Corps–loving liberal who worked on economic development for international agencies throughout her life. Ann wove a patchwork of United Nations diversity into her family by twice marrying men from different cultures. She authored a dissertation on the Indonesian peasant economy, titled "Peasant Blacksmithing in Indonesia: Surviving and Thriving Against All Odds," which focused on the transition from rural agricultural economy to the industrial economy; in the introduction of her life's work, she acknowledged her children, "Barack and Maya, who seldom complained when their mother was in the field" (Dunham 1992). Like his mother, Obama is a bit of a dreamer, yet more grounded and pragmatic, and he has also worked for progressive causes all his life.

During a 2008 symposium held in Ann Dunham's honor at the University of Hawai'i, Alice Dewey described her as "a woman of the people," who will be remembered for her passion, practicality, and global outlook. Today as we debate the merits of the American military's Human Terrain System, which pairs soldiers with anthropologists in Iraq and Afghanistan, we must recall that anthropology as a discipline has been at the front lines of progressive activism since the days of colonial expansion (Shweder 2007; Asad 1995). The origins of cultural anthropology were deeply rooted in attempts to soften the blows of colonialism in the Old World, as they were to understand the native populations in the New World (Boas 1940). At the 2008 symposium, more than 200 attendees were hoping to catch the progressive spirit that compelled Obama's mother.

Ann Dunham specialized in rural economic development and worked on early efforts to create microfinance opportunities for villagers in Indonesia so they could pull themselves out of poverty. This was long before lending microcredit came into vogue in development economics or even in mainstream banking, now popularized by the Bangladeshi Nobel laureate Muhammad Yunus (2007). Obama's sister, Maya, has said of her mother that she was truly at home in the world; she was a wanderer before she became a professional anthropologist. "Both of us—my brother and I—were very lucky to have been raised by a woman who honored and respected local ways of doing things, but was also global in her thinking," she said.

Ann had researched the Indonesian rural economy for many years. She worked as a program officer for the Ford Foundation and as research coordinator for Bank Rakyat Indonesia, but she was most at home in rural villages. Her personal knowledge and contacts allowed her to persuade banks to extend loans to poor peasants, who were just as important to her as high-ranking bank officials. Dewey said, "I think she was the hardest-working person I've ever met, and did it without seeming to be. If we have Barack as president and he works that hard, we're fine" (Essoyan 2008). Another audience member at the panel discussion held at the University of Hawai'i at Manoa said her reason for attending was to learn about Ann's role in shaping Obama's political philosophy. Other women related to Ann's cultural sensitivity, common sense, global worldview, and progressive vision for underdeveloped nations.

Ann Dunham also managed to deftly combine her interests in women's development with economic anthropology, while simultaneously being a practitioner in the field. Historically, anthropology has been at the leading edge of multiculturalism in the social sciences; feminist anthropology focused on international development was a fairly new line of inquiry when Ann decided to pursue it as an academic and professional career (Lewin 2006).

In a letter written from the field sometime before she started writing her dissertation, Ann Dunham described to Alice Dewey her pioneering projects in feminist anthropology and international development:

Other than worrying about plans for fall, life is good here. Maybe you remember that I am handling projects for Ford in the areas of women, employment and industry (small and large). Jakarta was made the Regional Southeast Asia office last year, so that we are also working in Thailand and the Philippines. This year I have major projects for women on plantations in West Java and North Sumatra; for women in kertek factories in Central and East Java; for street food sellers and scavengers in the cities of Jakarta, Jogja and Bandung; for women in credit cooperative in East Java; for women in electronics factories, mainly in the Jakarta-Bogor area; for women in cottage industry cooperatives in the district of Klaten; for handloom weavers in West Timor; for shop girls along Jl. Maliboro and market sellers in Berigharjo (still tentative); for slum dwellers in Jakarta and Bandung; for street food sellers in Thailand (with Christina Szanton as the project leader); etc. In addition I am still team-teaching the Sociology of the Family course with Pjuawati Sayogyo at Bogor Agricultural Univ., and I am project specialist on a research project that she is coordinating on The Roles of Rural Women on the Outer Islands of Indonesia. . . . All this means I am on the road quite a bit, doing a lot of quick-and-dirty anthropology for purposes of setting up and monitoring projects. I am hoping to take Maya with me (in lieu of home leave this year) and stop off in Thailand on the way there and Delhi on the way back.

We can grasp from Ann's letter that she was practicing a kind of global activism in the emerging East Asian economies, focused on rural development and women's lives.

When I asked who Ann Dunham's political and literary heroes were, her colleague Kay Ikrangara, who now works for the Academy of Educational Development in Jakarta, said Ann was really an activist and a peacenik influenced by the philosophies of Mahatma Gandhi and Martin Luther King. Both Ann and Kay were married to Indonesian men and worked together in Jakarta in the early 1970s. Eventually, both became applied anthropologists for international development agencies and remained friends over three decades.

Ann Dunham was five years older than Hillary Clinton, and the two women might have been generational cousins. The optimism that drove Ann Dunham also runs through Hillary Clinton's narrative. Both shared a post–World War II global view of the world, and they both grew up with parents who were politically conservative. Most importantly, Ann Dunham and Hillary Clinton later adopted progressive activism. Hillary Clinton's *It Takes A Village* (1996) could have been the title of Ann Dunham's dissertation on microfinancing in Indonesian villages. When Obama arrived in Washington, D.C., as the freshman senator from Illinois, Hillary apparently informed him to keep a low profile, a piece of advice he did not take seriously. Stephan Richter of *The Globalist* has suggested that Obama may have realized early in the 2008 presidential campaign that his real advantage was that he was pretty close to "the very son that Bill and Hillary never had—combining his charm with her brains" (Richter 2008).

Barack's sister has revealed interesting details about her brother's early ambitions as they were shaped and supported by his mother. "There was always a joke between my mom and Barack that he would be the first black president. . . . So there were intimations of all this early on. He has always been restless. There was always somewhere else he needed to go," she told a reporter from the *New York Times* (Steinhauer 2007). Early on, Maya witnessed a complex young man who was struggling to find his cultural identity. Although Barack's racial confusion was assuaged by an ethnically mixed population in Hawai'i, when he looked in the mirror he saw himself as a black man, the most accessible social label available to him at the time. Barack's inner turmoil exacerbated as he approached his teenage years. His feelings of alienation stemming from his diverse background pulled at him in different directions and competed with his lofty ideals about his place in the world. The twofold question that every teenager struggles with—Who am I? Where do I belong?—may have been difficult for him to resolve; it was this early searching for a cultural identity that provided Obama with a unique perspective on the American experience.

As the cultural model of a new hybrid identity, emanating from the microcosm of Hawai'i, Obama was involved in a struggle to incorporate the white middle-class conditions of his birth and upbringing with his African lineage and heritage. He had to incorporate the strong support and influence of his American mother and grandmother in his daily life with the unexplainable, almost mysterious pull of his African father's mythic image. In myths, as in real life, the hero must come to terms with these dueling inner forces—the strong image of the mother and the father—in order to emerge victorious from his struggles (Campbell 1949).

"He couldn't sit back and wait for the answers to come to him. . . . He had to pursue those answers actively. People from very far-away places collide here, and cultures collide, and there is a blending and negotiation that is constant," said Maya, who still lives in Hawai'i (Steinhauer 2007). When I spoke with her later, she agreed with my suggestion that Hawai'i may have given her brother a sense that a lot of different cultures and perspectives can live in harmony, and that Barack developed the ability to feel at home in many different worlds.

As we glimpsed in the early childhood portrait of Barack and his mother, he projected a bold, extroverted, and congenial temperament, while his mother provided the human scaffolding that every young child craves. However, the social and cultural context of Hawai'i surely engendered an optimistic and hopeful tone for Barack's journey, fostering a cool, steady, and calm exterior. This social environment gave Obama the skills to work with people from different cultures with ease, something his anthropologist mother had perfected as a professional technique while living and working in Jakarta, Indonesia.

A Pragmatic Grandmother

Most Americans heard about Obama's grandmother, Madelyn Dunham, for the first time during the race speech in Philadelphia; she was one of the unsung heroes of his campaign. She was the rock in his foundation that made him a political rock star. His grandmother was a strong, down-to-earth, matter-of-fact woman from the Midwest who became his de facto guardian and caregiver from the age of 10 to 18 years, a function his mother could not fulfill as she was working and living in Indonesia.

Madelyn Dunham has been described in the media as the "typical white person" who loved Barack Obama "as much as she loved anything in this world," but may also have displayed a tinge of fear of black men who passed by her on the street and pressed her for money (Obama 2008). When I interviewed Barbara Nelson, who knew Madelyn Dunham well, I was amazed to learn of the day-to-day roles and functions that Dunham performed in Obama's life. In addition to doing most of the domestic chores and managing the household, she worked at the Bank of Hawai'i and was present at most if not all of Barack's basketball games at the Punahou Academy.

Every morning Madelyn would get up early and take the bus to downtown Honolulu to the banking district. On many occasions, Barack would visit her office after school; he would often sit at the table outside her office doing his homework. She was Barack's grandmother, legal guardian, and after-school caregiver, all in one, filling multiple and critical functions for his budding personality. She provided the stability and the constancy he needed for healthy development as a growing boy. He inherited from her the spirit of American pragmatism amidst the idyllic ambience of the Hawai'ian Islands.

"Cherchez la femme," wrote a reporter from the *Asia Times*, suggesting that if you want to uncover Obama's secret, look for the women in his life (Spengler 2008). This was an interesting insight, followed by a political analysis of his late mother's life and career and an examination of his wife, Michelle Obama's involvement with the campaign, but it completely omitted the grandmother who supported his private-school education and was there for him like an anchor during the turbulent adolescent years.

The role of grandparents in the lives of American children is now increasingly evident. As changes in the American family have affected many households, grandparents have become parents twice over, especially for

African American children. Approximately 9 percent (7 million) of all U.S. children under age 18 live with their grandparents, and almost 30 percent are cared for by their grandparents in dual wage-earner households, according to the latest U.S. Census (U.S. Census 2010). The American family has been transformed from rural, extended farm families to nuclear families to single-parent households and alternative families; this transition is reflected in Obama's own family history. His grandmother remained the solitary witness through the passage of time who had seen his birth, his growth and development into a politician, and his rise to the presidency.

Given her importance in his adolescent life, I asked Dennis Ching, who worked for Madelyn Dunham at the Bank of Hawai'i, if there were any early signs of Obama's political rise under his grandmother's supervision. Ching said that the Dunhams had a small, tightly knit group of politically savvy friends who regularly played bridge. "Madelyn Dunham was very good at strategic thinking; you could see this at work and in her card games. She was a smart cookie, you know. I think she taught him to think strategically," said Ching. As a state senator, Barack Obama took to playing poker with a close-knit group of politicians in Springfield, Illinois, and though Madelyn may not have taught Obama how to play cards, she definitely taught him to make the best of the deck that life had dealt him, said Dennis Ching. Given the absence of his biological father and given that his mother had an itinerant career, Obama's grandmother was the one who taught him the Midwestern values of discipline, hard work, individual responsibility, love for country, and self-reliance. Her life struggles may have shone through Obama's rise as a politician in Chicago, Illinois.

In an interview in *Vanity Fair* Obama said, "She was the opposite of a dreamer, at least by the time I knew her. Whether that was always the case or whether she scaled back her dreams as time went on and learned to deal with certain disappointments is not entirely clear. But she was just a very tough, sensible, no-nonsense person." During his quietly turbulent teenage years, Madelyn "injected" into him "a lot of that very Midwestern, sort of traditional sense of prudence and hard work" (Purdum 2008). Some of these values manifested themselves in his life and career when he got older.

Madelyn hailed from the small town of Peru, Kansas, a population of only 5,000 people. In his memoir, Obama described it as the place where "decency and endurance and the pioneer spirit were joined at the hip with conformity and suspicion and the potential for unblinking cruelty" (Obama 2004a, 13). She grew up near large oil fields in Augusta, Kansas. Her father, Rolla Payne, managed one of the oil fields, and her mother, Leona Payne, was a teacher at the local school. Madelyn was the oldest of four children and displayed a sense of responsibility and maturity early. She addressed her younger siblings as "the kids," recalled her younger sister, Margaret Payne, now a retired statistics professor living in Chapel Hill, North Carolina.

In a family that stressed literacy and education, Madelyn was an avid reader. The Bible was a constant staple in the Payne household, even though it was not force-fed. Obama has written that his mother's side of the family "generally shunned the tent revival circuit, preferring a straight-backed form of Methodism that valued reason over passion and temperance over both" (Obama 2004a, 14). Although the family was Republican, they allowed Madelyn to travel to Wichita to listen to Franklin D. Roosevelt give a speech when she was a teenager.

The town of Augusta, Kansas, had only two black families in those days, but Charles Payne, Madelyn's younger brother, a retired University of Chicago librarian, has proudly reported that they attended the same schools as the white kids (Breed 2008). It has also been reported that Barack Obama has native Indian blood running through his matrilineal line, which was a "source of considerable shame" (Obama 2004a, 13) for his great-grandmother. Both his grandmother and mother, however, seemed to take pride in this fact; Madelyn "would turn her head in profile to show off her beaked nose, which, along with a pair of jet-black eyes, was offered as proof of Cherokee blood" (Obama 2004, 12).

Augusta was a sleepy little town before World War II, and as Madelyn and her friends approached their teenage years, they would catch a ride to Wichita to see all of the new bands at the Blue Moon dance pavilion— Glenn Miller, Tommy Dorsey, Benny Goodman, and Harry James. It was during one such excursion that Madelyn decided that she was getting married without her parents' permission, an intergenerational pattern that would repeat itself in her daughter's life years later.

Stanley Dunham, the boy she fell in love with, was from a nearby town of El Dorado, Kansas. Obama has described his grandfather as the boy with "slicked-back hair and his perpetual wise-guy grin" (Obama 2004a, 14). "It was not pleasant for my parents," Charles Payne has recalled (Breed 2008). The fierce independent streak was evident from the beginning, which would take Stanley and Madelyn Dunham across the country to the West Coast and all the way to Hawai'i.

Aside from the four-year interlude when Obama lived in Indonesia with his mother and stepfather, Obama spent his childhood in Honolulu—mostly in his grandparents' high-rise apartment. Obama has reminisced about his grandmother, Toot, watching him practice basketball from their 10th-floor apartment window.

Obama has openly acknowledged the debt he owes to his pragmatic grandmother. She is the one who took him on his first bus tour of the contiguous United States, stopping at Howard Johnsons along the highways. She showed him the Grand Canyon, Yellowstone, Disneyland, and finally, Chicago—the city where he would eventually put down roots and become a community organizer, start a family, and launch his political career. Obama's sister, Maya, has also acknowledged that the qualities that propelled Obama so far were rooted in Toot's midwestern values and work ethic. "From our grandmother, he gets his pragmatism, his levelheadedness, his ability to stay centered in the eye of the storm," she said, "and his sensible, no-nonsense (side) is inherited from her" (Breed 2008).

During a visit to his office in the Honolulu banking district, Dennis Ching told me that when Dunham retired from the Bank of Hawai'i in 1986, she wouldn't just sit back and take it easy; she continued to volunteer for various charitable organizations. She offered help to the local libraries and to the Oahu Circuit Court, where she became a court observer and an arbitrator for the juvenile court. One of the chief clerks who supervised her recalled that Madelyn was a sharp-witted, demanding, and stern woman; "I used to think, 'I don't know who's the supervisor here—me or her,'" the clerk said (Breed 2008).

After her husband passed away in 1992, Madelyn continued to play bridge with a small circle of friends, as many as six days a week, Ching said. Shortly after Barack Obama's fortunes began to rise in politics, she had a corneal transplant so she could see his debates on television, said Charles Payne (Breed 2008). In addition to volunteering and playing bridge, she wanted to know what was going on with her grandson and no doubt to track how he was playing his deck of cards.

In lifestyle, values, and ethics, Madelyn Dunham represented middle America, the heart and soul of the country Obama has been trying to revive. It is not a coincidence that Obama's grandparents were part of "the Greatest Generation," who fought a war to save the world from the brink of destruction and gave it a new life. For his grandparents, the history of World War II was central to their life narrative. They volunteered to fight in the war and later raised a grandson who would aspire to lead his own generation to greater heights. In this respect, Barack Obama is trying to replicate the valuable lessons that he gleaned from his grandparents' lives.

The author of *The Greatest Generation*, broadcast journalist Tom Brokaw, has written that, "It is, I believe, the greatest generation any society has ever produced" (1998, 2). Brokaw has suggested that the men and women who fought in World War II did not do it for fame and recognition; they were driven to do the right thing. When they came back from the war they rebuilt America into a superpower. The lessons imparted by this generation became day-to-day object lessons for Barack Obama's life; indeed, Obama selectively took from his mother's life, work, and travels whatever he thought was essential for building his identity, but he relied on the critical experiences of his grandparents to understand the American history on the mainland. Due in large part to their legacy, I argue, he settled in the Midwest and became a politician who could roll up his sleeves and readily connect with the folks in the heartland of the country.

Wife as Soul Mate

Although it is plain to see Barack Obama learned midwestern values from the trials and tribulations of his grandparents, and that these formed the core of his self from the age of 10 years onward, this same set of values may also have drawn him to Chicago and to his wife, Michelle, as he searched for a community on the mainland. Traveling from Los Angeles to New York he felt something was missing at the center of his life, something that was a critical component to the puzzle of his own identity. He began to explore the experiences and values that have shaped black America for more than two centuries and found where his true self, ethnic affiliations, and passions were rooted. As he began to understand his racial identity and got a job as a community organizer in Chicago, he learned more about what W.E.B. Du Bois (1903) had called "the souls of black folk," an inspiration he received from his friend, mentor, and future wife, Michelle.

His multicultural, international, and itinerant family experience complemented Michelle's parochial and somewhat sheltered upbringing on the

South Side of Chicago. And she inspired many students when she talked about her upbringing during her first visit to Mumbai, India, in 2010:

> My family didn't have a lot of money. My parents never went to college. I grew up in a little bitty apartment in a working-class neighborhood on the south side of Chicago. My parents worked hard to pay the bills and to keep a roof over our heads. But even though my parents couldn't give us material things, they gave us something much more precious—they gave me and my brother strong values. They taught us to treat others with dignity and respect. They taught us to push for excellence in every single thing we did. They taught us to be humble and to be grateful for everything we had. They taught us to put every last bit of effort into our education and to take pride in our work. They taught us that our circumstances didn't define us, and that if we believed in ourselves, if we made the most of every single opportunity, we could build our own destinies and accomplish anything we put our minds to. (Obama 2010)

Michelle offered Barack access to the African American experience and to its deep historical roots in this country, something Obama had read about when he lived in Hawai'i, but his own lived experience was far removed from the concerns of the African American community. He deepened his African American affiliations and connections through Michelle; with her he also found a community, a family, and a political persona. She became the mirror to his black soul, the soul of Africa that he had inherited from his father but had been cut adrift when his father abandoned him.

Michelle Robinson LaVaughn grew up in a squarely middle-class home on the South Side of Chicago. Born on January 17, 1964, she is almost three years younger than Barack Obama but attended Harvard Law School earlier than he did because she was academically focused and showed early promise. Her father, Fraser Robinson III, was active in the local democratic politics, while working as a city water plant employee. Her mother was a full-time homemaker who did secretarial work at the Spiegel catalog store. The Robinson family traces its roots back to the pre–Civil War African Americans in the Deep South.

She was socialized in a rather conventional two-story home on Euclid Street in the South Shore neighborhood. She has described her home life as typical of many American families, where "the mother is at home, the father works, you have dinner around the table" (Bennetts 2007).

The family attended the local church, was well connected to the local community, and vacationed in a rustic cabin in the neighboring state of Michigan. Both Michelle and her older brother, Craig Robinson, excelled academically and skipped second grade.

She showed early intellectual aptitude and later attended Whitney Young High School, Chicago's first magnet high school, where she was on the honor roll for four years, took advanced placement classes, was a member of the National Honor Society, and served as student council treasurer. She was also a high school classmate of Santita Jackson, the daughter of Jesse Jackson and the sister of Jesse Jackson Jr.

Michelle graduated from high school as salutatorian in 1981, went straight to Princeton University, and graduated in 1985. Her undergraduate thesis, which has drawn some media attention, was called "Princeton-Educated Blacks and the Black Community." In it she observed that she was shocked "by college students who drove BMWs. I didn't even know parents who drove BMWs" (Johnson 2007). At Princeton, she was active in the Third World Center (now known as the Carl A. Fields Center), a support group for minority students, which included cultural and social events, a day care center, and tutoring services.

Michelle studied sociology and African American studies, graduated cum laude with a bachelor of arts degree, and chose to become a lawyer. She graduated from Harvard Law School in 1988. While at Harvard she again showed concern for minority rights when she petitioned the university to hire more minority faculty members, worked at the Harvard Legal Aid Bureau, and assisted low-income clients by representing them in housing cases.

A few years later, Michelle met Barack Obama at the law firm of Sidley Austin, where they worked together. The two were among the few African Americans at the law firm, where she was assigned to mentor him as a summer associate. Their relationship started with a business lunch and then a community organization meeting where he first impressed her with his passion for improving the community. The couple's first date was to the Spike Lee movie *Do the Right Thing*. The couple married in October 1992, and they have two daughters, Malia Ann (born 1998) and Natasha (known as Sasha, born 2001).

Obama had already been a community organizer for three years in Chicago after graduating from college. He found a high level of satisfaction and a moderate degree of success from this type of work. In order to engage in work of lasting importance, however, he needed to go further; his commitments had to be stronger and deeper. In the struggle to find a vocation that would have lasting impact and that connected his past and foreseeable future, he became a civil rights lawyer serving the people of Chicago.

Thus, Michelle Obama completed the triumvirate of women who made Barack Obama who he is today. By providing a kind of stability and domesticity that his mother could not provide, Michelle significantly added to Barack Obama's maturation and development. Across the racial, ethnic, and historical divide, these women had one thing in common: all three were very strong-minded and independent women. Obama's mother was a humanist—a dreamer, a romantic, a traveler, and an anthropologist. His grandmother was a pragmatist—a down-to-earth, reliable, and even-tempered banker. Michelle Obama, with her roots firmly established in the South Side of Chicago, offered him a transparently black identity and the dream of a future with political ambitions. Barack Obama, lacking a stable father figure, relied on these three women to complete his self-development and is quintessentially a mama's boy.

In his relationship with Michelle, Obama established a sense of place, time, and rhythm in his daily life. He put down roots, engaged in raising a family, and became a Chicagoan. In the words of Studs Terkel, Obama became one of the regular guys—a lecturer, a writer, and a politician (Democracy Now 2007). Obama had known Chicago as a bachelor before attending Harvard University, but back then he was a community organizer. Like his mother, he defined his identity by helping the poor, and like his father, his purview included the African American community. His mother had spent a summer in Chicago as an au pair; she had also been accepted to the University of Chicago as an undergraduate, though she never attended. Thus, the South Side of Chicago had many different and multilayered meanings for Barack Obama, tying up many loose ends in his family history.

Marrying, settling down, and having a family and kids are all hallmarks of firming up an adult identity. While he established his racial identity in Chicago, his eyes were always on the broader landscape of American life. He became a lecturer, but despite offers to become part of the permanent faculty at the University of Chicago he decided to enter politics—but now we are getting ahead of the story. Suffice it to say that although the Dunham women, Madelyn and Ann, gave Barack Obama a head start in life and provided the foundation for his early self-development and maturation, he cemented his identity in Chicago with Michelle Robinson, who turned out to be not only his mentor and friend but also a wife and soul mate.

4

Global Schooling in Jakarta

Education is not a preparation for life; education is life itself.

John Dewey (2006)

The compelling changes in our economy, the dawning of the Information Age, and the horrible events of September 11, 2001, and their aftermath have created an unprecedented need to focus on international knowledge and skills. To solve most of the major problems facing our country today . . . will require every young person to learn more about other regions, cultures, and languages.

Colin Powell (2003)

With the onset of globalization, Internet technology, and rapid travel, it is now well recognized that the value of global schooling—learning focused on different languages, cultures, and people—is essential for succeeding in the 21st-century economy. However, when Ann Dunham decided to uproot her family to a sleepy *kampong* on the south side of Jakarta, Indonesia, and place her young son in an Indonesian school, she was simply driven by a sense of adventure. Excited by the prospect of falling in love again, she had married an Indonesian man, Lolo Soetoro, and moved her family to live in a place that was remarkably different from what she had known in Kansas, Washington, or even Hawai'i.

In a revealing passage Obama described how his mother disclosed to him that she had accepted Lolo Soetoro's marriage proposal. The four-year-old boy wanted to know if she really loved his soon-to-be stepfather. There was no intimation in Obama's autobiography that he may have felt any resentment toward his stepfather for taking his mother away from him. He did reveal that "lolo" in Hawai'ian means "crazy," which his grandfather thought was funny. Yet, according to Obama, Lolo was a good man and "possessed the good manners and grace of his people" (Obama 2004a, 30). However, as the story unfolds, Barack Obama, or Barry Soetoro as he was known then, turns into the little man who will protect and defend his mother from any threat that might come to her and offers some important insights about their acclimation to Indonesian society.

As a result of the move to Jakarta, Barack Obama became the beneficiary of global elementary schooling for approximately four years from the age of six to ten years. As he said in a speech to university students, "Indonesia is part of me" (Obama 2010). Although he did not attend any international schools, the schools he did attend were and continue to be significant local institutions of learning, imparting elementary and high school education to Indonesian children even today. The first was the private Catholic school, St. Francis Assisi, in the southern end of Jakarta, the first neighborhood where Obama's family settled and where they lived for approximately three years. The second somewhat elite, nondenominational school, which Obama attended for about a year, was located in the more affluent neighborhood of Menteng Dalam, Besuki SDN Menteng 1. It was near the U.S. Consulate and catered to children of wealthy and well-connected families.

I followed the trail that had been laid out by Barack Obama in his autobiography. I was in search of the teachers and friends who may have played a critical role in his life during these early formative years. I also wanted to examine his early cultural environment, the neighborhoods, streets, parks, and homes where he grew up, and the local religious and cultural institutions—churches, schools, and mosques—where he may have studied and prayed with his Indonesian peers.

A senior editor for the *Jakarta Post* noted:

When Barack Obama and his mother arrived in Jakarta in 1967, Indonesia was just emerging from major political upheaval and a deep economic crisis that had made it one of the most impoverished nations in Asia. The city's few high-rise buildings only highlighted the poverty around them. Those who had cars, perhaps more for status than for transport, competed for space on asphalt roads with public buses, motorcycles, three-wheeled rickshaws, pedestrians and hawkers peddling food, cigarettes and whatever else they could sell. (Bayuni 2009)

In the late 1960s, the country was densely populated but could not feed its own people and needed huge infusions of cash from development agencies. Several hundred thousand citizens were accused of being members of the Indonesian Communist Party, and many of them had been massacred by the pro-American General Suharto, who had grabbed the reins of control from the leftist President Sukarno. Indonesian society was barely managing to lumber on the path of democracy and development.

Several weeks before I arrived in Jakarta, a group called the Friends of Obama, a nonprofit organization, had erected a statue of the 10-year-old Barack Obama in Menteng Park near the Besuki School. This was a widely publicized event; the daily news in Jakarta had shown the unveiling of the statue, and even CNN International had sent reporters to the park. The statue, depicting Obama with his left arm stretched out, a butterfly resting on his fingertips, was supposed to encourage kids to think big and dream big. Yet the statue had created an unexpected controversy with the local population.

A fellow traveler, a local businessman sitting next to me on the flight from Bangkok to Jakarta, had noticed my American accent and shared the news story with me.

"Are you from America?" he asked.

"Yes, it's my first trip to Jakarta," I replied.

The flight was an early morning business shuttle from Bangkok to Jakarta, filled with bankers, consultants, and IT workers, so the man surmised that I must be working on a project in Jakarta.

"Are you traveling for work?" he inquired.

"I am traveling on a research project," I replied.

Before I could describe the nature of my research project, he asked, "You know that Barack Obama lived in Jakarta when he was a child?" His smile widened as I nodded with agreement.

"Yes, I think he spent four years here," I said. Wanting to learn his impressions of young Barry, I asked if he knew anyone connected with Obama's Indonesian family, to which he replied with an indifferent shrug. "I only know what I have read in the newspapers," he said.

"I am from the same region as Obama's stepfather. I am also Javanese," he claimed. I asked, "Are you also a Muslim?" Knowing full well that the majority of Indonesian men are Muslim, I expected him to reply with an affirmative nod, but I wanted to find out how secularized his views might be on religion and Islam specifically. "You know Lolo Soetoro practiced a brand of Islam that was very secular," I said, drawing on a line from Obama's autobiography.

He explained, "Yeah, Java and Bali have always been more secular in their outlook and have many other active forms of religious life. Jakarta has lately become more Islamist, women wearing head scarves and men regularly going to the mosque to pray."

By now he seemed to realize that I might know more about Obama than I was revealing. He returned to his morning newspaper, and I sensed a reticence on his part to taking the conversation deeper. So I volunteered that I also had grown up in a secular society, a multireligious and multicultural society with close ties to the Muslim community in India. Although Indonesia has the largest Muslim majority, India has the largest Muslim minority population.

The man again offered a smile of approval as if to display his sense of ease. "You know that Indonesians are very proud of Obama's win, even though he left too early, when he was just 10 or 11 years old. But he went to the schools in Jakarta. His mother continued to live here and work here for many years afterwards," he continued.

He shared more news bulletins from the Indonesian press about the wonder boy named Barry Soetoro. Almost all of these stories celebrated the little boy who once roamed the streets on the south side of Jakarta with a carefree attitude. Indonesians seemed proud that he had become president of the United States, one of the most powerful positions in the world. There is now a movie about Obama's years in Jakarta, *Little Barry*, a fictionalized narrative by a young, up-and-coming filmmaker.

"You know his friends have built a statue dedicated to him near the Besuki School. You must visit there," he insisted as we began to deplane. Displaying his sense of hospitality, he gave me directions to the Besuki School as a way of welcoming me to his country.

So, I took his advice. After I quickly cleared customs at the Jakarta airport, I hailed a Blue Bird taxi to Menteng. The Blue Bird is the national symbol of Indonesia, representing Garuda, the flying giant bird of Hindu mythology; like the American eagle it can be found on countless national monuments and commercial entities.

The cab driver, whose English was relatively fluent, maneuvered through the congested Jakarta streets on the hot summer day, while providing a tour-guide view of some of the important landmarks. We sped past the Sukarno-Hatta monument, the National Monument, paid homage to General Sudirman's statue near downtown, and saw from a distance the Hindu flying monkey-god Hanuman leaping into Jakarta's skyline, trying to wrestle bad demons. More than an hour later, we arrived at a semiresidential area directly behind the diplomatic enclave, which also houses the U.S. Consulate, called Menteng.

An Indonesian Public School

As we pulled onto a narrow street off the main highway, crowded with vendors and local stores and restaurants, the driver pointed to the name of the street—Jalan Besuki.

"This is the street. The school is located down this way. Just a short walk from here," said the driver.

My mind still fixated on the totemic landmarks that define the city of Jakarta, I was ready to be pleasantly surprised by the Obama statue, but there was no statue in sight. As I strolled down the street, my eyes first caught a glimpse of a 20 × 16 plaque with a frame made out of brushed nickel and cast iron and an impressive-looking engraved image of Barack Obama. Studded to a marble stone column at the entrance of the school, the image of Obama was offering his usual smile to the passersby. It seemed I was at the right school; the ease with which I found the school was a good omen, I thought.

The plaque read: "Barack Hussein Obama II, the 44th President of the United States of America, attended this school from 1969–1971." This was a donation from the same nonprofit group that had erected the statue, the Friends of Obama, which included the founder, Ron Mullers, an Indonesian American who runs a restaurant and a bar in Jakarta, and Dalton Tanonka, the Hawai'ian native and news anchor.

It would take another 10 to 15 minutes to walk to the statue, a street vendor told me. "It is not part of the school. The statue is in a public park where children play," he said. The street was crowded with vendors, pedestrian traffic, and the noise of parents going in and out of the school. I thought it would be better to make a separate trip to the statue after I had visited the school.

At the school's gate there was a uniformed guard. As I examined the plaque, I noticed that the guard stopped everyone at the gate and asked questions before letting them enter the school's premises. A group of children were playing with marbles in one corner of the veranda, another group of children were sitting in a circle with a teacher, and parents were moving in and out of the veranda with their children. When I announced my appointment with Principal Hasimah, the guard escorted me to her office.

Walking through the lobby, I could not help but notice many of the Obama posters that graced the hallways of the school. High on one wall, a poster depicting a smiling Barack Obama accepting the nomination at Mile High stadium seemed well positioned to inspire the schoolchildren.

Another corner of the wall chronicled Hillary Clinton's visit to Indonesia after she became secretary of state: shaking hands with Indonesian president Susilo Bambamg Yodhoyono, holding a town-hall meeting with elated schoolchildren, and greeting female teachers clad in traditional garb with head scarves.

During this trip, reaching out to the world's most populous Muslim country, Hillary Clinton said, "'Indonesia has experienced a great transformation in the last 10 years. If you want to know if Islam, democracy, modernity and women's rights can coexist, go to Indonesia" (Landler 2009). Even conservatives like Paul Wolfowitz have praise for Indonesia: "Indonesians have achieved this success largely on their own. But having chosen a path of freedom, democracy, and religious tolerance, they would like to see that recognized" (Wolfowitz 2009).

Obama underscored the point by sharing a personal anecdote on his day-long trip to Jakarta in November 2010:

But even as this land of my youth has changed in so many ways, those things that I learned to love about Indonesia—that spirit of tolerance that is written into your Constitution; symbolized in mosques and churches and temples standing alongside each other; that spirit that's embodied in your people—that still lives on. *Bhinneka Tunggal Ika*—unity in diversity. This is the foundation of Indonesia's example to the world, and this is why Indonesia will play such an important role in the 21st century. (Obama 2010b)

The evidence of America's soft power, one of the Obama campaign's selling points to the global community, seemed to be omnipresent throughout the school. The image of the first black president of the United States on the wall of an elementary school in Southeast Asia clearly suggested that America's goodwill knows no bounds or that the old American glory had not faded yet. Almost 40 years ago, the same allure of American power had caught hold of Obama's imagination. Americans used to hold joint military exercises with the Indonesian army, something his stepfather had full knowledge of while working for the American oil companies. At the time, his mother was teaching English to Indonesian businessmen at the U.S. Consulate. It was in Jakarta, in the nascent years of his development, when a child's mind is very impressionable and malleable, that Obama had grasped the hard and the soft arms of American power, the military as well as the business influence, respectively.

Developmental research shows that very young children begin to grasp the rules, structures, and authority relations that gradually mature into a political orientation and an expectation of norms regarding individual and collective behavior. By 13 or 14 years old, children have a fairly well-developed loyalty to a presidential figure and begin to grasp the various powers of the government. In an essay called "The Father in the White House: American Children and the Remaking of Political Orders," the cross-cultural psychologist Jaan Valsiner claims that the process of political socialization has sped up with the onset of Internet technology (Valsiner 2006). The father image of the American president is more accessible than ever before. Part and parcel of the stockpile of global images that circulate around the world, Obama has quickly become a household name, just as the younger Obama would have looked up to an American president like John F. Kennedy in his youth.

Concerned with her son's education, Ann Dunham had selected the Besuki School. It was the more affordable option compared with other international schools, but the public school had an esteemed reputation in the local community. In 1934, it was founded by the Dutch colonial administration as the Carpentier Alting Stichting Nassau School, the school was reserved for the children of the Dutch and Indonesian upper classes. The Indonesian government took over the school's administration in 1962. Former students included children and grandchildren of senior politicians, such as Bambang Trihatmodjo, the son of President Suharto.

After independence in 1945, all the public schools were founded on the five principles of Pancasila (the Sanskrit word for "five principles"), which also served as the basis of the Indonesian constitution (Nishimura 1995). The principles name inseparable and mutually qualifying rights, which have only a vague resemblance to the American Bill of Rights but are often compared to it:

1. Belief in the One and Only God
2. Just and civilized humanity
3. The unity of Indonesia
4. Democracy guided by the inner wisdom in the unanimity arising out of deliberations amongst representatives
5. Social justice for all the Indonesian people

With the emergence of the Suharto government in 1965, the Pancasila was fully revived in public school education. When Ann Dunham arrived in Jakarta with Barack Obama, the force of the Pancasila in civic education was in full effect, reflected in the curriculum, textbooks, and teacher training.

Largely due to the political philosophy of Pancasila, public school education is the beacon of secular values in Indonesia even today, over and above the more Islamist or fundamentalist trends, which have their roots in the traditional interpretation of Islamic scripture and a narrow reading of the constitution. Thus, the Besuki School has historically catered to children of families from many different religions. The evidence of this trend is most clearly demonstrated in the allocation of different prayer rooms for children of different religious backgrounds, the Muslim majority and the Christian, Buddhist, and Hindu minorities.

As I waited in the lobby of the school, a teacher named Emi Katemi, who spoke fluent English, introduced herself to me; she was expecting my arrival and was going to serve as my translator. Dressed in a modern pantsuit, with a matching head scarf and a pair of custom-made reading glasses, Emi Katemi clearly projected the image of secular Indonesian values. I realized I was witnessing the embodiment of modernity and Islamic values as they are transmitted and socialized to young Indonesian children and their families.

During my introductory meeting, Principal Hasimah further underscored the importance of Pancasila as the basis of modern education in Indonesia, something I had researched for the trip; her formal introduction to the principles of Indonesian education further added to my cultural understanding of the concept. According to her, the principles of Pancasila might have had a lasting and positive impact on Barack Obama in the context of day-to-day schooling, as he would have recited it regularly. Obama and his classmates would have used the Pancasila principles as a kind of pledge of allegiance. Thus, the secular principles of Indonesian democracy, where multiple faiths flourish side by side, were indelibly impressed on Obama's mind from a very young age.

Interestingly, Obama did not neglect to highlight the importance of this constitutional principle on his quick jaunt through Jakarta:

Such is Indonesia's spirit. Such is the message of Indonesia's inclusive philosophy, Pancasila. Across an archipelago that contains some of God's most beautiful creations, islands rising above an ocean named for peace, people choose to worship God as they please. Islam flourishes, but so do other faiths. Development is strengthened by an emerging democracy. Ancient traditions endure, even as a rising power is on the move. (Obama 2010b)

At the end of our meeting, I toured the school, attended a meeting of the alumni association, and mingled with the students and staff members. Accompanied by a translator, I examined the classrooms where Obama studied, the playground where he played, and the mosque or the prayer room where he prayed during the afternoon. I would make several repeat visits.

Currently, the Besuki School follows government-instituted international standards, matched with the Australian curriculum. Students from the Besuki School compete in science and math competitions with Australian children and have an exchange program with several Australian schools. The Besuki School is a coeducational institution, with reportedly an equal ratio of boys and girls from the first grade to the sixth grade.

The two-story building consists of a large open courtyard, the size of a basketball court, enclosed by classrooms on all four sides. It is built in the Dutch colonial style adapted to the needs of the tropical climate, with open verandas, hallways, and staircases; large airy windows that open out to a balcony; and stepped tiled roofs made of red clay designed to withstand the summer heat. A Dutch steeple designed by the original founders still stands atop the red clay–tiled roof as a reminder of the school's history and legacy. My guide pointed this out several times as a sign of the authenticity of the school and as a matter of pride for its Dutch heritage.

The main structure and design of the building has not changed since Obama was here as a student, although a major renovation has been added to the Islamic prayer room and many of the classrooms and teachers' offices have been wired to the Internet. "When Obama was here there was a prayer room here, but it was much smaller," explained Emi Katemi. "Also we did not have any ICT [information and computer technology]." I made a note to myself that this was another indication of how tradition and modernity go hand-in-hand in Indonesia and how technology and religious revival had occurred simultaneously; they were not antithetical to each other.

Looking across the open courtyard, with children playing basketball during recess, I could imagine how Barack Obama learned to handle the basketball on this playground and developed a love for his favorite pastime. I decided to mingle with the children and shoot a few hoops myself.

During the casual basketball play, a few of the children volunteered that Obama is their new hero and one day they hope to go to America to study, to be like him. I thought of the Michael Jordan commercial, "I wanna be like Mike," from a decade ago when the Chicago Bulls were on a roll. Now, it seems everybody around the world wants to be like Obama!

At one end of the courtyard, a walkway led to Obama's third- and fourth-grade classrooms. The classrooms and their floor plans have remained essentially the same for more than five decades. Each classroom housed about 30 desks and chairs, directly facing the blackboard. Each child was assigned a mailbox and a work area, not unlike an elementary classroom in America or any other urban metropolitan area. Students' artwork and projects were pasted on the walls of the classroom, with detailed plans for each subject or topic area to be studied, natural science, art, languages, etc. The classrooms were neat, were air conditioned, and had a dozen or more computer stations. Pictures of Barack Obama and his family were on display in each classroom.

When I asked to visit the prayer rooms in the school, Emi Katemi did not hesitate. "Oh, yeah, you're welcome to go to the prayer room. Just remember you have to take your shoes off before you enter," she instructed me. As I followed her, we climbed up an open staircase from a corner of the courtyard to the second floor of the school, directly above Obama's third-grade classroom. When we reached the prayer room, she explained, "We have prayers every day at noon, which is part of the regular school day. All children must pray at this time. We also have a prayer program on Fridays, which children must attend. Besides that children must participate in other activities, like how to read the Koran, and learn to pray and so on."

The prayer room contained wooden Islamic arches, with an Arabic scripture inscribed on a gold-plated masthead—"Allah, oneness of God." Approximately 30 prayer mats covered the floor. A schedule of activities was outlined on the bulletin board, and teachers were assigned to different religious activities for different days of the week. The prayer room also displayed trophies the children had won in intramural Islamic prayer recitation competitions sponsored by the Indonesian government.

"Here at this school, when the prayer room was much smaller, Obama learned to read the Koran. A small mosque may have been constructed around 2002, but there was an Islamic prayer room at the school when Obama attended, where he learned to recite the traditional Islamic prayer," explained Emi Katemi. He may have been socialized at home by his stepfather in reciting the Islamic prayer, but at the school he would have been required to attend the religious education class. "He would have attended the prayer classroom at noon," Emi Katemi clarified.

At my request, Emi Katemi opened one of the Korans and started to read from the opening passage. She described how a student would learn to read the scripture from the basic sounds and syllables from the holy book: *b-ismi-llāhi r-rahmāni r-rahīm*. "In the name of God, most gracious, most merciful . . . " she started to translate. Her lyrical Arabic sounded soft yet penetrating. Soon the room started to fill with children arriving for their noon prayer. Curious about gender roles in religious instructions, I asked if both female and male teachers could teach the Koran. Emi Katemi said, "Of course, men teach to the boys and women teachers teach it to the girls." Any teacher, whether or not the teacher is a cleric, can teach the Koran to students. This is true in all of Indonesia's public schools.

When I met with several members of the Friends of Obama at the Besuki School, their stories about Obama's childhood in Indonesia came alive through our conversation. Obama's friends are also members of the alumni association of the Besuki School, 300 people who meet regularly at the school for various events and functions. At one such alumni meeting, I spoke with several former classmates of Obama, who knew him and remembered that "he was taller than most Indonesian children in his class."

He was generally a naughty kid, according to his friends, and sometimes used to get into trouble because he would chase after girls. "One time we tied him to a tree and [another time] put him in the toilet and locked him up, just for the fun of it," said one classmate. "He was a cute kid, very funny and different from all of us. He was a bit chubby and black so he stood out," said another classmate. "He was mostly a good sport, although sometime he would get into altercations," said another.

When asked about his religious affiliation, several of his classmates said, "His mother was Christian, but Obama used to pray with us in the Islamic prayer room. His stepfather was Muslim. It was not a big deal then." The classmates all prayed and played together, many were Muslim children, some were Christian, and a few were Buddhists and Hindus. "There was a separate prayer room for Christians and Muslims, as there is now, but we were all friends," reported his classmates.

Accompanied with Emi Katemi, I interviewed the Christian teacher at the Besuki School, who supervises the prayer sessions for Christian students. At present, there are four students who pray in a Christian way in the separate prayer room. Instead of prayer mats on the floor, they sit on chairs at desks, where they fold their hands and recite the Christian prayers. The prayer room displays a prominent cross, a statue of Jesus Christ, and a list of Christian values on a laminated poster board, drawn from the Ten Commandments.

"Where are you from?" asked one of Obama's friends.

"I grew up in India, which has a large Muslim population. But now I live in the United States," I replied.

"Well, for people like you we have the Pancasila," said one of Obama's friends.

"All religions are welcome here in Indonesia," said another.

"Occasionally, Obama's mother would drop him off at the school because she worked at the U.S. Consulate nearby," added another friend. Obama has described some of the details of how visiting the U.S. Consulate with his mother was an occasion for him to catch up on American comics, take a dip in the refreshing pool, and relish a Coca-Cola on special occasions. During these years, his caregiver was a Javanese man named Pak Saman, who was also his mother's assistant at PPM Management Institute, where she taught English part-time. PPM is an executive business-training center, founded in 1967, for Indonesian businesses, schools, and government. After having worked at the U.S. Consulate for two years, Ann joined PPM in 1970.

Pak Saman looked the part of a Javanese man, short, stout, and very tough, not unlike Obama's stepfather, Lolo Soetoro. Every day Pak Saman drove Barry from home to his school and back on a *becak*, a traditional three-wheeled rickshaw. On these daily trips, they would often stop off at the U.S. Consulate, at the tennis courts where Lolo played regularly, or at a friend's house for a playdate, depending on Ann Dunham's schedule.

I had an opportunity to interview Pak Saman at length at the PPM. His proximity to the Soetoro family was unparalleled. He was involved in the day-to-day handling of Barry's schedule and cared for him when his parents were at work or busy with their daily routines.

Pak Saman remembered Barry as a very active child, who would get into altercations with other children and was often ready to defend himself. Fortunately, his stepfather was known as "the army man"; his friends were impressed with Barry and were afraid of his stepfather. Every time Barry would have a fight with a boy from school, Pak Saman would say "his father is an army man." The boys would automatically step back or simply run away. The other boys often called him "the dark boy with curly hair." Barry was known to fight back verbally, and sometimes he would defend himself physically; he was capable of fighting against several kids at once, recalled Pak Saman.

At the school, Barry had an assertive and strong personality. He had the ability to attack strongly, kind of like what he does now in politics, said Pak Saman. Another reporter has described a similar pattern, where Barry was the object of insults and rocks being thrown at him while he was visiting the town of Yogyakarta with his mother. Ann's friends were horrified at the risks she was exposing her young boy to, but she apparently said, "No, he's okay. . . . He's used to it." Barry for his part seemed "unfazed, dancing around as though playing dodgeball with unseen players" (Scott, 2011, 107).

Barry was a brilliant person, Pak Saman added. He could remember the numbers of license plates on cars even as a child; when his father changed cars, Barack remembered the previous number plates and the ones before that and so on. Barack was an intelligent person from a young age, said Pak Saman. Pak Saman remembered that once Barack Obama drew the different crocodiles from Africa, Asia, and the Pacific and knew how each type had a different-shaped head. He had studied them in a geography book, but recalled the details by sheer memory.

Pak Saman and Lolo Soetoro were both Javanese warriors by temperament and genealogy. Pak Saman recalled that Lolo was a champion tennis player who had a strong forehand. He was a very good rifle shooter and had been sent to the Papua New Guinea jungles by the Indonesian government to do geographical mapping (Operasi Tjenderawasih II, or Operation Cenderawasih, Border Survey Team) a fact Maya also confirmed. He had the scars to prove it.

Pak Saman vividly conjured up memories of Lolo's house, filled with different weapons—knives, machetes, and arrows—from his time in Papua New Guinea. He remembered a time when Lolo gave Barry a set of boxing gloves as a birthday gift. Barry's face lit up upon receiving them, and he put the gloves on every day and tried to box. He was a strong athletic boy and physically imposing compared with Indonesian children.

On a few occasions, Barack would go to the mosque with his stepfather. Lolo was not a religious man at all, remembered Pak Saman, and was married to a Christian woman who celebrated at least some of the Christian holidays, including Christmas and Easter, even while living in Jakarta. This may be the reason Obama never converted to Islam, recalled Pak Saman, in any formal sense of the term.

Barack did not go through any rite of passage or perform any traditional ceremonies that a young Muslim boy of his age might go through, such as *sunnet* or circumcision. Barry had been circumcised previously, confirmed Pak Saman, who used to bathe Barry sometimes and get him ready for school in the morning. Pak Saman rejected the idea that Barry ever converted to Islam or passed through any ritual ceremony while living in Jakarta. In fact, Obama left Indonesia just about the time he might have gone through some initiation rituals marking the transition from boyhood to manhood.

Pak Saman also confirmed, as did Obama's sister, Maya, that Barry was never legally adopted by Lolo. There was no doubt, however, that Lolo had great affection for his stepson, recalled Pak Saman. For his part, Obama seemed cognizant that his biological father lived in Kenya, yet he had great admiration and respect for his stepfather.

Pak Saman revealed that Ann Dunham was a tough mother, at times bordering on being domineering. "At that age, Obama used to be really afraid of her," he said. Ann Dunham was Pak Saman's supervisor at the PPM, and when she needed someone to look after Barry, she selected him because he was a good worker and a loyal and trustworthy person. She paid him an extra salary to do the household work and for child care services. Pak Saman's love for the Soetoro family was evident, however. He readily complied with my request for an interview and was very gracious. He was one of the few persons Barry visited when he returned to Jakarta with his mother after graduating from Columbia University.

Pak Saman also discussed Obama's daily routine. In addition to waking him up at 4 a.m. to study English from an American correspondence school, Ann Dunham made sure that he had a fixed routine when he came home from school. Pak Saman revealed that, typical of other Indonesian children, Barry was required to take regular afternoon naps after school, which may have been almost a necessity in the hot tropical climate. Ann made sure that he ate properly, being sure to include different kinds of food, and had enough time to play with children from diverse backgrounds. He was forced to drink his milk and take extra tonics in the morning and evening, generally before and after school. He was not allowed to go out and play until he had finished all his homework. At times when he would slack off, Ann was known to spank him; Pak Saman attested to hearing him cry in the privacy of his room after he was physically punished for not finishing his homework.

Ann Dunham was the main authority figure in Barry's early years, a woman whose worldview by far exercised the strongest influence on Barry's emerging mind. Although he had a stepfather who was a strong male role model, Barry's personality, daily habits and behaviors, sense of right and wrong, and way of looking at things were indelibly shaped by his mother.

Slamet Januadi, one of Obama's other boyhood friends, was the son of their landlord's chauffeur. Slamet, who still lives in the same servant quarters next to the former Soetoro residence, confirmed that Ann Dunham was indeed a stern mother and a strict disciplinarian, although she encouraged Barry to play with children from all economic backgrounds, not to discriminate based on social status, and to get along with everybody.

While sitting on the lawns of the Istiqlal Mosque, the largest mosque in Southeast Asia, Slamet shared stories of their childhood games and the pranks they would play on each other. Shortly after Maya's birth, a couple of days after she was brought home from the hospital, the two boys were playing on the front lawn next to the gravel driveway.

"So Barry, do you know where babies come from?" Slamet asked nine-year-old Barry jokingly. Barry did not seem to know about the birds and the bees, so his friend explained how babies are born. Learning this for the first time, Barry appeared horribly shocked and disappointed. Slamet thought that he was sharing something highly confidential with his childhood friend. "No, silly, your sister came from your mother's vagina. Remember this forever; this is our little secret," explained Slamet. He then revealed to me that, "Barry firmly held to the belief that both his mother and father have a penis. So, Maya must have come from somewhere else, not his mother's tummy." Slamet educated Barry with a crude explanation about the differences between the sexes and how babies are made. "This is our little secret. If you tell him this story, he will still remember me," said Slamet with a sense of gleeful pride.

I was immediately struck by the frankness of his expression. This seemed to be an interesting story for many reasons. First, growing up in an Islamic society Obama may have been socialized to repress sexual differences. An open discussion about sexuality may not have been permitted and simply avoided. Although in the late 1960s, when Obama lived in Jakarta, the society may have been more relaxed compared to

Islamic constrictions on sexual mores today (Indonesia has become more conservative), nevertheless, his awareness about biological differences between men and women may have developed later, after he was 10 years old or maybe during his teenage years. Generally in most Westernized societies, boys learn about such basic sexual differences early on and develop a male-oriented sexual identity in the prepubescent years.

Second, Indonesia has a matrifocal kinship structure, where women have a significant amount of power over men in the domestic world. Women's status tends to be higher in Indonesia compared with other more patriarchal Asian countries. Even infant mortality and nutritional indicators tend to be better for young girls than boys. The sex-role differentiation between Indonesian boys and girls is not that clearly demarcated or rigidly drawn in early childhood (Megawangi 1997). For all of these reasons, Alice Dewey, Ann's mentor and colleague, told me that Ann may have felt more at home in Indonesian culture; she felt more empowered as a woman there.

Barry's other experience with alternative gender roles may have come from the family's gay cook who, as Obama disclosed in his autobiography (Obama 2004), may have engaged in cross-dressing behavior. Obama's sister, Maya, confirmed this interesting fact, revealing in a matter-of-fact manner that Trudi, as the cook liked to be called, may have carried on an affair with a local butcher as suggested by another story (Onishi 2010). At the fringes of Indonesian society alternative lifestyles and sexual orientations have long been permitted, partly as a reflection of the historical intermixing of different cultures, religions, and races on the archipelago.

Thus, in this rather fluid cultural milieu Obama's attribution of the male organ to his mother may be due to his early socialization, where he was trained to not perceive any hard gender differences between his mother and stepfather in terms of sex-role differentiation, masculinity-femininity, and who wielded power and authority in the household. Both parents seemed to possess the levers of power in the family, which again suggests that his mother was at least as strong and powerful as any of the male role models in his early years. In Obama's case, the lack of a biological father in the family would offer one of the most straightforward explanations for this early family dynamic.

This family dynamic would also suggest from a purely psychoanalytic perspective that Obama's resolution of his underlying oedipal feelings vis-à-vis his father figures was at best delayed or not fully resolved. However, in the post-Freudian and postfeminist era, Obama's early socialization would be seen by many social theorists as possibly a healthy outcome for Obama's psychological development (Chodorow 1999; Gilligan 1993). A feminist might argue that Obama grew up in a less stereotypically patriarchal family, where men and women had an equal amount of power. Liberal feminist theorists might also suggest that this episode from Obama's childhood shows that the shaping of his personality by his mother offers a window on his leadership style, which has an overtly empathic, feminine, and listening quality; this is why even as a black man Obama was able to win votes from white women in large numbers. This explanation, however, might completely undermine the deleterious impact of father absence in his early life.

Kay Ikranagara, a colleague of Ann Dunham's at the PPM who still lives in Jakarta, said, "I think Ann Soetoro always thought that her greatest contribution to the world would be Barack and Maya." Ikranagara met Barry as a child and later when he was a senator. She remembered him as a "plump kid with big ears" who was an extrovert, very outgoing, and friendly with everyone because he had lived around different kinds of people and cultures. She believes this is the main reason why he truly has the ability to listen to people from all kinds of backgrounds.

Indonesian children have a lot of freedom to run around. People's homes are generally open, and kids have fun running in and out of their neighbors' homes and doing lots of mischievious things. Ikranagara recalled, "What my son Inno remembers is that Barry took him and his sister, Maya, up to the attic where they were not allowed to go. They were not allowed to touch the swords or *keris* [belonging to Lolo] up there. The swords are supposed to be full of all kinds of ghosts and spirits, but he took them up there. He touched the swords and did all kind of wicked things that an older boy would do."

Julia Suruyakusuma, a close friend of Ann Dunham for many years and a columnist at the *Jakarta Post*, said Ann was an engaged mother. When I interviewed her in Jakarta, she clarified that she did not know Ann Dunham during the early years, but met them later when Maya was almost six years old; she also did not know Lolo Soetoro well. Suruyakusuma elaborated further:

When I got to know Ann Dunham she was strong minded and firm in her views. We were both actively involved in the raising of our only sons; Barry and Aditya are of the same age group. We were both very similar in that we had our professional lives and we shared strong intellectual interests. She was a people's person; he is very much like that. Barack gets that trait from her. She was a pretty dominant woman, though not in a bad way. She was liberal but a strict disciplinarian, a diligent and hard-working person. I related to her; we had a lot in common. We were similar in that way.

Then she said something even more insightful:

Her image is very different in Indonesia than in the United States. Here she is the caring humanist, an ex-pat, who is interested in local cultures and people's lives. In the United States she may be often seen as part of the counterculture. She probably had a strong influence on Obama; he is not aware of it now. As the president, his mind must focus on so many other things that he does not think about it much.

As a former student of psychology, Suruyakusuma correctly noted that most people are not consciously attuned to their mother's influence on their life. She further mused that it might be interesting to think about how Ann's strong individuality might have shaped Obama's personality, and how he may have also reacted to her headstrong personality by staying back in Hawai'i. This is a decision Barack Obama made when he declined to go back to Jakarta after living in Hawai'i with his grandparents, a decision he found truly liberating.

Yet, in a recent interview, now that he is a father of two children himself, he admitted that this separation would have been a hard thing for a young child: "I think that was harder on a ten-year-old boy than he'd care to admit at the time," said Obama with candor. "When we were separated again during high school, at that point I was old enough to say, 'This is my choice, my decision.' But being a parent now and looking back at that, I could see—you know what?—that would be hard on a kid" (Scott 2011, 135).

I asked Suruyakusuma about the impact of Indonesian Islam on Barack Obama, given that she has written extensively about secular Islam in her book *Sex, Power and Nation* (Suruyakusuma 2010). She said, "Islam in the 1970s was a liberal Islam. It was syncretic Islam that got along with other religions. Islam has changed in recent years. We keep asking 'Will the real Islam please stand up?'" She agreed that Obama was socialized with a real sense of a secular Islamic identity when he lived here. "We have asked the question of Islamic identity several times in this country, and the voting public has always said that Indonesia is a democratic, secular, and open society," said Suruyakusuma. "Women wearing the Islamic gear, the hijab, are not necessarily doing the Islamic thing. They don a persona, give an impression of being religious, but they are not necessarily religious. People go through a nominal Muslim identity, but Indonesia is not a Muslim state at all," she said categorically. Anthropologists such as Alice Dewey, who have worked in Indonesia for many years, call this the "statistical Islam," in reference to how one might state one's religious identity on a census form.

I then shifted the conversation from filial love to love of political figures and asked Suruyakusuma about the recent controversy surrounding Obama's boyhood statue. She thought it was amusing and heartwarming that there is a statue to the child Obama in Menteng Park. She said, "Indonesians have a love-hate relationship with America. You can see this playing out in our relationship with Barack Obama. Just as soon as we had erected it, people started to protest about it. People have been complaining that Obama is not an Indonesian hero."

Obama's election changed the tone of Indonesia's relationship with the United States, but the structure remains the same. Suruyakusuma said, "We look at Obama with pride. He is our export to the United States. We feel in some ways he is ours because he spent four years of his life here." As someone who cried profusely at Obama's election, mostly because "I was thinking about his late mother," Suruyakusuma added that although overall she was pleased with the Obama statue, she thinks it is adulation taken too far.

Suruyakusuma echoed some of the sentiments I heard from Obama's other classmates, who talked about the recently erected statue and the controversy surrounding it at a meeting of the Friends of Obama at the Besuki School. A group in the Menteng area had been protesting that Obama had not done anything for the Indonesian people and did not deserve to have a statue in a public place. This group was petitioning the local government to remove the statue from Menteng Park.

I felt I had to visit the statue before completing my trip and see for myself what the big fuss was all about. However, before heading off to Menteng Park, I had to visit the St. Francis Assisi School, where Obama had spent three critical years from 1967 to 1969 during the early transition from home to school.

A Private Catholic School

Located on the south side of Jakarta, in an economically deprived part of town, St. Francis Assisi School is a Roman Catholic institution; in the late 1960s, it was run by a stern Dutch priest. However, compared with the Besuki School, the privately run Assisi School has expanded into a much larger campus since Obama attended it. It has an active church community and a nonprofit clinic run by the Catholic sisters whose living quarters are attached to the school. Here, children recite a Christian prayer at the beginning and end of each day.

As Barack Obama described in his autobiography, the school is within walking distance of the old Soetoro residence on 16 Haji Ramli Street, a home that, until recently, still belonged to the Soetoro family (Obama's younger sister, Maya, decided to sell the property in the early 1990s). The school appears to be an oasis for children in the midst of the hectic daily life in Jakarta.

As you turn in from the main street, Jalan Drive Saharjo, the narrow gulley leading to Haji Ramli Street crosses over a 20-foot-deep open sanitation line, a landmark Obama had identified in his autobiography; the pungent odor of the sanitation line is simply unforgettable. For a brief moment, I felt transported back to my own childhood in New Delhi, India, where in certain sections of old Delhi such an odor is commonplace, especially during the monsoon season. As the cars, scooters, mopeds, and pedestrian traffic moves past the local shops and street vendors, one has to maneuver carefully through the narrowing gullies and traffic bottlenecks. Everyone operates with a different sense of purpose on these roads, ever mindful not only of their own bodily orientation but also of others on the street. A passerby might turn out to be a stranger, a friend, a neighbor, or even your schoolteacher, whom you would have to greet with the appropriate deference.

I felt I had just penetrated the invisible outer wall of the kampong (village); now I had to gain entry through the next layer of the community. In the late 1960s, when Obama arrived here with his mother, Menteng Dalam was a ramshackle kampong at the outskirts of Jakarta mostly inhabited by middle-class and blue-collar Indonesians who were recovering from the bloody coup of 1965 and struggling to get on with their lives against the insults of abysmal poverty and hard living conditions.

In those days, most of the streets were dirt-baked; during heavy downpours the streets would clog with mud and adjoining front yards and verandas would flood. Ann Dunham was probably the only ex-pat woman who would have dared to live in such a neighborhood for fear of feeling completely out of her element. However, because she had decided to marry an Indonesian man and uproot her life, she was ready to live through the rough times in the way the native Indonesians did.

Several of Obama's former friends and neighbors confirmed that Ann Dunham, with her parched white complexion and dark flowing hair, was a unique figure in the kampong. The elected head of the kampong, Coenraad Satia Koesoemah, a former executive with Garuda Airlines who is now in his 80s, said that Ann's youthful appearance was matched by her gracious and loving heart. She used to teach English to poor children and adults in Coenraad's living room, a memory he still cherishes fondly. "Barry used to play with my children in this living room," he said, pointing to the area where we were sitting.

Coenraad recalled that Ann Dunham was an ex-pat who dared to live among the natives, which at the time was not easy. He said, "When I saw Barack Obama debating Hillary Clinton on the T.V. for the first time, I was reminded of Ann Dunham; she used to have strong views and an even stronger personality."

Almost everyone I interviewed in the kampong had affection for Ann and was fascinated with her life. Thus, Barry, by extension, was remembered as a local child of the kampong, which is now called the Barack Obama kampong. After much petitioning to the local governance committees, Coenraad got the new name approved in anticipation of Obama's Indonesian visit.

Coenraad also revealed that during these early years, Obama had a regular companion who was like an older sister; her name was Liah Soetoro. Only a few years older than Barry, she was distantly related to the Soetoro family and lived with them to help socialize Barry into the Indonesian language and culture. "Barry, this is Liah. She will be your companion. She will stay with you so you learn the language and if you need anything, you simply ask her. This is how Ann introduced them," said Coenraad. Liah and Barry were often seen together in the kampong, according to Coenraad. In the local newspapers, Liah's relationship to the Soetoro family has been disputed, but she may have been instrumental in teaching Barry the local customs and helping him find his way through the mazelike streets of Jakarta.

One of my first stops in Menteng Dalam was the office of Yustina Amirah, the principal of the St. Francis Assisi School. This school also had a uniformed guard, and I had to check in at the security gate before entering the school compound. I met Amirah in her quiet and neatly organized office, where we were able to block out some of the noise of the children playing outside; high above her desk was a laminated poster depicting Barack Obama speaking to a large audience. When I asked her how she had became an educator at a Catholic institution, she said that although both of her parents were Muslims by faith, and more than half of her family members are non-Christians, she had married a Catholic man, converted to his religion, and then became an educator. She said this type of intermingling of world religions and faiths is fairly common in Indonesia and has been part of Indonesian culture for centuries. Her disclosure made my job of probing about Obama's religious background and education fairly simple and gave me insights into the multireligious and multicultural community where Obama was first socialized.

St. Francis Assisi School was founded by Dutch missionaries. From the convent in Den Bosch, Netherlands, the now 81-year-old founder, Bart Janssen, closely followed the wave of publicity around Obama and his school. He recalled, "I am going back 40 years ago. The elementary school Assisi began in 1967 with the name SD Strada Assisi. The elementary school started with two classes, the 1st and 4th grade. The principal was Mr. L. W. Pareira, who taught the 4th grade while I myself and Mrs. Israella Darmawan took care of the 1st grade. In this small beginning, the school attracted 30 students for each grade. In the beginning the students did not wear uniforms."

At the opening of the second year, Barry Soetoro was admitted. "Each morning his mother brought him to school. She was a white American woman, and her husband was from Indonesia. He had the name Lolo Soetoro and lived close by the school. Barry was dressed neatly with stockings and shoes, was never late, and always brought with him a packed lunch, which he ate and finished off during the break."

Janssen, who has kept in touch with the three teachers who taught Obama in elementary school, fondly remembered that he "knew Barry as a brave boy, happy, easy to get along with—and he always adapted to circumstances. He was listening attentively, disciplined, and showed enthusiasm when following his lessons. As soon as he arrived it was obvious that he stood out among fellow students through his attitude and especially through his physical appearance."

The school now consists of a multistory cinderblock structure. For an urban school, Assisi has spacious classrooms, open playgrounds, wide open walkways, full-size basketball courts, several auditoriums, a well-maintained Catholic church, and lots of green trees. The main walkway, which runs through the school for several hundred yards, is enclosed by the administrative offices on one side and classrooms on the other side, and the large church is at the far end of the school.

As I roamed the school, I felt protected and cloistered. It felt like I was walking inside an open mall located in a kampong; children were running about and playing with their friends, and the parents were actively engaged in conversations with the teachers and staff members. There was a hubbub of activity in every classroom; as it turned out my visit to the St. Francis Assisi School coincided with the parent-teacher conference week. The level of parental engagement I witnessed was lively and strong.

I met all three of the teachers—Israel Darmawan, Firmina Sinaga, and Cecilia Sugini—who taught Obama during his elementary school years. All three teachers live in different suburbs of Jakarta and are now retired, but they gathered at the school for a visit and an interview with me. They all remembered Barack Obama as Barry Soetoro, his Indonesian name. Darmawan, Obama's first-grade teacher, recalled that when she first heard the name Barack Obama she did not recognize who he was. Then she realized that he was indeed her student Barry Soetoro from many years ago. Darmawan often receives reporters who want to interview her about little Barry's childhood.

Sugini and Sinaga, who taught him in second and third grade, respectively, remembered meeting Obama's stepfather only rarely during the nearly three years Obama spent at Assisi. However, all three teachers remembered vividly that his mother was a constant presence in his life; even with the passage of time the traces of Ann Dunham's image did not fade in their memory. They recalled that she used to bring him to school every morning and stand by the gate at the entrance of the school to pick him up; this was before she started working at PPM and hired Pak Saman to look after him. She used to look after Obama's studies, they all concurred, and she attended many of the parent-teacher meetings at the school.

It was during these elementary school years, when he was nine years old and in the third grade, that Obama wrote an essay titled, "What Is My Dream" for a class assignment. Sinaga still recalls the essay:

My name is Barry Soetoro. My teacher's name is Mrs. Firmina Sinaga. My mother is very beautiful with long hair. My mother is my idol, my hero. I love to live in Indonesia because it has good weather and good views. I go to school by walking. I want to be President one day. I want to visit around the world after I become President.

When I asked her how she managed to remember the essay 40 years later, she replied, "I remember the main points he wrote down. After people started to ask me about him, the memory simply came back to me." As the meeting with the three teachers was organized on the spur of the moment, Sinaga would not have had time to coordinate her narrative with the other teachers, so I assume her rendition of the story was original and accurate to the best of her abilities; it was not like any of the stories I had read in the Indonesian newspapers.

Darmawan added, "He wrote that he wanted to be president because he wanted everyone to be happy." She clarified that he did not specify which country or nationality he wanted to be the head of, but the story seemed unique enough to warrant the attention of the teachers; they discussed the story among themselves at the time. They also recalled that he was left-handed and that he had just become adept in writing Indonesian bhasha when he penned this childhood narrative. Mrs. Darmawan recalled in vivid details that Obama used to imitate Suharto while watching him give speeches to the Indonesian masses.

From the Netherlands, Janssen also remembered Obama's style of leadership:

> Since a young age his leadership qualities were obvious. The same happened also in the second grade with Mrs. Sugini and also in the third grade with Mrs. Sinaga. According to both teachers his behavior in these grades was no different than his behavior in the first grade. Very remarkable was that when Mrs. Sinaga gave the task of writing a composition in the Indonesian language, he wrote that it was his dream to become President. Now he has realized this ideal.

I asked all of the teachers if there was a particular event that might have triggered this ideation or creative thinking. His teachers recalled that he was a good student overall, and especially strong in math. He was a good leader, and though he was not fluent in bhasha, he would often direct other students on the playground, telling them to stand in a straight line and not to cut ahead of others while waiting. Basically, he was telling other children not to cheat. He was popular with the other children, although he was different and stood out because of his dark skin and curly hair. Obama showed no signs of tension within his family, but the teachers had heard from the gossip around the village well that there was friction between his parents.

They recalled that his younger sister, Maya, was born in the house on Dempo Street after the family had moved away from Haji Ramli Street; shortly after this move, Barack Obama went back to Hawai'i, maybe after a year. Obama may have also spent a summer vacation and Christmas holiday in Hawai'i during third grade. Then they did not hear about him again, except through the old neighbors near Haji Ramli Street.

I had read the story about Obama's childhood dream during the 2008 primary campaign season when the Clinton camp had chastised the Obama camp that their candidate had hatched a grand design to become president from an early age. The idea that Obama aspired to become president since the third grade was somehow seen as a negative characteristic. As I verified this story with all three of Obama's elementary school teachers, each of them added a different element to the story, as if to complete the story with the fragments of what they remembered. I began to piece together the different parts of the story as a gestalt of Obama's life in Jakarta.

When I asked Pak Saman about this story, he also recalled that Obama used to imitate Suharto in front of the T.V., try to speak like him, and copy his mannerism, tone, and speech, as if he were becoming a great leader himself. One time when the whole family sat down for dinner, Lolo asked Barry: "When you are a big boy, what do you want to be?" It must have been when he was about 10 years old and in fourth grade at the Besuki School recalled Pak Saman. "I want to be P.M. when I grow up," replied Obama. Pak Saman claimed to have observed such an intimate family scene several times between Barry and his stepfather while he worked for the Soetoro family. "Barry gave the impression, even at such a young age, that he had the capacity to become anybody he wanted to become," said Pak Saman. The way Obama used to defend himself demonstrated that he had the potential from a very young age to take a stand and defend it. He was good at communicating his thoughts to people and had a strong, assertive, and persuasive personality.

Pak Saman clarified that in the Indonesian context the term "P.M." could have meant that Barry wanted to be part of the paramilitary or military police, very much like his stepfather, or it may have been that he wanted to be president or prime minister, like the Indonesian leader Suharto. Irrespective of the interpretation of the term "P.M.," the story conveyed by several informants is consistent in outline, theme, and emotional tone.

Pak Saman also recalled that Ann used to think highly of her son's academic abilities, waking him up early to study. A doting mother, she would often boast about her son's ability to adapt and adjust to foreign environments. In her eyes, her son could do anything he put his mind to, including becoming president some day. "Sometimes when she talked about Barack, she'd say, 'Well, my son is so bright, he can do anything he ever wants in the world, even be president of the United States.' I remember her saying that," reported another Indonesian associate (Scott 2011, 131).

After learning of these stories from multiple points of view, I was somewhat struck by the plain innocence and consistency of the stories. These stories also aligned with Obama's own narrative as he outlined it in his autobiography. When Obama arrived in Indonesia with his mother, she was his idol. She was the center of his universe, his principal caregiver, though, as he disclosed, "Walking off the plane in Djakarta, the tarmac rippling with heat, the sun bright as a furnace, I clutched her hand, determined to protect her from whatever might come" (Obama 2004a, 32).

What seems to have emerged in fascinating details through a child's mind was an early awareness of a multidimensional political reality, interconnecting different members of his extended family in Indonesia with Hawai'i, and broadly connecting Asia and Africa with America; thus, Obama's mind was wired to think globally from these early formative experiences. Most American children have not witnessed Third World politics close up, unless they step out of their insular or protected world. In Indonesia, Obama developed a global view of America because this was his everyday family reality. He began to view America and ex-pat Americans from the outside in, almost like an ethnographer with an anthropologist's eye. As the child of an ex-pat mother who was gradually turning into an anthropologist, he could be both empathic and critical.

The tension between his mother and stepfather, although a source of anxiety, must have added another layer of complexity to his worldview. Although his mother appeared to be critical of America's strong business influence through the big oil companies, his stepfather accepted the changing business and political environment and began working for the American oil firms, specifically, Union Oil Company of California. He started to draw a handsome salary to keep the family intact and to be successful in the new Indonesian economy. Obama seems to suggest that though he understood his mother's naively idealistic view, he was more sympathetic with his stepfather's hard-headed view of the emerging social and economic reality.

As his stepfather said, his mother could always go back to America, but the Indonesians had to struggle on with their everyday lives.

Obama recently described his mother as "naively idealistic and sophisticated and smart. She was deadly serious about her work, yet had a sweetness and generosity of spirit that resulted occasionally in her being taken to the cleaners. She had an unusual openness, it seems, that was both intellectual and emotional" (Scott 2011, 4). His sister, Maya, agreed, "At the foundation of her strength was her ability to be moved" by the simple suffering of everyday folks (Scott 2011, 4).

As Obama described in his autobiography, before he returned to Hawai'i, he was gradually shifting from his mother's orbit toward his stepfather. With Lolo Soetoro's guidance he was learning about how the real world worked and how power shaped Indonesian and global politics. His mother never fully appreciated or took a liking to politics. Obama was beginning to identify with his stepfather and was moving away from his mother's somewhat romantic worldview.

Power had taken Lolo when he was suddenly yanked back from Hawai'i and sent to Papua New Guinea. The coup of 1965 had changed the rosy view of the world Lolo had while living as a student in Hawai'i. Obama seems to suggest that as he spent more time with his stepfather the dynamics of power were also pulling him away from his mother's somewhat purely humanistic views about the world. During the 2008 presidential campaign, Obama denied that he had had any childhood fantasies about wanting to be president; this is not a dream he had ever had, he said. However, a dream disclosed in a childhood essay written at the age of nine or ten years is not something he would necessarily remember consciously. We can recall only a small portion of our memories from early childhood, although these memories and events continue to shape our worldview. In many ways, it is more meaningful and telling that Obama does not remember his early memories in all of their detail, yet his teachers or caregivers recall the same story. Since the details provided by these people add up and generally match Obama's own retelling of his years in Jakarta, it is difficult to simply disregard this story as apocryphal.

In a recent news report, Slamet offered a slightly different version of the story (Onishi 2010). He recalled that one day Obama asked a group of boys whether they wanted to grow up to be a president, a soldier, or a businessman. A president would own nothing, a soldier would possess weapons, and a businessman would have money, the young Obama explained.

Slamet and his brother readily volunteered that they wanted to become soldiers, which is indeed what they did by joining the Indonesian army when they grew up. Another boy who became a banker in real life said he wanted to be a businessman. Barry patiently waited his turn and then revealed that he would become the president, order the soldier to protect him, and use the businessman's resources to build something. The boys immediately protested that he cheated because he did not tell them all of the rules of the game. Yet all of them became what they had wished to become as children, uncovering the simple yet profound impact of children's fantasy play on their imagination and destiny.

Obama's Worldview

The education Obama received in these early years shaped his emerging theories of the world, his worldview, and his character. At the Besuki School and the Assisi School, from first through fourth grades, Obama's curriculum included a wide array of subjects, including moral and religious education.

Religion and character building (*Pendidikan Agama*) are central to Indonesian public schooling. *Agama* refers to religious education within the context of modernist secular Islam and the teaching of morals, ethics, and politeness. *Pendidikan* refers to the process of education. The end goal of religious education is the creation of a noble character, one who is capable of upright moral values and endorses the ethical standards of a society. Indonesian democracy recognizes six official faiths as part of its religious demography: Islam, Catholicism, Protestantism, Buddhism, Hinduism, and Confucianism; citizens are free to choose a religion or any other religion not mentioned, such as animism, Judaism, or Shintoism.

At the Assisi School Obama engaged in daily Christian prayers,while at the Besuki School he recited the Pancasila, or the five principles of Indonesian secular democracy, as well as learning the traditional Islamic way of praying and reading the Koran. Thus, as per the Indonesian curriculum, Obama participated in religious education at both the Assisi and the Besuki schools.

Religious education is encompassed within the overall vision of Indonesian education, which is the realization of intelligent persons who are able to act and react to changing challenges of their era. Indonesians are seen as adaptive and bright—spiritually, emotionally, socially, intellectually, and kinesthetically—and as competitive citizens. The promotion of all types of educational systems—formal and informal—is envisioned by the Indonesian constitution.

Basic education is conducted in both public schools and religious schools called *madrassa* (*madrassa ibtidaiyah* for elementary school and *madrassa tsanawiyah* for junior high school). Although public elementary schools are managed according to policies established by the Ministry of National Education and operationally controlled by autonomous local/district/town administrations, the madrassas are managed by the Ministry of Religious Affairs through its local (district/town) offices throughout Indonesia. Obama attended a public school, not a madrassa, a fact verified by my own field research and by other journalistic accounts.

His education included classes in civic education (*Pendidikan Kewarganegaran*), where *Kewarganegaran* means civic life or citizenship, or how to become an engaged and informed citizen of Indonesia. This subject is intended to develop learners' awareness and knowledge with regard to their status, rights, and obligations in community, state, and nation and to improve their quality as human beings. Obama's own behavior and reflections about this period show a breadth of view and an acute awareness and knowledge of his Americanness, a sense of self, and a feeling of patriotism, which led him to defend his American identity on many ocassions.

Obama was also enrolled in a class in Indonesian language and history (*Bahasa* Indonesia); *Bahasa* literally translated refers to a written and spoken language. On the archipelago of Indonesia, the principal language is Indonesian, a dialect of Malay. Obama learned to speak the *Bahasa* Indonesia and was fluent by the second and third grade, but after leaving Jakarta it fell somewhat by the wayside. Although Obama studied social studies, history, and politics, he showed little formal interest in these subjects as a young boy.

He also studied basic mathematics (*Matematika*) and all of his teachers reported that he was strong in numeracy. Although he studied natural sciences, this was not reported to be his favorite subject. He took an interest in Indonesian arts and culture, for example, subjects like puppetry and mask making, and he enjoyed drawing and painting as a regular hobby. He was good at drawing stick figures and cartoons and was often seen sketching action heroes like Superman and Batman during leisure time. Consistent with his interest in action heroes, Obama was a very active child and engaged in sports with vigor.

Thus, we can see from this profile that during his early years in Indonesia Obama grew up within a multilingual, multireligious, and multicultural environment; his family members spoke different languages, practiced different religions, and came from remarkably different social and cultural worlds. His budding theory of mind by 10 years of age was shaped by a diverse array of societal, cultural, and historical contingencies and parental influences. This shaped not only his understanding of religion but also his view of poverty and underdevelopment.

Finally, and most importantly, as a child Obama had a front-row seat to America's role in shaping a newly emerging independent nation in the Asia-Pacific region at the onset of the postcolonial era. It was not a coincidence that his mother married two men from developing countries, both of whom belonged to nations with long colonial history; she was a peacenik and sympathized with the counterculture movement. As a student in Hawai'i, Ann was exposed to the forces of globalization much earlier than her peers on the mainland, before there were buzzwords to identify the mechanisms of an emerging global culture through finance, capital markets, and outsourcing.

Both Obama's African father and Indonesian stepfather were sponsored by their governments to study in the United States, to help advance the cause of freedom in their own countries, and they were actively involved in government operations in different capacities. They deeply cared about the local conditions in their own nations and were committed to changing the world.

Furthermore, both of Ann Dunham's choices of life partners reflected an affinity for non-Christian men, who practiced a brand of modernist or secular Islam, which was a far cry from any Islamist jihadist zeal that pervades the political discourse these days. Ann Dunham was drawn to Islam, perhaps, for the alternative viewpoint of the world it offered or for some other unknown reasons; there is no evidence to suggest that she ever converted to Islam in Indonesia or prayed in the Islamic way. In Indonesia's multireligious society, it was easy for her to retain her secular humanist views while practicing certain Christian rituals and holidays. There is no evidence to suggest that Ann was ever forced to convert to Islam by Obama's father or stepfather, or to put on the veil, a burka, or a hijab. Furthermore, the men she married loved life in the modern sense of the term; they were bon vivants, as the French describe it. These men were well-versed and experienced in secular Western values; in some ways they practiced American liberal values. They had been schooled in the West and applied some of the same logic and frameworks to their own local cultures. They were especially carefree about Islamic religious constrictions regarding eating and drinking; both Obama's father and stepfather lived life with gusto, married multiple times, loved women from different cultures, and took a liking to hard drinking.

His mother's commitments to these men to a large extent shaped Obama's social world in the early years. Obama inherited a dizzying array of cultural and geographical divides, which under normal circumstances might have broken a person of lesser strength or temperament. From the moment of conception, Obama's family was starkly divided along lines of race, culture, history, geography, and religion. His mother was from Kansas and his father was from Kenya; their cultural and historical origins were a world apart. Like the characters in Nadine Gordimer's fiction who live in racially divided apartheid in South Africa, they were drawn to each other by the intensity of their remarkable differences; on the face of it, they had very little in common.

If Obama had simply focused on the cultural differences between his mother and father, he might have found little common ground between them, or he might simply have descended into madness. Thus, he had to look for a higher purpose or a common humanity between the world of his father and that of his mother. He had to reconcile the disparate and often contradictory worldviews they came from, and by shaping an ethnic or cultural identity as an African American male he found a workable solution to bridge the cultural and geographical divide. As a black man in America, he found the connective tissue that held the various parts of his inner and outer self together in a seamless whole.

In Indonesia, he learned how different religions historically accommodated each other in a syncretistic manner, especially how Christianity lived side by side with Islam. His mother was a secular humanist with a Christian upbringing, but his stepfather was a secular Muslim. They lived in the largest Muslim democracy on the planet. Indonesian public school education offered a window on secular Islam and how peaceful coexistence of multiple and competing faiths was not only possible but achievable. In these early years, Obama may have been drawn to Islam because it was the religion of his grandfather, father, and now stepfather, albeit in its secularized form and modern outlook. Even if he was not drawn to it, he could not avoid being part of the secular Islamic culture at home, in school, and in the daily ambience and rhythm of the city life. Even today, he can conjure up the lingering memories of listening to the Islamic prayer at sunrise and at sunset.

Finally, Obama began to see the impact of the industrialized, developed economies on the lives of people in the developing world. Within the context of poverty and underdevelopment, Obama witnessed Indonesian society coming of age, which occurred partially under the influence of American business and diplomacy. As we have seen, his mother worked for the U.S. Consulate and various development aid agencies, and his stepfather worked first for the Indonesian government and later for major American oil companies. The manner in which Obama grasped the competing interests of his mother and stepfather resolved some of these naturally occurring tensions, but it had a long-term impact on his identity and politics.

In his autobiography, he clearly stated that his mother did not reciprocate Lolo's attempts to get her to curry favor with the American and Indonesian businessmen at social events, parties, and golf outings. New money was pouring into Jakarta, especially after the bloody coup that had elevated Suharto to the presidency, and more and more American and Indonesian businessmen were cutting deals with each other. While working for American multinational oil companies, Lolo saw this as a real opportunity to advance his career. However, Ann Dunham did not wish to be part of any such deal-making, and refused to participate in any formal or informal social networking on his behalf. The American businessmen were not her people, she said repeatedly. Although Lolo aligned himself with the new money and the flow of capital that Americans had to offer to Indonesians, Obama's mother was more interested in the progressive strain of American culture that favored international development and aid. This is the crux of what may have divided Ann Dunham and Lolo Soetoro, a clash of worldviews finally broke up their marriage; shortly after Obama returned to Hawai'i, their marriage further deteriorated. Later, when Ann returned to work on her doctorate in 1975, she did not live with Lolo.

Thus, Indonesia played a critical role in shaping Obama's worldview in early childhood. His time in Indonesia was the only extended time he lived within a nuclear family with a live-in stepfather and a mother. These family dynamics shaped him indelibly; his sojourn coincided with his home-to-school developmental transition, considered critical for all school-age children. It was in Jakarta that Obama began his elementary schooling. It was in Jakarta that Obama was first exposed to Islamic culture as a way of life. It was in the dusty streets of Indonesia, an underdeveloped country, that Obama was first exposed to abysmal poverty and misery, the likes of which he had not seen before. It was also in Jakarta, near the Besuki School, where Obama saw firsthand the raw power of American business and geopolitical strategy in transforming the world, in this case a fledgling Southeast Asian democracy.

In Indonesia, the youthful Obama saw massive and programmatic social and cultural change at the micro- and macroeconomic levels, which served as a counterpoint to his idyllic life in the Hawai'ian Islands. He may have grasped the nature of social change in Jakarta and the power of large-scale social transformations. As he observed the aftereffects of the political change brought on by American policies in Southeast Asian and the Pacific region, he witnessed the nature of political power in changing the lives of ordinary citizens.

In a revealing passage in his autobiography, Obama described how his mother finally learned from Lolo's cousin Trisulo about the coup in 1965 that occurred just a few years before their arrival and the atrocities that followed in the name of national unity. On September 30, 1965, in the dead of the night, six Indonesian army men were kidnapped and killed. The Communist Party had been suspected of the crime, which was immediately struck down, but a bloodbath ensued that people still describe as the bloodiest in the history of the archipelago. Rivers were red with blood and decapitated bodies of hundreds of thousands communist sympathizers clogged the open waterways.

The cousin explained that Lolo had been dragged back home from Hawai'i and had disappeared for a year on a government assignment in the jungles of Papua New Guinea. When Trisulo described how many students simply went missing or were massacred, all because of the coup, which most likely was supported by the CIA in an attempt to keep Indonesia from becoming communist, Ann Dunham's world went topsy-turvy. She had not seen the nature of political power in such a raw and transparent manner. At some unusually low points, she may have also felt that she made a mistake in moving to Jakarta.

Obama described his mother's reaction in graphic detail:

> *Power.* The word fixed in my mother's mind like a curse. In America, it had generally remained hidden from view until you dug beneath the surface of things; until you visited an Indian reservation or spoke to a black

person whose trust you had earned. But here power was undisguised, indiscriminate, naked, always fresh in the memory. (Obama 2004a, 45)

Ann Dunham, who worked on egalitarian and humanitarian projects most of her life, never fully came to terms with the nature of unadulterated political power.

After returning from Papua New Guinea, Lolo had arranged for his wife and stepson to come live in Jakarta. Lolo struggled a bit in the beginning, but then he started to work regularly. As money started to flow, things got better; Lolo moved the family from Menteng Dalam to Menteng Dempo, an upscale neighborhood with better schools, streets, and parks. Barry also changed schools from Assisi to Besuki; a car replaced the motorbike, a television and other gadgets replaced the backyard zoo, but the distance between his mother and stepfather grew larger not smaller. During this period Obama's sister, Maya, was born on August 15, 1970.

Pak Saman remembers this period well. Ann Dunham used to work two shifts at the PPM in those days, 4:00 to 6:00 p.m. and 7:00 to 9:00 p.m. She would often stay late to help students who needed extra assistance with language instructions. Traveling home late at night was not easy because of the unavailability of reliable public transportation, so Lolo insisted that Ann get a ride home from a friend, rather than travel alone after dusk. However, oftentimes a student would not drop her off at home but instead at the nearest street or intersection.

This situation tended to anger Lolo. On several occasions, Lolo would get rough with a student who drove Ann home and beat him up pretty badly in a drunken rage; the person would often leave bloodied and bruised. Pak Saman clarified that Obama did not know about these fights and altercations because he was often fast asleep in his bedroom.

Pak Saman recalled that after Maya's birth, Barry began talking about going back to Hawai'i. He also said that Ann Dunham wanted to return to work, but Lolo Soetoro wanted to have more children. As a result of different priorities, they gradually began to drift apart.

Ann Dunham left Soetoro in 1972, returned to Hawai'i, and reunited with her son Barack for several years, offering Obama a latent sense of oedipal victory over his stepfather. Soetoro and Dunham saw each other periodically in the 1970s when Dunham returned to Indonesia for her fieldwork, but they did not live together again. They divorced in 1980 and she began using the name Ann Dunham Sutoro, with a modern variation of her former husband's surname. Pak Saman worked for the Soetoro family until 1973 and didn't meet Ann again until 1986, when she returned to PPM for a visit.

After completing multiple visits to both of Obama's schools and visiting his former homes on Haji Ramli Street and Dempo Street, I was ready to pick up my trail to the statue of Obama as a boy. With the help of a teacher at the Besuki School, I ventured into the neighborhood near the U.S. Consulate, through winding paths and narrow streets lined with modern gated homes and imported cars, until we made it to a well-maintained and leafy park that appeared to be the size of Boston Commons. One corner of the park was turned into a children's zone, where I found a life-size statue dedicated to Barry Obama, with a Nobel Peace Prize medal around his neck.

The curious bronze statue was a tourist attraction for foreigners. Many local residents, however, weren't pleased with it. Indonesians didn't want the statue in the park, said Yunus, the park keeper. "I'm not against Obama," said Protus Tanuhandaru, one of the Indonesian founders of a Facebook page that collected fans calling for the figure's removal. "But it's wrong to have a statue in a public park of someone who has contributed nothing to Indonesia" (Beech 2010).

Slightly smaller than the Little Mermaid in the harbor at Copenhagen but twice the size of the Mannequin Pis in Brussels, the Barry Obama statue in Menteng Park was a fascinating sculpture for the childlike wonder it evoked in the audience. Tourists often stopped and looked. They read the inscriptions and touch little Barry's hands and feet as if to capture some of the magic he possessed. They looked at the expressions depicted on Obama's face—a serene, happy, and curious gaze, staring into the distant horizon.

On one side, the inscription inspired the observers: "The future belongs to those who believe in the power of their dreams." On the other side it outlined Obama's journey from Menteng to 1600 Pennsylvania Avenue: "A young boy named Barry played with his mother, Ann in Menteng Area. He grew up to be the 44th president of the United States and Nobel Peace Prize winner, Barack Obama."

A few weeks after I flew back from Jakarta, as a result of the mounting pressures from the group protesting that the statue should not have been placed in the public park, it was moved to the courtyard at the Besuki School. It now stands where I had seen the school children playing marbles under the watchful eye of the guard. I saw the pictures of the school administrators wrapping the statue of the 10-year-old Barry and carrying it to its new location in a procession-like ceremony. Approximately 57,000 petitioners found the statue objectionable on the grounds that Obama is not an Indonesian hero, or at least not yet, and he has not done anything substantive for Indonesian people to deserve such an honor.

As a metaphor of Obama's childhood in Jakarta, the statue embodies the magical and mystical time he spent there. It also reflects the uneasy alliance Indonesians feel with the United States; many of the editorials in the leading Indonesian newspapers covered the controversy the statue had generated. However, many of the Obama supporters and detractors believed that for now the Obama statue belonged in the courtyard of the Besuki School and not in a public park. Perhaps with the passage of time and with changes in his foreign policies, the Obama statue might be returned to another important public venue. In the meantime, on his recent trip to Jakarta, Obama pushed economic cooperation as well as Islamic outreach.

On the Move: Barack Obama riding a tricycle during the early years in Hawai'i. (Barack Obama family collection)

Standing Guard: Barack Obama on Waikiki beach in a lifeguard stand next to the famous pink Waikiki hotel, The Royal Hawai'ian, in 1967. (Barack Obama family collection)

Strolling at the Beach: Barack walks along Waikiki beach shortly before he and his mother moved from Hawai'i to Indonesia to live with her second husband, Lolo Soetoro, in 1967. (Barack Obama family collection)

Mother and Son: Stanley Ann Dunham holding the young Barack, scaffolding him with her strong arms while he was sitting on a fence. (Barack Obama family collection)

Language Teacher: Obama's English teacher, Mrs. Barbara Nelson, around 1980. (Courtesy of Barbara Nelson)

Pauahi Hall: Obama's homeroom building at the Punahou School. (Courtesy of Dinesh Sharma)

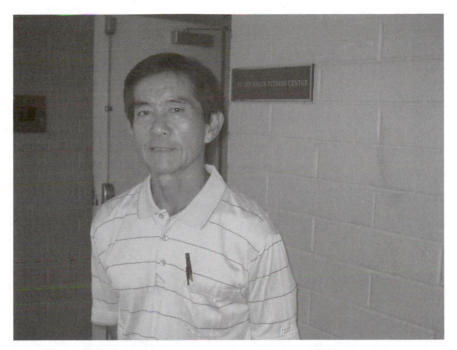

The Kumu: Obama's homeroom teacher, Mr. Eric Kusonoki. (Courtesy of Dinesh Sharma)

Brother and Sister: Maya and Barack in 2008. (Barack Obama family collection)

Grandparents' Apartment: Punahou Circle Apartments, 2010. (Courtesy of Dinesh Sharma)

A Family Friend: Governor Neil Abercrombie of Hawai'i in Washington, D.C., in 2010. (Courtesy of Dinesh Sharma)

The Dunhams: Dunham family, with precocious Stanley Ann; her father, who named his only child after himself; her mother, Madelyn, the firm influence in the home. (Barack Obama family collection)

Father: Barack Obama Sr., a Kenyan economist, met his future wife while they were students at the University of Hawai'i. He abandoned the young Barack at the age of two to continue his studies at Harvard. (Barack Obama family collection)

Granny: Barack Obama poses with his paternal grandmother during his first trip to Africa, around 1987. (Barack Obama family collection)

Ann Dunham at PPM: Obama's mother with Mr. Anton Hilman at PPM School of Management. Both were teachers at the school, 1975. (Barack Obama family collection)

Ann Dunham and Friend: Ann Dunham with a friend at PPM School of Management, Jakarta, 1975. (Barack Obama family collection)

The Church: Catholic Church at Obama's school, St. Francis Assisi, Jakarta, 2010. (Courtesy of Dinesh Sharma)

The Street: Haji Ramli Street leading to Obama's childhood home in Jakarta, 2010. (Courtesy of Dinesh Sharma)

The Prayer Room: Islamic prayer room at Obama's public school, SDN Menteng Dalam, 2010. (Courtesy of Dinesh Sharma)

The Mosque: Mosque near Obama's childhood home where he grew up, Jakarta, 2010. (Courtesy of Dinesh Sharma)

First Home: Obama's childhood home at Haji Ramli Street, 2010. (Courtesy of Dinesh Sharma)

A Plaque: Obama's plaque at the public school, SDN Menteng Dalam, 2010. (Courtesy of Dinesh Sharma)

A Statue: Obama's childhood statue, which was located in Menteng Park near his school in Jakarta, 2010. (Courtesy of Dinesh Sharma)

Three Teachers: Elementary school teachers who taught Barack Obama in first, second and third grades, respectively: Mrs. Sinaga (left), Mrs. Darmawan (middle), and Mrs. Sugini (right), 2010. (Courtesy of Dinesh Sharma)

The Nanny: Pak Saman, Obama's caregiver who worked for Ann Dunham, with a faculty member at PPM, Dr. Bramantyo, 2010. (Courtesy of Dinesh Sharma)

Second Home: Obama's childhood home in Menteng Dempo, Jakarta, 2010. (Courtesy of Dinesh Sharma)

Family Room: Obama's family room at Menteng Dempo, Jakarta, 2010. (Courtesy of Dinesh Sharma)

Classroom: Obama's classroom at the public school, SDN Menteng Dalam, Jakarta, 2010. (Courtesy of Dinesh Sharma)

Obama's Public School: SDN Menteng School courtyard, 2010. (Courtesy of Dinesh Sharma)

Obama's Catholic Elementary School: St. Francis Assisi School, Jakarta, 2010. (Courtesy of Dinesh Sharma)

5

A New Spring in Hawai'i

In youth we clothe ourselves with rainbows, and go as brave as the zodiac.

Ralph Waldo Emerson (2003)

Hawai'i is still young, still imbued with a spirit of experimentation, an apprecia-tion of nature's gifts and a pride in place and in self. If this be the prevailing spirit, then the promise of Hawai'i becomes reality, the life on the land will be represented by i ka pono; and Hawai'i will give birth to a more truly egalitarian and pluralistic society, and to a new cosmopolitan race of mankind.

Tom Coffman (1973)

Obama's transformation from Barry to Barack forms an interesting rite of passage in the annals of presidential history. In this chapter, I examine Obama's years in Hawai'i, where he spent eight years at the well-known Punahou School, and make the case that his transformation from boyhood through adolescence to young adulthood owes a lot to his early school-ing at an elite preparatory school in Honolulu, not too far from the Uni-versity of Hawai'i, where his parents met in the early 1960s, his mother completed her doctorate in anthropology, and his father graduated with a bachelor's degree in economics with honors. Interestingly, the name of the school is derived from the Hawai'ian term *ka Punahou*, which means the new spring. Obama also grew up not too far from the Pearl Harbor naval base, the site of the previous sneak attack on the United States before 9/11, which took more than 3,000 American lives and thrust his grandfather into World War II.

In the 1970s, when Obama returned from Indonesia to Hawai'i, the rapid pace of globalization had not yet reached the Hawai'ian shores, and Internet and cell phones were several decades away from connecting the world. However, Obama gradually soaked in the multicultural, multiethnic, and international influences at Punahou; here he began to train his mind in the arts of writing, rhetoric, and debate, with a keen international or global focus. In time, these early influences would shape a new type of American leader, which very few could have foreseen or predicted.

In Obama's world, the wide chasm that separated Hawai'i from Indonesia physically by way of the Pacific Ocean was connected by a bridge made up of his social and cultural experiences with his transnational family. His mother, sister, and stepfather provided the emotional and connective tissue that linked his family in Jakarta with his grandparents' new apartment in Hawai'i. The transition from Jakarta to Hawai'i was not easy, but in the media-driven consumer culture of Hawai'i he began to nurse the wounds he suffered in Jakarta, including the impending breakup of his mother's second marriage, the constant burden of appearing different, the daily insults of the grinding poverty, the often congested streets, and the different levels of environmental pollution, all of which seemed to take a toll on the young Barack. Yet these constraints seemed to magically melt away in Hawai'i and as a result of his grandparents' guardianship. He could watch his favorite T.V. shows, go to the beach, play basketball, and hang out with his newfound friends at the local Baskin-Robbins or the Rainbow Drive-Inn. In the privacy of his grandparents' apartment he could also retreat into his inner world and figure out his place in the world.

He took to reading and basketball with a passion. Basketball began to define his outer self and his network of friends, while reading led to his inner discoveries. In these two activities, he found himself and began to develop his higher cognitive abilities and a sense of social purpose and belonging. In the privacy of his grandparents' apartment and at the Punahou School, he wrestled with the questions surrounding his racial identity, as he has written in his autobiography. He did not fully resolve his racial identity until well after he moved to the mainland, but in Hawai'i he arrived at the coordinates of the fundamentals of his self, which guided him in his search for a self as a young adult on the mainland.

Alan Lum, who played basketball with Obama and who now teaches at the Punahou School stated that Obama did not reveal his inner struggles to his peers, "[b]ut when you think about it, . . . he was trying to define himself as an African-American on a campus where we only had maybe five African-Americans." (The total student body was 1,600 students.) "You don't have any models . . . basically you have to figure it out on your own," said his former classmate (Calmes 2009).

One of the few female African American students, Joella Edwards, has reported being teased and feeling alone while at the Punahou School. She was relieved to see another black student in several of her classes. However, Obama was somewhat shy, reserved, and highly intelligent, she claimed, and not easy to reach (Edwards 2008).

I argue that the ease with which the mature Obama seems to transcend race is deeply rooted in his socialization in the Hawai'ian cultural milieu, where no ethnic group has a majority. The current demographics include the following mix of ethnic groups: Asian American 38 percent, white 27 percent, multiracial 21 percent, Pacific Islander 9 percent, Hispanic and Latino 8.7 percent, African American 2.4 percent, other 1.4 percent, and American Indian 0.2 percent (U.S. Census 2010b). Obama's early environment portrays the emerging demographic reality on the mainland. As of 2009, the other states with a majority of minorities include California, New Mexico, and Texas.

At Punahou, which is in many ways a microcosm of Hawai'i, Obama learned to feel comfortable in his skin. Most students at Punahou are of mixed ethnicity. This is reflected in a variety of skin colors and pigmentation, but everyone is an American. In this respect, Hawai'i and Obama both grew up together and were ahead of their times. Hawai'i became a state in 1959, and Obama was born just two years later in 1961; both may be leading the mainland or the rest of the nation toward a future on the horizon, Obama as a president and Hawai'i, as a global village.

Hawai'i as a Global Village

The year 1959 was an important milestone in the history of the Obama and Dunham family. A constellation of cultural and geopolitical forces would lead to a brief romance and eventual marriage between Barack Obama Sr. and Ann Dunham. The year Hawai'i became part of the United States, Barack Obama Sr. moved to Hawai'i as an exchange student. Just a year later, the Dunham family moved to Hawai'i, drawn by a business opportunity.

After Alaska entered the Union as the 49th state, Hawai'i was still in the running for the statehood. The Alaska-first strategy proved to be right, dispelling any concerns about managing a demographically diverse outpost as a noncontiguous state. It sealed support for Hawai'ian statehood from Senator Lyndon Johnson and Senator Sam Rayburn, two influential politicians who wanted to garner democratic supporters from Alaska and potentially Hawai'i.

Many in Congress were concerned that granting statehood to Hawai'i was a bad idea because Hawai'i faces the East whereas America was a thoroughly Westernized nation. The ethnicities on the Hawai'ian Islands were the main concern. Arch-conservative Strom Thurmond, who as it turned out had fathered a mixed-race child himself, expressed his concerns about the different races and ethnicities in Hawai'i. Thurmond even summoned Rudyard Kipling to make the case that "East is East and West is West and never the twain shall meet."

Alice Dewey, an anthropologist who has a keen eye for the kinship and marriage patterns on the islands, told me that there are very few pure racial or ethnic groups in Hawai'i, where interracial marriages have been the norm. In 1961, the year Obama was born, approximately two thirds of Hawai'i's population was ethnically mixed nonwhites, and there were very few blacks or African Americans in Hawai'i. After the second and third generation of mixed marriages, it became very difficult to tell who belonged to what race or ethnic group. Hawai'i is a blended state, especially when it comes to color, and the mainland may be gradually heading that way socially and demographically.

Even though there were no majorities on the islands, the business and governance was still run by the whites or *haole*. The trading, commercial, banking, and land companies were all run or dominated by the whites. The city's building and tourist boom was still in the planning stages. Coinciding with the era of the jet age, Hawai'i would soon become an ideal destination for travelers and honeymooners. After statehood, plantations turned into resorts, and many owners of large plantations turned into rich businessmen overnight. People who had been waiting to be part of the United States finally found their footing, and many more newcomers came to be part of the post-statehood boom.

The first settlers of the Hawai'ian Islands were Polynesians, who reached the islands on wooden canoes after journeying across the open seas. The Polynesians were expert navigators and conservationists and knew how to get along with nature. These original settlers were later discovered by Captain James Cook, one of the first European navigators to reach the islands and who documented his findings.

Only eight days after the American declaration of independence, Cook began his voyage toward the Northwest Passage and happened to find the Hawai'ian Islands on his route. The natives first thought he was a god, but they later discovered his human frailties, and during his third visit they killed him. Cook was eventually buried on the islands but his secret discovery was revealed to the world by his shipmates. Once the path was opened, sailors came to the islands in large numbers. Virtually unknown to the world in the 1700s, Hawai'i became a crossroads for the Asia-Pacific trade route in the 1800s. During the California gold rush, Hawai'i was already a bustling port city with a large amount of seafaring traffic.

Charmed by European sailing ships and early technology, Hawai'ians took in strangers with open arms and married them to upper-class Hawai'ian women who produced half-white children, *hapa-haole* or *hapa*. There were no negative connotations in Hawai'i against being half-white; it was an accepted phenomenon. The acceptance of foreigners fits perfectly into the indigenous scheme of things; the belief in incorporating different value systems was part of the aloha spirit. The word *aloha* comes from the word *alo*, which translates as "presence," "face," or "sharing" of the *ha*, which is "life" and "breath," with relatives and loved ones.

Aloha consists of the following behavioral traits: *akahai*, kindness with tenderness; *lokahi*, unity with harmony; *'olu'olu*, agreeableness with pleasantness; *ha'aha'a*, humility with modesty; and *ahonui*, patience with perseverance. In ancient times, aloha meant taking in family members of blood, adopting *hanai* relations, and welcoming newcomers into the circle called *ohana* or extended family.

Ohana or extended family is still the central concept at the heart of Hawai'ian society. It includes any affiliation group that stresses family-group obligations over and above the individual. Most Hawai'ians love families and children. A home without children is a home without life. In a recent study, political scientist Yasumasa Kuroda examined the aloha ideology in practice and found that several of the key constructs from the aloha ethic were central to Obama's winning message (Kuroda 2009).

However, foreigners accepted aloha while belittling what they perceived as the backward ways of the Hawai'ian natives. Before long Western notions of private ownership and the need to make a profit took root in the Hawai'ian soil and mentality. It is an often repeated observation that the missionaries who came to "do good" on the islands often ended up "doing well"; in fact, financially they did very well for themselves. As foreigners married Hawai'ian royals and their offspring followed suit, the newcomers to the Hawai'ian Islands became land-owning entrepreneurs and industrialists.

For more than a century, as people from all over the world came to the Hawai'ian shores, mixed marriages increased, and cultures were constantly in flux; it created a unique blend of Hawai'ian Americans. People with four or more ethnic lineages were called *chop suey*, a mixture of noodles and vegetables, or *poi dog*, the local name for a mutt or a mixed breed. Not surprisingly, children who were ethnically unmixed or belonged to a single ethnic group began to complain, "Why aren't we part of someone else or some other ethnic group?"

Although the push to make Hawai'i a state was begun in the 1850s by King Kamehameha III, who wanted to negotiate with the U.S. government, his plans were approximately 100 years too early. It took the Pearl Harbor attacks during World War II and the emerging economies in the Asia-Pacific region for the U.S. government to fully realize the strategic importance of Hawai'i as a state. During World War II, Hawai'ian-born troops of Japanese ancestry made huge sacrifices and fought valiantly alongside Americans from the mainland. After the war ended successfully, their struggles were recognized as Hawai'i became an official state. Several of those who fought in the war were later elected to the U.S. Congress and the Senate.

In the postwar years, Hawai'i's new generation exerted its influence in a uniquely multicultural environment. While their parents kept their traditions alive, the new generation felt the need to fit into the larger American culture. They understood that in order to get ahead as Japanese, Chinese, Filipinos, Koreans, and Portuguese they all had to stick together. Thus, in the postwar years Hawai'ians minimized their ethnicity at the altar of achieving white, Anglo-Saxon Protestant individuality and became in effect WASPs. However, by the time Barack Obama began studying at the Punahou School, the trend was swinging back again toward claiming one's ethnic pride in being Hawai'ian.

During the 1950s and 1960s, the Cold War was the operative geopolitical reality; Hawai'i reveled in its role as the mediator of conflict resolution and diplomacy between the U.S. government and the Asia-Pacific region. The East-West Center, started as a place of research exchange for international scholars, soon became a model for creating a Peace Corps in reverse. In the sunny and beautiful surroundings of Hawai'i, many diplomats, journalists, and scholars from different backgrounds came to the Manoa campus and created new plans for peace.

Those who fell in love with the island life did not return, and many stayed in Hawai'i to start families. One such family included Barack Obama Sr. and Ann Dunham, who had met in a Russian class. Neil Abercrombie, who knew them both, recalled that on the face of it they had very little in common; they were an improbable couple.

Barack Obama probably remembers very little of his father's image and voice from the age of one or two years, when his father abruptly left to attend Harvard University. Like the islands of memory, the small interactions he had with his father at that early age remain submerged in his subconscious without any trace or any possibility of retrieval; yet his father's image continued to exercise an unexplainable pull on his mind. His first real memory of his father is from the age of 10 years in Hawai'i when his mother arranged for an extended visit after he returned from Indonesia and enrolled at the Punahou School. Barack's father visited his classroom, did a show-and-tell presentation, and gave a speech to his classmates about Kenya and his native village.

Barbara Nelson, who met Obama's father and mother only this one time at the Punahou School, remembers this meeting well. She noted the continuity between the names of the father and the son, Barack Hussein Obama. Nelson was present in Mabel Hefty's fifth-grade classroom when Obama's father visited the school right before the Christmas break in 1971. Eric Kusonoki, Obama's homeroom teacher, also confirmed this fact. Nelson eventually struck up a lifelong friendship with Obama's grandparents.

With the support of his grandparents, Obama spent most of his middle childhood and adolescence in the neighborhood around Punahou Circle apartments. His grandparents, who lived near the elite preparatory school most of their life, insisted that he attend Punahou School, which had an outstanding reputation as a local institution in Hawai'i. Obama later described the school as an incubator for Hawai'ian elites. Although the school had not yet produced a president for the White House, it had produced many well-known leaders in all walks of life.

Punahou as an Incubator

Cloistered in a leafy, affluent section of Honolulu, the campus of the Punahou School is an impressive collection of 44 buildings spread out over 76 acres. Even by the standards of the elite preparatory schools in the northeast on the mainland, Punahou is a remarkable school for its tropical ambience and stately surroundings. I was struck by the grandeur of the campus when I went in search of Obama's Hawai'ian roots. As the cultural and social context for shaping Obama's personality, the Punahou School indelibly shaped not only his interests, attitudes, and cool temperament, but it also offered him something more—a global purview with a special emphasis on the emerging economies in the Asian-Pacific region.

The elite academy, built by the missionaries in 1841, is the oldest and largest private school west of the Mississippi River. Originally established with a charter to educate the children of missionaries and native Hawai'ians, the school gradually grew into a prosperous incubator for the children of wealthy civil servants and Hawai'ian elites. At present, the school includes "three libraries and learning centers; computer areas and language labs; an impressive physical education facility (that includes a gymnasium, 50-meter pool, Mondo track, playing fields, racquetball and tennis courts, and weight and training facilities); and art facilities that include jewelry, ceramics and glassblowing" (Punahou School 2010). Indeed, while walking on the campus I had the distinct impression that I was taking a tour not so much of a high school but what seemed like a historical landmark.

On the oldest wall in the school, a more than 100-year-old crest indicates that the Punahou School was originally called the Oahu College. During an interview, the head of external relations stressed to me that Punahou's academic standards can be matched to any college or university on the mainland; many of Punahou's students indeed enroll in advanced placement classes. As I admired the nicely painted stucco walls on the century-old architecture, freshly manicured lawns, and tall palm trees, I could feel the weight of the school's history and legacy. This legacy was deeply ingrained in Obama's early education and character development. Obama recalled that when his grandfather took him to school he told him, "Hell, Bar, . . . this isn't a school. This is heaven. You might just get me to go back to school with you" (Obama 2004a, 58).

The economic gap between the apartment building where Obama lived and the day school where he spent most of his waking hours is noticeable even today. Although he lived in a squarely middle-class environment, within Punahou's gated community with its five-feet-high walls, he was sheltered and nurtured in a way that "should not be left to the luck of the draw, but should rather be every child's birthright," Obama said later in a lecture to the student body (Arakawa 2004).

In this serene environment, where time lumbers on rather comfortably and children go to class in flip-flops and sometimes even barefoot, the mind develops leisurely. Here, Obama learned the skills to chart his own path to the corridors of higher learning at Columbia, Harvard, and the University of Chicago. As I walked along the same path he took from his homeroom to the gym and chapel, I began to grasp his remarkable journey.

On the way to the school, I stopped at Obama's old home, the apartment building on Britannia Street. Here, I spoke with some of Obama's former neighbors and building managers and collected a pamphlet in the lobby that described the major milestones of his life story. A collection of family pictures on display in the apartment's lobby presented a portrait of Obama's different life stages up to his becoming president. Most of these pictures have been circulating on the Web—a gestalt of his humble beginnings, a family portrait drawn from intimate family photos assembled by his sister, Maya. The family pictures conveyed feelings of love, care, and affection. I was immediately reminded of my conversations with Maya about how her mother had raised them as one family unit in both Indonesia and Hawai'i despite the long distances that often separated them.

The pamphlet I gathered at the apartment told the romantic version of the Dunham family history. The family moved into the apartment in 1962, after landing in Hawai'i in 1960. The pamphlet described Obama's life story as spanning "miles and generations, races and realities." The pamphlet also described how after his now famous speech at the Democratic National Convention in Boston in 2004, his grandmother told him, "You did well, I just kind of worry about you. I hope you keep your head on straight." The narrative went on to describe how "for the future President his grandparents were an anchor, though it was not always easy living with them. . . . But when it mattered the woman whom he and his sister, Maya, called 'Toot' was always there for them. Toot would say, 'So long as you kids do well, Bar, that's all that really matters.'"

When I asked to see the exact apartment where Obama had lived, the building manager said in a heavy Chinese accent, "The apartment is already rented out, occupied by another tenant. Sorry, can't help!" The building is owned by a Chinese American investor, who did not want to lose the rent. The apartment where Obama lived was no longer open for viewing. Although the state of Hawai'i and the building management might someday be interested in turning it into a landmark or a museum, for now it's just another apartment.

The neighborhood where Barack Obama grew up is a modest area of Honolulu called Makiki, stretching for a few miles, with downtown skyscrapers to the west and rainy Manoa Valley to the east. It is remarkably different from the touristy Waikiki Beach or the Punahou School. Even today it consists of cinderblock walkup apartments built in the late 1960s and a hodgepodge of modest bungalows. A few blocks from his grandparents' apartment is the Kapiolani Hospital, where Obama was born, and the basketball courts where he refined his game.

Makiki is home to second- and third-generation enterprising immigrants, where Obama's neighbors "were mostly store clerks, restaurant workers and small business owners—many aspiring to government jobs" (Lin 2008). Local businesses still drive the economy, consisting mostly of beauty salons, bars and karaoke lounges, and a slew of fast-food restaurants, including the Baskin-Robbins ice cream store on King Street where Obama worked in the evenings and summers.

The demographics of Makiki have been humble, mainly working class, and multiethnic (e.g., Japanese, Chinese, Korean, Filipino, and Micronesians). The neighborhood has remained mostly the same over the past 30 years since Obama attended high school here, though new apartments and condominiums have overtaken some of the shops and cottages. Yet a quick jaunt down Punahou Street from his grandmother's apartment to the Punahou School provides a glimpse of the old landmarks. "Ever a stewpot of races and ethnicities," Obama's humble Makiki upbringing played a central role in his multicultural outlook (Kay 2010).

Obama's old apartment is surrounded by religious institutions, temples, and different places of worship. Across the street from the Punahou Circle apartments is the Central Union Church, easily seen from the apartment building. A right turn down Punahou Street leads to the First Church of Christian Scientists on route to the Punahou School.

Next door to the Punahou Circle apartments, immediately on the right, is the Shinshu Kyokai Buddhist Temple, and only a block away is the Olivet Baptist Church, both located on Beretania Street. The True Jesus Mission of the Latter Rain is the other next-door neighbor on Punahou Street, standing in close proximity to the apartment building. A half block east is the Church of the Latter-Day Saints on South Beretania Street. Finally, there is the Full Gospel Church, with an entirely Korean congregation, on Young Street, just around the corner from Barack's old apartment.

After visiting Obama's former apartment building, I continued to the Punahou School. As I walked onto the campus with wide-open athletic fields, golf carts slowly transported visitors around the campus. The presence of security crews conveyed a sense of order and security. Equally impressive were the old limestone buildings decorated by palm trees and blossoms, the site of Obama's homeroom. The administrative buildings overlooked the playgrounds and open lawns, offering a picturesque view of the entire campus. Obama's grandfather may have been correct when he said the school resembled a paradise; certainly, it is a paradise compared to a lot of the poorer schools on the mainland. I had to blink my eyes a number of times to make sure that I was not daydreaming.

It is here that the young Obama learned the talents and people-skills that he is now famous for: the calm, cool, serene exterior; the modulated tone of voice, anticipating what the others are feeling and thinking; and how to impress people from diverse walks of life. All of this brought to my mind the often-quoted Zen saying, "If you are calm like the lily pond you can pierce through the murkiest waters." Punahou indeed is well-known for its lily ponds, one of which is located right next to the chapel. Here, Obama learned to be calm and still in the midst of turmoil and learned to penetrate the murkiest of waters even during times of distress. He was required to attend chapel every week for eight years as part of his moral education. Thus, in addition to acquiring the three Rs in the classroom, at the chapel he gained insights into his budding identity while sitting in prayer.

The mission of the school promotes Christian values, intellectual or academic excellence, a high level of athletic competition, cultural diversity, and a sense of social responsibility. Consistent with its missionary founding, the school stresses community service and a vision of the larger public good as its principal value. Certainly, this is consistent with many of Obama's campaign messages. Echoes of community service are sprinkled throughout his speeches, without a doubt rooted in his early education.

Although Punahou has always been very socially involved in the local community, it has become increasingly more active in many social projects. Community service was always important, but now it is mandatory. Working in the community is part and parcel of the missionary legacy of the school, something deeply impressed on Obama. Contrary to popular belief, community service is not something Obama suddenly acquired overnight when he landed on the South Side of Chicago; it was drilled into him at the Punahou School. Community service is the key to his early value-based education, which he obviously took to heart. Although he got in touch with his specific "calling" when he decided to settle in Chicago as a community organizer, the seeds for a public service career were sown much earlier.

Character education is central to Punahou's philosophy; though the concept was not formally introduced until 1994, it was actively practiced when Obama was a student. The character education program emphasizes a social and ethical value each month. In a two-year cycle, the value themes can cover a wide range of ideas and actions: respect, responsibility, compassion, faith, commitment, love, wisdom, health, humor, honesty, cooperation, humility, peace, patience, creativity, courage, environmental awareness, and freedom. Some of these values built on Obama's mother's informal lessons, but they clearly went beyond what Obama had learned from his mother in terms of Midwestern values of hard work and honesty, as described in his autobiography.

Most of this knowledge has now been codified into educational manuals on social and moral development, which provide a glimpse of the kind of moral upbringing Obama received at the Punahou School. In these manuals, created specifically for the character education program, teachers are provided with a definition of the values from many different traditions and in many different languages. A statement of purpose about each of the values is communicated through age-appropriate folktales from around the world and stories from the major spiritual traditions. Biographies of heroes and heroines whose lives exemplify each of the values are introduced; Washington, Jefferson, Martin Luther King, and Gandhi are part of the discourse. Ideas for community service projects and discussion questions are designed to engage the students directly. Each month certain chapel sessions are devoted to a specific character education theme, and teachers are encouraged to integrate these themes in all academic disciplines while adding and sharing their own experiences.

The school also prides itself in possessing a smart body of teachers and students. It is considered cool to be smart and intelligent at Punahou. Several of the teachers I spoke with were very well trained and widely traveled; some were Fulbright Scholars and had international experience in classroom teaching. Obama's favorite teacher was the late Mabel Hefty, who had been to Kenya on a sabbatical before he joined her classroom in the fifth grade.

Punahou's student body also displays a superior range of ability, interest, and talent; more than half of the current students are exceptional on standardized measures. Many of the graduates are merit scholars, score high on SATs, and are enrolled in advanced placement classes for college credits. Punahou students are well known in many fields, including science, technology, sports, and politics. In fact, on the islands one's identity is more grounded in which high school you attended rather than where you went to college; by way of introduction, people typically ask where you went to high school, Punaho, 'Iolani, Roosevelt, or Kamehameha. Both Punahou and 'Iolani are elite private schools founded by early Christian settlers, sitting at the top of the hierarchy of schools in both educational excellence and athletics. Kamehameha is a private school founded specifically to educate the native Hawai'ians, and Roosevelt is one of the oldest public schools on the islands.

Punahou prides itself on diversity, reflecting the richness of Hawai'i and the Asia-Pacific region. It stresses global education from a young age; for a child like Obama, who had lived in Indonesia for four years, this was an added benefit. Punahou has several intensive language programs that cover different language areas of the world. When I asked Obama's sister about her memories of the school, Maya said it was an exceptional experience. She remembered taking classes in photography and Russian literature, while also learning how to write a resume.

Although we do not have access to Obama's exact curriculum, based on Punahou's course catalog from 1971 to 1972, we know that he was enrolled in the following subject areas: art, math, music, reading/language arts/English, science, social studies, physical education, and shop. When I asked Maya specifically about the curriculum, she said, "It was a kind of education where classes were small enough that each individual child got nurtured, where tests weren't as high stakes, where there were projects and papers, and the whole child was attended to."

"There was something about this school that embraced me," Obama has said, "gave me support and encouragement and allowed me to grow and prosper" (Tani 2007). Although Obama was a solid B student in terms of grade point average, at a school with less stringent standards he might have had a higher grade point average. He excelled at literature, reading, and writing and at the time wanted to be a writer and actually published in the school's bulletin, as confirmed by his homeroom teacher Mr. Kusonoki.

As a preparation for entering high school, Obama most likely enrolled in some advanced placement classes, such as "Government and Living in the World of Change" and "Christian Ethics" when he was in eighth grade. Christian ethics taught biblical faith in the context of everyday life, and the course on government dealt with processes and problems of government at the local and national level. The course may have introduced Obama to international relations and the challenges facing individual citizens in changing the world, a theme he would revisit at Columbia University, where he took keen interest in international relations.

Yet Obama did not show overt signs of political activism or an interest in politics; instead, his social popularity was driven by sports. His prowess on the basketball court seemed to not only elevate his status among his peers but also to give him an aura of friendliness and sociability. He was a well-known and well-liked student. Although basketball may have given him an early taste of social success and the high that comes from winning on and off the court, his experience on the Punahou basketball team was bittersweet, as he spent much of the time on the bench. Still, it was on the basketball court that Obama practiced the skills to be a team player. These skills he would use throughout his life, especially during intense periods of decision making.

Making of a Global Leader

How a leader is shaped involves a complex interplay of personality, socio-cultural, and historical forces. A lot of research has been conducted on the ontogenesis of creative leadership (Sternberg 2008; Gardner 1996). In Obama's case, given his diverse background and early upbringing, a developmental and cultural view is essential, something that has not been fully explored. Although the social and environmental conditions may be too varied to predict how a leader will ultimately turn out, shape his era, or lead a majority, in Obama's case one can study the unique set of conditions that led to his leadership development.

Indeed, the set of conditions that fed his creative leadership are rather remarkable. We have seen that his parenting was unique, especially by his liberal mother and grandparents. His environment was unique in that he traveled extensively at a young age and settled in diverse and multi-cultural settings. The extensive amount of travel not only stimulated his brain but also his senses; he was moving back and forth between very different cultural worlds at a young age and trying to reconcile them in his mind. This may have predisposed him to think globally from a young age because his perspective had to encompass the world.

As we have seen, his early schooling was also exceptional for the breadth of view it offered. His schooling in a secular Islamic democracy, which was quickly emerging as a satellite state of the U.S. business and geopolitical interests, gave him a critical perspective on U.S. power relations in Southeast Asia. Added to this, the Hawai'ian perspective gave him insights into the challenges the United States continues to confront economically from the rising economies in the Asia-Pacific region.

Given his mixed-race parentage and upbringing, especially in Hawai'i, which has very few blacks, Obama was socialized to believe in a special destiny and purpose for his life. He was socialized to believe from a very young age that he has a very unique purpose in life by virtue of his mixed race and the conditions of his birth.

His mother and grandparents raised him to believe he was meant for higher things in life and that his raison d'être was to do extraordinary things, to be different, and to be a trendsetter. This may have been a way for his mother and grandparents to assuage the loss of a father at the beginning of his life or a way for the Dunham family to collectively make meaning out of their daughter's fateful decisions to marry Barack Obama Sr., then Lolo Soetoro, and the eventual breakup of both of her marriages. Be that as it may, his mother and grandparents drilled into him that he could do great things if he believed in himself and worked hard enough. Your brains came from your father, his mother would often say, look at how your father had struggled, coming from a poor background, a poor country, a poor continent, but he went far in life; your biological father is your role model, his mother often said to him.

"She had only one ally in all this, and that was the distant authority of my father. Increasingly, she would remind me of his story. . . . He hadn't cut corners, though, or played all the angles. He was diligent and honest, no matter what it cost him. He had led his life according to principles that demanded a different kind of toughness, principles that promised a form of power. I would follow his example, my mother decided. I had no choice. It was in the genes" (Obama 2004a, 50).

His mother's object lesson for Barack was full of idealism, to make a positive difference in the world and in other people's lives. Her own life

was an example of this mission statement, backed up by Barack's pragmatic grandmother, who was a practical nondreamer, and his grandfather,
who was an itinerant bohemian. In addition to the examples they offered
Barack, they all gave him love and support. Obama's grandfather Stanley
thought the world of his grandson. "He loved that boy like his own son,"
Abercrombie told me emphatically. "I knew Stanley well as a friend, and
he used to carry that boy around town on his shoulders like his own son,"
said Abercrombie. Barbara Nelson, who knew the Dunhams, concurred
with this observation about Stanley's love for his grandson.

In addition to all of these unique family patterns that constituted a
driving force in Obama's ultimate destiny, there was a kind of permanent
psychological trauma in Obama's life, a cross he has had to carry for himself, a weight that nobody else could carry for him. This is of course the
neurosis related to his father's loss. This trauma was the main psychological issue that ate at him; this was the mystery that he had to uncover for
himself before his development could proceed further.

The basic psychological hunger due to his father loss drove him
through his childhood and youth, and it may drive him even now. The love
for a father he hardly knew drives Obama psychologically, socially, and
politically. As a reformer and a politician, Obama has turned this neurosis
at the heart of his life story and personality into a love for the American
people, love for his country, and a love for transforming the world. In
attempting to transform the pain, hurt, and loss at the center of his life, he
has tried to remake the world.

All psychological development begins with a sense of loss; this was
the great insight of psychoanalysis and modern psychiatry. In Obama's
case this sense of loss was indeed profound. Yet he pressed forward by
accepting things as they are. Thus, as Obama moved forward, his vision
was deeply shaped by the early experiences that were central to his life.
Psychologists have often said that a reformer is a larger-than-life personality who loves to play out his complexes on the public stage; although
this may be true, the world still needs good reformers more than good
psychologists.

Thus, for Obama the "more perfect union" he wishes for is the fractured union between his parents made whole again, or acceptance of
unions between blacks and whites where his parents could have lived
out their normal lives without any worries or concerns about how others perceived them. He wishes for a more perfect union between black

America and white America, or a union between Africa and America so that a man from Kenya, his father, could live out the normal course of his life with a woman from Kansas, his mother. In Obama's inner iconography, then, Africa is the remote fatherland and America the much more familiar motherland.

In this family drama, Obama is the prodigal son who has the charisma, mass appeal, and knowledge to fix the great divide at the heart of American life. However, because a person cannot fully be explained by his psychological complexes, a politician like Obama is not simply reducible to his childhood trauma and early personality. But although it is not sufficient to grasp the trauma that underlies Obama's driving motivations, it is certainly necessary for a full understanding of his character.

Thus, while Obama appeared to be an above-average student academically throughout his early schooling, he inherited certain special gifts, a kind of wise beyond his years confidence and reserve in the face of adversity, a sky is the limit, hopeful view of the world, and a gift of oratory. I argue that these enduring traits were passed on to him not only by his progressive mother and his grandparents but these traits he also developed in an aspiration to become like his Kenyan father.

If we realize that Obama is indeed our first multicultural president, not the precursor but the product of the civil rights movement, we may actualize the promise of the Obama generation. A longtime educator who developed the curriculum at Punahou has noted that although we can't draw a straight line from what Obama did and saw in Hawai'i to what he would do as a world leader, there is no doubt that the cultural milieu of a youngster's formative years plants millions of seeds that bear fruit in later life.

I obtained a very revealing portrait of Barack Obama in his formative years from his homeroom teacher Eric Kusonoki. The Punahou School always provided the same dean and homeroom teacher for the four years of a student's high school education. The goal was to keep the stability and constancy in a child's life. A homeroom teacher represents the most important educator in a growing child's life, a *kumu* in Hawai'ian. Outside the circle of parents and extended family, the stability of this relationship with a *kumu* is critical for schooling.

This homeroom practice remained constant throughout the years Obama was a student and is in effect today. Obama's homeroom had about 25 students, and although the homeroom teacher did not distribute any grades or tests, his or her role was to advise the students and serve as a guide and mentor. The children had the option of coming to the homeroom before school started. Obama took advantage of this privilege. Home-room regularly opened at 8 a.m., but Barack would often report at around 7:30 a.m. and sometimes even earlier.

He had a favorite spot in the homeroom: one could usually find Barry close to the door, but near the teacher's desk, relaxed but sitting sideways, and usually rocking back and forth in his chair. While Kusonoki turned on the radio, opened up the newspaper, and got his morning coffee, Barry would talk about his day, current events, or whatever else was on his mind that morning. Kusonoki volunteered all of this information generously without much questioning on my part because he remembered Barry very clearly. Since he has often been asked to comment on his now famous mentee, he has had to reflect and recollect some of his thoughts.

I discovered that Kusonoki had never met or talked to Obama's mother, grandfather, or grandmother, even at the annual school day or during open house. They may have been there, but he never met them during the four years Obama was in his homeroom. Was this a pattern of early independence training or benign neglect on the part of his grandparents and mother? It is not clear, but certainly as a result of this family dynamic Barack began to look after himself quite early.

Barry was always respectful and courteous, greeting his homeroom teacher with a polite "Good morning, Mr. Kusonoki." Barry was always kind to everyone. Kusonoki suggested that he had a charisma about him even in high school. He was very pleasant, well mannered, and sincere; this made him popular with students and teachers. He had the same walk, a swagger, a pleasant mannerism, and the same congenial personality that we see in him today when he is greeting people at the ropes or giving a speech.

This congenial personality forms Obama's "bargaining self," according to Shelby Steele (2007), which has helped him to navigate his arduous path through American politics as the first black man to reach the presidency. Obama has made the hard-to-attain goal look easy. According to some personality psychologists, the underlying traits that drive Obama's congenial and likeable political persona are agreeableness and conscientiousness, rare qualities in a politician who wishes to change politics as usual. Cordiality and compromise characterize his interpersonal relationships. He is humble (as politicians go) and gracious—even with respect to adversaries and people he dislikes (Moore and Immelman

2008). Agreeableness can appear to be too accommodating or cooperative at times, too eager to reconcile differences. Conscientious personalities, on the other hand, are cautious and deliberate. Obama has a dignified bearing, is attentive to details, and is deliberatively attuned to the long-term implications of his policy initiatives. Clearly, these traits define certain important aspects of Obama's political persona.

"When I saw him on the stage in 2004 at the Democratic National Convention speech, a group of us could not believe it. He has the same walk and mannerism as he did in high school," reported Kusonoki. "We always believed Barry would be successful due to his people skills," said Kusonoki. "He was always a very good listener. It was never about 'I' or 'me' as it is with some kids these days. He would not take the stage right away; [he would] always wait and hang on the side or stay back and analyze the situation before reacting to a discussion or decision. Hence, he got along with everybody and was very popular."

Kusonoki was a bit surprised when he read in Obama's autobiography that he had questions about his identity as a black man or about being black in Hawai'i. "We're all different, but it does not make a difference. We're Japanese, Chinese, Polynesian, and African American. We are happy and curious about your origin of difference but not hung up on it," said Kusonoki. "His identity questions may have come up when he went to the mainland to go to college, which happens to a lot of us when we go away to college from the islands to the mainland," explained Kusonoki. Obama went to Los Angeles after graduating from Punahou, which is very different from the Hawai'ian Islands, much more segregated in terms of blacks and whites and ethnically not as intermixed; there is less diversity and differences can be more pronounced. While Hawai'i definitely contributed to his presidency, ultimately it is a great coincidence of history, the meaning of which still has to be determined that he grew up in Hawai'i, said Kusonoki.

Kusonoki confirmed that basketball was also very important to Obama, and he was on the court a lot. It was his "real passion," and during his senior year Punahou won the state championship. When I asked about Obama not being on the starting team during his senior year, Kusonoki responded that he worked really hard at basketball; for him it was all about the team winning the championship. The team was more important. "He never complained to me that he did not get to play or that he was on the bench most of the season," revealed Kusonoki. Kusonoki also suggested that Barry was always very humble. He did not mind that he did not have the best clothes or the newest sneakers. "He is still very much like that, simple shirt and suit but always classy," said Kusonoki.

Hawai'i offered a rich multicultural environment within a uniquely evolving racial and ethnic demographic mix. This was deeply imprinted on Obama's mind. Although Chicago was where he cut his teeth in community organizing and politics, Hawai'i forms the core of Obama's inner self; it shaped the deepest layers of his personality. The spirit of aloha, with a tolerance for all cultures born from the deep wellspring of Polynesian culture intermixed with evangelical Christianity, touched Obama's heart, mind, and soul. At the onset of his U.S. Senate campaign, Obama said, "The essence of Hawai'i has always been that we come from far and wide, that we come from different backgrounds, and different faiths and different last names, and yet we come together as a single *ohana* because we believe in the fundamental commonality of people" (Pang 2004).

It was with this aloha spirit in mind that Mabel Hefty, Obama's fifth-grade teacher, invited Obama Sr. to speak to their classroom. When I interviewed Barbara Nelson, a longtime educator at Punahou, she remembered the Obama father-son duo very fondly. She observed them interacting with each other in Mabel Hefty's classroom. She heard his father speak in his clipped British accent.

Later Nelson was Obama's English teacher during his junior and senior years. She attended most of Punahou's basketball games and would often sit in the bleachers with Madelyn, Obama's grandmother. Nelson was friends with Madelyn and Stanley Dunham outside the Punahou School and socialized with them regularly at dinners, card games, and other functions.

She recalled that Obama at a young age was emerging as a champion, someone who was driven to win on high-minded principles and ideals. According to personality psychologist David Keirsey, who has worked with thousands of companies and many different organizations, including the U.S. military, Barack Obama is an idealist (Yoffe 2008). Obama's specific personality type is an extraverted, intuitive, feeling, and perceptive type (ENFP), represented as a personality mandala (see Figure 1). In common use, a mandala consists of a plan, chart, or geometric pattern that represents the cosmos metaphysically or symbolically, a personal microcosm of the universe seen as a representation of the human personality. Some psychologists believe a mandala is a reflection or facsimile of the unconscious self (Jung 1973), consisting of the underlying personality profile and a leadership style (Yoffe 2008). Each one of us lives in a multidimensional space. A person's life trajectory and personality mandala are two very effective ways of understanding his or her life in an evolving yet also multidimensional space.

Obama prefers to perceive the world through its possibilities intuitively and translate these possibilities through interpersonal and intrapersonal relationships based on feelings. Because Obama is an extravert, all of this takes place in lively interaction with the outside world while his keen perceptive attitude guides him with a never-ending flow of alternatives to the changing social and electoral landscape.

As an idealist, Obama likes to champion big causes and is convinced that he can easily motivate people around him. He believes he can inspire people to action and can move institutions to act in a way that is beneficial for the country, and as part of the American creed he thinks we need leaders who can inspire us to greater heights. As evidenced by his memoir, Keirsey believes that idealists like Obama have a deeply introspective core. Animated by their authenticity, which is the basis for their self-confidence, they are "aware of themselves as objects of moral scrutiny" (Yoffe 2008). As reformers, idealists tend to shy away from holding a high office, but like Thomas Paine, Mahatma Gandhi, and Martin Luther King Jr., tend to build large movements of people. Obama is the first black president who has built a large grassroots movement, but according to Keirsey, he is one of the more idealistic presidents we have seen in a very long time. "At their best they bring a refreshing alternative style to top management and decision making," Keirsey said (Yoffe 2008).

In Obama, who has inspired the country as a politician, these management traits took many years to refine. As a young man, Obama was a beautiful writer, very professional in his dealings with people and somewhat of a stage performer, recalled Barbara Nelson. At Punahou, Obama was socialized with the motto that "it's smart to be smart and it's smart to be cool," said Barbara Nelson, "because all students are socialized to behave in a smart, brainy manner, and to be cool about it." This is why Obama now appears somewhat aloof to his supporters and many detractors, who see him from a distance as he discusses arcane and complex policy ideas without fumbling a word or a phrase.

He was taught from a young age that the sky is the limit. Students at Punahou are taught that there is nothing that they cannot do if they work and apply the right combination of skills. Although ethnicity was important, it did not form the basis of social networks at Punahou. "Everyone is a mixture of different ethnicities," Nelson said, "so no groupings are exclusive; everybody shares a part of some other person." Thus, Obama's ethnic and racial background was never a barrier or a point of discrimination, according to Nelson.

In Hawai'i, many different generations live close to each other. Mixed marriages are more common on the islands than on the mainland, even though it still raises concerns among the older generations regarding their traditional cultural values. Within the same family, however, different people may follow rituals and practices of a different culture or ethnic group and not force each and every family member into a monocultural tradition.

Hence, when young people who are minorities or part of a majority group move from Hawai'i to the mainland, they may suddenly feel different because of their ethnic status, a concept that may not have fully entered their consciousness before leaving the islands. The island mentality in Hawai'i leaves a deep imprint on most of its inhabitants.

In Obama's case, in Hawai'i he blended in and was like everyone else, according to Barbara Nelson. In fact, the Fijian and Samoan students were darker than he was, she added, and may have had more pronounced aboriginal features. In sharp contrast to how his skin color was perceived on the streets of Jakarta, Obama's darker color may not have made any impression on his Hawai'ian peers, according to Barbara Nelson. In fact his mixed color and hue may have been considered more attractive.

His peers often jokingly called him the "handsome dude." He had a good sense of humor and often found the comical side of things; generally, he did not take things too seriously unless he felt he had to. Thus, he never wore his identity issues on his sleeves and people close to him may not have noticed that he felt alienated.

When the discussion centered on issues of humanity, the poor, and the downtrodden, for example, Obama would become serious and assume a different demeanor. He was a good listener and, more than his peers, would clearly hear others when they voiced their opinions. Sometimes, his own perspective would almost be missing in the discussion while listening to others. "He would make himself internally calm and still that you forgot he was there listening to you," said Barbara Nelson.

Nelson described to me in great detail Obama's emerging leadership style with his peers and his decision-making skills. She observed him in the English literature class for several years, and he stood out in her mind as one of the exceptional students for his ability to elevate the discussion to a higher level. She said, "He would often hang back and listen to others first. He was never the first one to jump in right away."

Always the consummate interpreter and synthesizer, Obama would take the bits of information often expressed as opinions by others in the heat of the discussion and integrate them into a larger whole. She recalled that he always began his comments with a statement like, "It seems to me, what we are saying is . . ." and then he would move the discussion to a more integrated level and to a more relevant domain. She said she can still picture him sitting "in my classroom, slouched in his chair with his long slender legs stretched out, but attentively listening."

She also recalled one specific classroom episode in great detail. She had asked her ninth- and tenth-grade students to think about a specific question: "What is most to be feared?" Many of the students responded with a wide array of answers right away: death, hell, abandonment, loneliness, and total darkness. She recalled that Obama did not respond at first and kept listening to everyone's response. Then he leaned in, looked at everyone, pulled in his thin legs, and folded them under his chair. He began to speak, "Words, words are to be feared the most. Every individual has an arsenal at his disposal, even the words you say to yourself or what a parent says to a child. Wars are started by words." Everyone was speechless. They seemed stunned by his response and began to think about what he had just uttered. His words clearly stayed with them for the rest of the class.

Even more impressively, his words also rang in his teacher's ears for many years. Several years later, when Obama was running for the U.S. Senate, Nelson penned and published a poem in part inspired by her former high school student. In the author's notes, Nelson stated: "Interestingly, this former student is now a very wise, articulate U. S. senator."

The power of words, imagery, and rhetoric are central to Obama's persona (Berry and Gottheimer 2010); however, it also carries a danger, according to Keirsey. The idealist's belief in "word magic" can be taken too far (Yoffe 2008). The ancient idea that words can make things happen by simply saying it can lead to disillusionment among the listeners or the audience; this is indeed the basis of a critique of Obama's leadership style.

Obama was often a catalyst during the open classroom discussions. He was a catalyst for moving the debate from a groupthink mindset to a higher level of abstraction. "Since he analyzed the situation first, rather than jumping in, he would often say things most students were not thinking about. It was a unique style of taking charge of the situation," Nelson said, and she believes this is how he makes decisions. According to Keirsey, an idealistic leader like Obama can best be seen as a catalyst because he inspires those who encounter him to do their best (Yoffe 2008).

One concrete example of Obama's leadership style came during the health care debate, when Obama let the open discussion proceed for almost a year before he let his opinion be known publicly in terms of where he firmly stood on the range of issues that eventually became part of the legislation. He was the catalyst for the debate but mostly remained behind the scenes. The same pattern was evident on the Afghanistan issue, where he took more than three months to commit additional troops, while he gathered the opinions of others in his cabinet. There is a consistency in Obama's decision-making style. He has been reserved and thoughtful from his early years. Not one to be impulsive or make rash decisions, Obama clearly premeditates before he acts, seeks group consensus before he publicly declares his intentions, and studies the issues in great detail to gain command of the various aspects of the debate before people find out where he actually stands. This very style of decision making has also led to successes against Al Qaeda in Pakistan and Afghanistan.

Obama's pattern of decision making was evident much earlier, on the high school basketball court, especially during the years leading up to the Punahou School's winning the state championship. On the basketball team, because he was not part of the starting five, he would often analyze the situation better than the coach and would know how to execute a play better than the coach. When given the opportunity he would spring to action and score for the team. That is how he makes decisions now, suggested Barbara Nelson. Clearly, Obama plans before he executes. He is not someone who shoots from the hip or reacts without careful and meticulous planning. However, on the flipside, his constituents may often think he is vacillating on the issues or taking too long to make decisions on the critical issues of the day.

Curious about the linkage between Obama's classroom behavior and his style on the basketball court, I asked Barbara Nelson to explain further.

She asserted that she watched him play for almost four years so she can say this with some confidence. "He would often have a higher-level perspective on the game from the sidelines. When he would step on the court, he would often double pump or run a fake pattern and dunk the ball. This is how he arrives at decisions now," Nelson said.

According to Keirsey, Obama possesses a "diplomatic intelligence"; he naturally and instinctively seeks common ground, wants to "forge unity," and arrive at "universal truths" (Yoffe 2008). Whether he is able to realize his objective is contingent on external factors, but foremost it is his intent to achieve a consensus on a wide range of issues. Given Obama's shifting family environment, he naturally evolved into a "peacemaker," who takes multiple perspectives into account before taking any sides. His opponents claim his leadership style is naive and gets little accomplished. In the end, a deliberative style of decision making may get more accomplished by furthering the debate on a whole host of issues simultaneously, while achieving some of the big things in the process.

Obama's interpersonal skills, which he learned in Hawai'i as a biracial person living in one of the most ethnically saturated and multicultural milieu, informed his social vision. Obama has the "people smarts," the hallmark of Howard Gardner's interpersonal intelligence, an ability everyone needs but is at a premium for a politician (Gardner 1983). Anybody who deals with other people has to be skilled in the interpersonal sphere, but a successful leader who can create a grassroots movement clearly has high interpersonal intelligence. Here, Obama shares qualities with his political heroes, Abraham Lincoln, Martin Luther King, and Mahatma Gandhi, all of whom displayed a heightened interpersonal intelligence and led large social reform movements.

The evolution of these skills may have taken time to mature, as Obama's half-sister, Maya, witnessed a complex young man searching for his cultural identity. Although Barack's racial confusion was assuaged by an ethnically mixed population in Hawai'i, when he looked in the mirror he saw himself as a black man, the most accessible social label available to him at the time.

The identity crisis that every teenager struggles with may not have been easy for Obama to resolve. It was this early struggle to achieve an identity that gave Obama a new perspective on the American experience. Maya claimed that Punahou, and Hawai'i in general, gave her brother a sense that a lot of different cultures and perspectives can live in harmony, and as a result felt at home in many different worlds. This milieu in Hawai'i, and to an extent Indonesia, gave Obama the ability to face different worlds with ease even as he struggled within to find his place in the world.

As Obama traveled through the mainland, making stops in Los Angeles, New York, Chicago, and then Harvard, the idealism he acquired in multicultural Hawai'i was tempered with a strain of American pragmatism (Kloppenberg 2010). However, this took many years of indoctrination in some of the best American colleges and universities and many hours of community service in Chicago's inner city and ghettos. Yet the years spent in Hawai'i in the youthful spring of his life continued to shape Obama's journey.

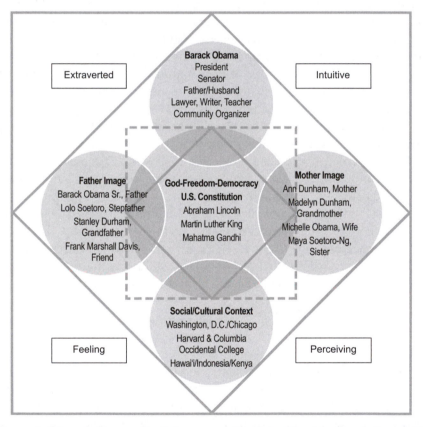

Figure 1. Obama's Personality Schema as a Mandala. Mandala (Sanskrit maṇḍala "essence" + "having" or "containing," also translates as "circle-circumference" or "completion." In common use, mandala has become a generic term for any plan, chart, or geometric pattern that represents the cosmos metaphysically or symbolically, a microcosm of the Universe from the human perspective. Some psychologists view the mandala as a representation of the unconscious self.

6

Hybrid Identity on the Mainland

No man is an island, entire of itself; every man is a piece of the continent, a part of the main.

John Donne (1624)

You cannot spill a drop of American blood without spilling the blood of the whole world....We are not a nation so much as a world.

Herman Melville (1850)

Ronald Takaki cofounded the African-American Studies Department at the University of California, Los Angeles, and later taught Asian-American Studies at the University of California, Berkeley. He was delighted by Obama's rise as a presidential candidate but died at the age of 70 years in the months after the 2008 general election. As Takaki shared in an op-ed piece from 2008, like Barack Obama, he also grew up in Hawai'i. Unlike Obama, who went to Punahou, Takaki attended 'Iolani, the other private school on the island, which competes with Punahou in academics and athletics. Both Obama and Takaki came of age in a part of the United States where everyone felt valued as a member of a minority group because there were no majority groups in Hawai'i. Like many Hawai'ians, Takaki left the islands for the first time when he attended college on the mainland. Obama also made the same journey. However, their sense of rootedness in Hawai'ian culture shaped their worldviews and the possibilities of what America is and could become in the near future.

The comments made by Takaki, who once advised President Clinton on his race speech, resonate with many others who have lived and worked in Hawai'i and have ruminated about Obama's upbringing. Hawai'ian journalist Jerry Burris analyzed the issue in great depth and concluded that Obama's dream of a blended nation really begins in the multiculturalism of the Pacific (Glauberman and Burris 2008). A broadcaster and record producer, Ron Jacobs (2008) has said that Hawai'i made Obama a citizen of the world. Likewise, the presidential historian, David Maraniss (2008), has claimed that even "though Obama had to leave to find himself, it is Hawai'i that made his rise possible."

Language played a key role. As children, Obama and Takaki heard a variety of languages as they played and studied with children from different cultural and ethnic backgrounds. On the island of Oahu, Obama and Takaki's friends and neighbors spoke Japanese, Chinese, Portuguese, Samoans, Fijians, and Hawai'ian, but they were all happy to speak pidgin English as their common language.

After graduating from high school in 1957, Takaki attended the College of Wooster in Ohio, whereas when he graduated in 1979, Obama went to Occidental College in Los Angeles, California. Both experienced culture shock upon their arrival on the mainland.

Takaki said his fellow students asked him questions like: "What country are you from?" and "How did you learn English so well?" Yet his grandfather had come to the United States from Japan in 1886, long before many European immigrants. Takaki's fellow students could not and did not see him as an American, perhaps because they thought he did not look like an American and he did not have an American-sounding name.

Obama experienced something similar in terms of his name and identity. His African American friends thought he was an African or a Nation of Islam Muslim. His white friends were intrigued by his different-sounding name. Most of his friends were caught up with the hyphenated differences in his name and identity, though Obama seemed comfortable with a hybridized self. In fact, he seemed to thrive on it, being able to walk across different cultural, ethnic, and color lines with ease.

Looking back at their Wooster and Occidental experiences, both Takaki and Obama realized that their friends' cultural myopia was not their fault. According to Takaki (2008), in their U.S. history courses they had likely received a one-sided and highly slanted view of the history of African Americans, Asian Americans, Mexican Americans, and Native Americans in this country and were taught to see them through the filter of what has been called "the master narrative" of American history. This master narrative propagates the familiar story that the United States was settled by mostly white or European Americans. The facts are indeed more complicated as slave hands have touched every aspect of this country from its inception.

According to Takaki (2008), "The master narrative is so deeply embedded in our mainstream culture that it is a powerful current swirling beneath the surface of everyday conversation, the curriculum, the news and entertainment media, and political decision-making. This narrow definition of who is an American is something we take as a given." Race remains the original metaphor that Americans often deploy to construct their sense of Americanness. It lies at the heart of the American experience.

Although there may be cracks in the metaphor of race now, historically, it became a necessary condition for the cultural construction of America. In the process of creating a national identity, Americans defined themselves as white, and the "other," "the primitive," "the savage,"or "the alien" as the nonwhite. This has led to alienation and disenchantment among many of America's minority groups.

Sociologists often like to state that demography is destiny. Today, demographic changes are constantly challenging America's master narrative by expanding the diversity of the American people. Here the statistics reveal an underlying structural change. According to the 2000 U.S. Census, more than 7 million people claimed to be multiracial Americans and these numbers are likely to increase (Tauber and Singh 2009). Non-Hispanic whites have become a numerical minority in California, according to the U.S. Census (Dougherty 2010a). According to Takaki (2008), the trend in California is also occurring in Texas and New Mexico, and it will most likely happen throughout the U.S. population within our lifetime and in the lifetime of our children. We will all be part of a minority group in this country in the near future.

Takaki (2008) stated that the younger demographic segments just entering the voting age seem to be aware of the changing faces and colors of America. They interact with the diversity of students in their classrooms and the workplace. They have noticed that America is becoming more multicultural in demography, education, employment, and politics. The younger generation consists of all races and ethnicities, and there is an expanding notion of what constitutes an American.

For Takaki, Obama had already become a winner before he won the 2008 election by questioning and modifying the master narrative of American history. Obama's mixed-race complexion and his hybrid or foreign-sounding name had become American. Obama "opened a new identity not only for African Americans, but also for Asian Americans and Latino Americans," according to Takaki.

"Moreover, as a historian of multicultural America," Takaki welcomed "Obama's affirmation of America as a nation peopled by the world. He personifies diversity as America's 'manifest destiny.'" In his soaring rhetoric, Obama has tried to bind teeming diversity of its people into one nation.

As Americans increasingly deal with the rise of Asian economies in the Pacific region and beyond, the rise of the first president from Hawai'i has to be placed within the context of globalization. The flow of capital, markets, and labor has indeed shifted from the developed markets toward the emerging markets. Do Americans as a nation of immigrants have a distinct advantage in dealing with these tectonic changes that now redefine our world within and across our borders?

No Man Is an Island

The parallels between the lives of these two Hawai'ian-born men underscores the importance of Obama's first 18 years spent in the Asia-Pacific region. Many others who have grown up in Hawai'i describe a similar experience, living with a deep sense of the aloha spirit as an everyday reality, neatly encapsulated in the Punahou education where "no man is an island." Despite conflicts between the original Hawai'ians and the newcomers, many of the Hawai'ian born and those who are transplanted to Hawai'i still feel they are part of one big human family or *ohana*. Everybody must get along with everyone else; the idea that everyone is part of someone else is taken very seriously by people who live on the islands permanently.

At the same time, the feeling of isolation or being cut off from the mainland is also very palpable. "In the old days, you had nowhere else to go; even now it is not easy to just pick up and leave the islands," said Dennis Ching. Even if you leave, the internalized island mentality follows you wherever you go. If you're not happy and want to find your own paradise elsewhere, you will generally be in for a culture shock, suggested Dennis Ching.

Long before Obama became an inspiring leader, he went on a journey to search for his real self in the big cities of Los Angeles and New York City, seeking the intense city experience to test out his real values. He was indeed in for a culture shock, but he finally settled on Chicago as his adopted hometown because he wanted to be part of and work with its local communities. He had a big revelation when he arrived on the mainland. Unlike the Hawai'ian Islands, the mainland was much more fractured and divided than he had imagined. Obama decided he might do something about this by trying to bring different communities together in local churches and other civic meeting places.

As I've mentioned earlier, the formation of a cultural identity involves asking the twofold question: "Who am I? Where do I fit in?" In Obama's case, as with many college-age students from Hawai'i, he went through part of his adolescent psychosocial moratorium and identity crisis on the mainland. While living on the islands, he did become aware of his racial identity and the fractured nature of the American society, but this realization was somewhat compartmentalized and not as intense or pervasive as it would become on the mainland.

The segregated cities of Los Angeles and New York felt like speed bumps on his newly discovered path on the mainland. Obama felt an immediate shock, but his shock was founded on his blackness, his exposure to radical black voices, and his perception of a conflicted African American identity and the racial divide among blacks and whites. He discovered that the mainland was fiercely bifurcated, even on liberal campuses like Occidental and Columbia. Having grown up in a white household within a multicultural milieu, Obama could immediately understand and diagnose some of the long-term problems ailing cities like Los Angeles and New York, but solving them was another matter altogether. Obama did not even know where to begin.

The John Donne quote that opened this chapter captures the kernel of truth Obama carries within himself rooted in his Hawai'ian upbringing: "No man is an island, entire of itself; every man is a piece of the continent, a part of the main" (Donne 1624). When Thomas Merton, the American Catholic monk, later used this idea for a book with the same name, he highlighted the core psychological and spiritual problem of the human condition: we are all fundamentally interconnected and even in utter isolation and solitude humans are concerned almost obsessively with "the other" or "the different" (Merton 1955). Sociality, relationships, and community are the fundamental attributes that make us human; we are intensely social animals inherently driven toward others. Obama at his core embodies this island mentality and social ethic in his self and life story.

Long-term economic evidence suggests that island societies, like fully grown human adults, have only one of two strategies to adapt to rapid social change: remain an insular backwater of the world or embrace an expanding global worldview. The island factor, which is a cognitive attribute or a psychological capacity, suggests that countries and island states isolated from the trade and capital flows of the mainland economy and surrounded by different linguistic and cultural groups must adapt by opening up to the larger social world. The island mentality can be a booster by fostering a kind of survival strategy among people, societies, and cultures; even macroeconomic evidence bears this out. "The findings highlight the importance of a cohesive society with a strong sense of identity while being economically open to global competitive forces. This island mindset acts as a catalyst for enhanced economic growth" (Aubert and Chen 2008, 178).

Obama exhibits the island mentality and work ethic not only in his belief that we should all get along (we are all part of one big family or *ohana)* but also in the belief that Americans must not become insular and instead must become more outward looking as a nation while confronting head-on the challenges of the 21st century. Americans must engage not only their friends but also their enemies, as Obama noted during the inaugural address in January 2009. Embodying the aloha spirit is not a geopolitical strategy, but it may embody the essence of the soft power Americans must deploy in order to remain open to the rest of the world and to transform the U.S. economy and society from within.

Whether Obama's island mindset places him closer to Reinhold Niebhur, one of his favorite philosophers, or Robert Nye, the Harvard pragmatist whom Obama read during law school will continue to be debated. Is Obama a "naive realist" or a "pragmatic idealist"? Does he represent the pragmatic strain of American culture stretching back to William James and John Dewey? Or is he a community organizer at heart, one who understands America through its local communities, churches, and nonprofit organizations? "No man is an island," Obama said at a recent fund-raiser. "We're not here by ourselves. That's our vision of America. It's not a vision of a small America. It's a vision of a big America. I don't want a cramped idea of America. I don't want an idea of America that says 'no we can't' and 'we can't afford to look after folks who need help.'"

Obama's communitarian impulse is rooted in his developmental transitions, which occurred in environments that valued community relationships over the individual. First, at the age of two years he adapted to his father's loss; it was a time of separation and individuation marked by abandonment, fear, and loss. Obama does not remember this time consciously, but he would have become deeply trusting of and attached to his mother and to his extended family. His mother in turn would have become equally attached to him as their reason for existence during a trying and turbulent separation and divorce from Obama Sr.

Then, at the age of four years old, Barack Obama went to Indonesia and was forced to adapt to another extended family, environment, and culture. Although this would have been a source of anxiety for him initially, this transition also fostered a deep sense of confidence in him and the ability to deal with new and different people, foreign settings, and interpersonal challenges. His memories from this period suggest that he was deeply attached to his mother and would do anything to protect her from harm. She in turn was raising him to be highly self-reliant and independent.

Finally, at around the age of 10 years, he separated from his mother when he chose to stay in Hawai'i rather than return to Jakarta. As a young boy, he would have learned to be more independent, manage his own time, and grow up a little faster than his peers while adapting to his grandparents' lifestyle. In all of these developmental challenges, Obama's transitions seemed to have gone off well, albeit with a few psychological hurdles. Obama always felt uprooted, and there was the chronic problem of not having had a stable father figure.

In a recent interview, Obama openly admitted that these transitions may have been difficult for him as a young child. "I think that was harder on ten-year-old boy than he'd care to admit at the time. . . . When we were separated again at that point I was old enough to say, 'This is my choice, my decision.' But being a parent now and looking back at that, I could see—you know what?—that would be hard on a kid," Obama said (Scott 2011, 135). In essence, Obama conceded that he felt abandoned by his mother but there was nothing he could do about it.

Obama's adolescent transition to the mainland was similar to his earlier developmental transitions. Obama's move to the mainland took him in a seemingly opposite trajectory from that of his mother and extended family, who moved to Hawai'i because they craved the frontier lifestyle of the West and the Pacific and had a great appetite for risk-taking. Instead, Obama craved stability and needed to belong to a place, a city, a neighborhood, and a community. Like V. S. Naipaul's cultural travelers, Obama was determined to move from the backwaters to a major city, from the periphery to the center, so he journeyed to the mainland, wanting to feel grounded and secure in the process of becoming part of the mainstream experience (Naipaul 1984).

As a president, with many years of experience behind him, Obama explained his transition accordingly:

> It's not so much, I think, me rejecting what she did; I understood the appeal of it, and I still do. But it was a conscious choice, I think, on my part, that the idea of being a citizen of the world, but without any real anchor, had both its benefits but also its own limits. Either way, you were giving something up. And I chose to give up this other thing— partly because I'd gotten what my mother had provided when I was young, which was a lot of adventure and a great view of the world. (Scott 2011, 355)

However, feeling uprooted and adrift in a sea of anonymity is also part of the American experience; it is part of the DNA of the American people to just get up, move, and relocate to newer surroundings. Obama inherited the same wanderlust. There is a perennial tension in Obama's journey; he is a man of family wanderings and fractured worldviews, but he felt compelled to settle down. There is a Steinbeck quality to Obama's story, states Michael Powell in the *New York Times*, "Like so many migratory American tales: the mother who flickers in and out; the absent and iconic father; the grandfather, raised in the roughneck Kansas oil town of El Dorado, who moves the family restlessly, ceaselessly westward" (Powell 2008). Yet Obama has a dual or even a triple heritage from the different lines of his genealogy. As a young man he drifted from Hawai'i to Los Angeles and New York before touching down in Chicago. He has stayed in the same neighborhood of Chicago's Hyde Park for more than two decades. He is aware that his multiracial and multiethnic background can be seen as a sign of "the other" or "the foreigner." Thus, his adoption of the African American ethnicity has kept him grounded in a place, a community, and a family.

In the process of transitioning from the Hawai'ian Islands to the mainland, at least two significant events happened. First, Obama discovered his political voice while speaking at a student rally at Occidental College against apartheid in South Africa. Second, when he arrived in New York City, he received a call from a distant Aunt Jane announcing over a densely static telephone line that his father had passed away in Kenya.

Both events were significant and were highlighted as turning points in his autobiography.

At a student-organized antiapartheid rally, Obama found his capacity to connect with a mass audience. Public speaking gave him a high in front of a large audience, but the experience did not last long enough; he was quickly yanked off the stage by his friends. Yet even in the few words and phrases he spoke, his vision was already forming. He took a global view and seemed ready to take sides in the fight between right and wrong:

> "I say, there's a struggle going on! . . . It's happening an ocean away. But it's a struggle that touches each and every one of us. Whether we know it or not. Whether we want it or not. A struggle that demands we choose sides. Not between black and white. Not between rich and poor. No—it's a harder choice than that. It's a choice between dignity and servitude. Between fairness and injustice. Between commitment and indifference. A choice between right and wrong." (Obama 2004a, 106)

Where did Obama learn to publicly project his voice in such a clear and dramatic manner and draw out such stark distinctions between right and wrong? Was it in the dusty streets of Jakarta, where he used to imitate President Suharto arousing the masses, and where he first imagined that he could be president some day? Or was it in the English literature class at Punahou School, where he used to surprise his classmates with his brilliant insights and clever use of language? Did he train himself in the privacy of his grandparents' apartment, while he looked in the mirror and saw himself as a black Hawai'ian man with a gift of oratory inherited from his African father? The emergence of Obama's political voice at Occidental was determined by all of these multilayered influences—biracial family upbringing, international travel, and multicultural education. With time and maturation, his political voice would become more precise, but he would repeatedly draw similar contrasts between right and wrong, between justice and fairness, and between commitment and inaction.

As it turned out, just as Obama began to discover his political voice he realized that Occidental was too small for his emerging ambitions; thus, he quickly packed up and left for Columbia University in New York City. "'Literally, you could come to Occidental and not know the president was ever here,' says Jonathan Veitch, Occidental's president. This is about to change. The school is considering a statue, an Obama-inspired reading room and lecture series, among other things" (Audi 2009). The school's goal is to emphasize the fact that the beginning of a journey is as important as the end.

Obama said in a *Los Angeles Times* interview that Occidental was "a wonderful, small liberal arts college. The professors were diverse and inspiring. I ended up making some lifelong friendships there, and those first two years really helped me grow up" (Gordon 2007). Roger Boesche, one of Obama's intellectual mentors at Occidental, has said that he was "a very thoughtful student and a very curious student" (Gordon 2007). Obama took two of Boesche's courses: a survey of American government and an advanced look at modern European political thought. "You didn't take my European Modern class without wanting to think about deep ideas," said Boesche (Gordon 2007). In a recent meeting with his former professor, who is still on the faculty at Occidental, Obama complained that he got a B instead of an A on a paper on European political theory. Never one to forget a disagreement, Obama surprised his former teacher with his tenacity and sense of humor.

When Obama arrived in New York City, the news of his father's death cut his legs from under him: "Barry? Barry, is this you? This is your Aunt Jane. In Nairobi. Can you hear me? Listen Barry, your father is dead. He was killed in a car accident" (Obama 2004a, 5). At this juncture, Obama's life was thrown into a tailspin. But why, given that this was a man he hardly knew? Yet his father continued to exercise a strong pull on Obama's life. Obama was only 21 years old and still in the process of figuring out who he was. At the time of his father's sudden death, the man was still a mystery to his son. More a myth than a real person, Obama Sr. would play both a larger and a smaller role than one would expect in the life of this president.

At his father's passing, Obama's search for his real self intensified. He became a recluse, took to reading heavily, exercised a lot, and got busy figuring out what he wanted to do with his life. This is similar to how he adapted when he left Jakarta and returned to Hawai'i; he retreated into his inner world and by intensive reading figured out what he wanted to become, what his allegiances were, and what he really cared about.

The death of his father sobered him up; just as he was about to enter young adulthood, his father's demise put a punctuation mark on his life by reminding him of his own mortality and the rapid movement of time. He was forced to gather the few memories of his father by reading and reread-ing his letters, trying to find in them the hidden meaning and purpose of his own life. As a child, Obama learned about his father through the stories his mother and grandparents had told him. After each retelling, the stories would be burnished, smoothed over, and packed away for another occasion. Obama had a few photographs of his father, old black-and-white prints he had found while rummaging through cupboards and closets in his grandparents' apartment. These most likely stoked real memories beginning at the age of four years, the earliest period most of us can recall in our lives. For Obama, this was a time when his mother was about to marry her second husband. "I sensed without explanation why the photographs had to be stored away," he wrote in his autobiography (Obama 2004a, 9). However, on certain days when his mother was in the mood to talk, she would often tell him stories about his African father, who came from the distant shores of Lake Victoria. Listening attentively, he would often perk up and resonate with a fondness for his father, like children often do while listening to folktales and myths.

He was reminded again and again of the voice of his father, "My father's voice had nevertheless remained untainted, inspiring, rebuking, granting or withholding approval. You do not work hard enough, Barry. You must help in your people's struggle. Wake up, black man!" (Obama 2004a, 220). Now, the father who had been missing all his life was simply gone, just like the fantastical Grinch who had stolen his Christmas for a month when he had visited him at the tender age of ten years (Obama 2004a).

Obama was left mostly with faded images of his only visit, like old black-and-white films, grainy and opaque, appearing and then disappearing, burning a trace in his mind before melting away. In one of the images, he was ten years old and standing with his father next to the Christmas tree, holding an orange basketball. His father was happy to receive the tie that his son got him. His father's slight limp from an accident surfaced as he remembered walking in on his father and mother when they were dancing together for a brief moment. Then he noticed his father's increased frailty and a month later he was gone. While time had pushed on, his father's image—part real, part fiction—had remained frozen in time in the recesses of his mind. Precipitated by his father's early death, Obama was forced to revisit his early trauma, and he was haunted by a recurring dream that his father was somehow caught in a messy court trial and his son was trying to save him. He realized that the example of his father's life and work had provided him with the relational and rational foundation on which to build his own life.

From Barry to Barack

During this crucial period in his life, Obama dropped his American name and took on the name of his father, as if to complete the Lacanian oedipal triangulation and resolution (Lacan 1968; Reppen 1985). He now felt comfortable with himself and his budding identity. He visited black churches to pray and seek inspiration. His full adoption of the Kenyan name given by his father suggests both a clear break with the assimilationist trend at the time in the general African American population on the mainland and a sense of connection with his purely African lineage.

His adoption of the African name may suggest that he was ready to take on and interpret the African American traditions from the vantage point of an African, not as a descendant of slaves. As a new kind of African in North America, he represents both a discontinuity with the old racial debates and an engagement with the earlier metaphors as a way to move the debate forward. He may have consciously owned up to his triple heritage as the pan-Africanist Ali Mazrui has pointed out and to the various strands of his African lineage (i.e., African, Islamic, and Western) (Mazrui 1987). In this singular act, however, Obama seemed to have encapsulated his identity resolution, which would eventually push the debate on race relations forward on the mainland.

Shortly after I arrived in this country, as part of the first wave of immigrants from India, Alex Haley's *Roots* had become a popular television serial. A new African name, Kunta Kinte, which later acquired a mythic stature in African American literature, was added to my cultural literacy. My memory of Kunta Kinte, as played by LeVar Burton, is still fresh. Whenever I see LeVar Burton on PBS teaching kids how to read and write, I experience a flashback to the winter of 1977 when, as new immigrants, my family and I huddled together around the television and watched the saga of an American family.

During the 2008 presidential campaign, as the political signs began to pop up in our neighborhood, my kids would recognize and read aloud the names of the various candidates while riding in the backseat of the car. They got especially animated about the name "Obama."

"How do you say that name?" —both my son and daughter asked me.

"Buh-Rock oh-Bah-Ma. It's an African name, from Kenya," I explained.

Mainly because the name sounded different my kids were fascinated by it. Maybe because Obama rhymes with Mama it appeals to children: "Mama voted for Obama" (Zilber 2008). As one of the children's books described not long ago many people did not know who Barack Obama was, so they called him Baruch Yo Mama, Barack Alabama, or Barack O'Bama (Gormley 2008). Now the junior senator from Illinois has become the first African American president of America.

When anthropologists study different cultures, they are like children learning a new language. They spend a great deal of time studying different naming conventions. How are names acquired? What does a name signify? Among other things, a name may signify the name of a family, a place, a village, a tribe, or a clan. Historically, naming signifies continuity of a tradition or radical break with a tradition, especially in a country like America, which is a nation of immigrants. Almost all cultures have elaborate naming rituals involving newborns and their families.

When slaves came to the United States from Africa and the West Indies, they went through a name change and acquired a slave name, signifying an owner and a place. Although the factual basis of the life of Kunta Kinte may still be debated (White 2008), his biographical outline was as follows: Slave name, Toby; born ca. 1750; birthplace, Gambia, West Africa; tribe, Mandinka; owner, John Waller; county, Annapolis, Maryland; and religion, Islam.

After the Emancipation Proclamation in 1863, many African Americans changed their names to the name of their owner, to names like Freeman that reflected their new status, and to the names of presidents like Washington, Jefferson, and Lincoln. Through the civil rights movement in the 1960s, many more African Americans changed their names after converting to the Brotherhood of Islam and other African religions.

In the 2008 election, even political pundits behaved a bit like naive anthropologists, trying to trace Obama's genealogy and the roots of his African name. What does the name "Barack" mean? What is the origin of the name "Obama"? What about the middle name, "Hussein," which was never or rarely mentioned?

"Barack" is a Swahili word, derivative of the Arabic "Mubarack," which means "blessing." "Baruch" in Hebrew and "Mubarak" in Hindi, Urdu, or Persian have the same meaning. The surname "Obama" belongs to the Luo tribe of Kisumu, Kenya. Barack's father was named Barack Hussein Obama Sr. but presented himself as "Barry" when he enrolled at the University of Hawai'i in 1959. Barack Obama's grandfather, Hussein Onyango, converted to Islam when he worked for the British authorities as a colonial civil servant. Although his father was an atheist, Barack Obama has been a practicing Christian. All of this has now become fodder for children's books.

However, the middle name "Hussein" seemed to have touched a raw nerve, creating a tempest in a teapot and suggesting to some that Obama is a closet Muslim. Some of the conservative media outlets that have regularly rhymed "Obama" with "Osama" as a deliberate slip of the tongue have suggested that the country was being overtaken by our enemies, the Islamo-fascists, and that there was a sinister plot behind Obama's candidacy, which was to spell the end of American civilization as we know it. The satirical cartoon in the *New Yorker* on July 21, 2008, depicting both Michelle and Barack Obama in the Oval office dressed as terrorists underscored this general fear.

Clearly, a president with an African or foreign-sounding name has never been elected in this country, which created unease and discomfort among many in the general population, especially in the post-9/11 world. Yet, a group of young Obama supporters, representing the YouTube generation, converted their middle name to "Hussein" on Facebook as a sign of solidarity with their candidate, who, according to them, truly represented generational change (Kantor 2008b).

In contrast, several African American bloggers labeled Obama the "Kunta Kinte of 2008" or "Barack Toby Obama" in light of his break with Trinity Church due to increasing media pressures precipitated by Reverend Wright's controversial views (Watkins 2008). Jesse Jackson, in his off-air comments, said that "I want to cut his nuts out," because Obama was talking down to black people (Goldenberg 2008). Shelby Steele, who claimed that Obama was "a bound man" and could not win by accommodating to the majority had anticipated this controversy (Steele 2007).

When asked about changing his name from "Barry" to "Barack," Obama has replied that it was "when I made a conscious decision: I want to grow up" (Wolffe 2008)—to fully identify with the name of his father. It was when he arrived at Columbia University as a transfer student that he began to use the name Barack more regularly: "It was much more of an assertion that I was coming of age, an assertion of being comfortable with the fact that I was different and that I didn't need to try to fit in in a certain way" (Wolffe 2008).

Thus, in a generational election another African name was added to the mountain of names that make up the American experience. From Kunta Kinte to Barack Obama, we have come a long way in race relations in this country. Notwithstanding the prevailing postracial mood of Obama's election, even a chasm of centuries cannot erase the underlying symbolic and cultural logic connecting these two African American names to the history of this nation.

It is no coincidence that Obama aligned with the African American tradition even as he broke with it and attempted to reform it. He wanted to belong and feel connected to a local community. However, I believe his larger purpose may have been to stay connected with the world of his father and forefathers and with the soul and spirit of Africa.

After his father died, Obama's brief time in New York left him searching for a solution to his identity problem; he appeared alone, isolated, and depressed. Very few people remember him at Columbia University. However, soon he received another devastating call, this time from his half-sister, Auma Obama, informing him that one of his half-brothers, David Obama, had died. Obama recalls that event:

> I still wonder sometimes how the first contact with Auma altered my life. . . . Maybe it made no difference. Maybe by this time I was already committed to organizing and Auma's voice simply served to remind me that I had wounds to heal, and could not heal myself. Or maybe, if David hadn't died when he did, and Auma had come to New York as originally planned, and I had learned from her then what I would only learn later, about Kenya, and about our father. . . . I don't know. What's certain is that a few months after Auma's call I turned in my resignation at the consulting firm and began looking in earnest at an organizing job. (Obama 2004a, 138)

Obama decided to change the course of his life after the news of his father's and half-brother's death. Ultimately, it seems that he settled on his black identity while at Columbia University before moving to Chicago. Obama thought that New York City was too big, too overwhelming, and too divided. He settled on Chicago as his adopted hometown, and secured a job organizing some black neighborhoods. The more than two years spent in New York City seemed to have been his lost years, where he went through a profound identity crisis that led him to rediscover his true inner values; this also marked his identity resolution and the end of the psychosocial moratorium.

In Chicago, he was finally able to answer the twofold question central to his identity: I am a community organizer, and I belong in Chicago (Mendell 2007; McClelland 2010). Obama clearly began to identify with his father's name and legacy at the end of his undergraduate education and decided to work for the causes championed by his father and to a large extent already practiced by his mother in Indonesia. Thus, even in his absence Obama Sr.'s ideals and values left an indelible imprint on Obama's mind.

In an interview with the *New Yorker*, Tara Bay Smith, the author of *State by State: A Panoramic Portrait of America*, who grew up in Hawai'i and attended the Punahou School, stated:

> Obama embodies America at its best: a country where the concepts of native and foreigner, "pure" and "mixed," black and white, *hapa* and hundred per cent are so complex that the claim of belonging because of blood quantum or family tree must be set against the argument that what defines an American is not the place or the circumstances of his birth but his allegiance to his country's laws and ideals. Hawai'i, by virtue of its exceptionally diverse population, is a place where these questions are explicit. I am consistently heartened by Obama's hope for union in the face of seemingly irreconcilable differences, and his deep belief in the human capacity for change. (Mishan 2008)

Smith clearly believes that because Obama was born and raised in Hawai'i and his extended family members still live there, "he is expressive of its paradoxes, its opposite-of-monolithic character, and its ethnic nuances." Its history of high rates of interracial marriages, in which generations of Hawai'ian residents accepted American power and in turn created a demographically blended state, makes Hawai'i a true reflection of a back-to-the-future state, which ironically may be pointing the way forward for the mainland.

Hawai'i as the Demographic Future

Hawai'i represents the demographic end result of tectonic changes that are underway in the mainland; according to the U.S. Census, there will not be any majority ethnic group by 2042 (U.S. Census 2008). Following Hawai'i's lead, three other states are already heading this way—Texas, California, and New Mexico. Hawai'i may represent a model for an emerging American cultural identity, where everybody comes from a different part of the world but all are woven into the seamless cultural fabric of America.

According to the latest census, non-Hispanic whites may become a minority among newborn children in the United States, a demographic shift that is beginning to reshape the nation's politics and economy. Nonwhite minority newborns accounted for 48.6 percent of the children born in the United States between July 2008 and July 2009, suggesting a trend where minority births will soon eclipse births of whites of European ancestry (Dougherty 2010a).

According to a recent report by *Wall Street Journal*, "America's changing face has transformed race relations from the traditional divide of black and white to a more complex mix of race, language and religion" (Dougherty 2010a). Schools and social services are especially strained, and the emergence of immigration as one of the nation's most contentious issues as witnessed by Arizona's recent immigration law clearly shows that the melting pot is indeed stirred up and may be getting overheated.

The demographic push toward what the U.S. Census calls a "majority minority" future is partly driven by the aging of the baby boomer population. The non-Hispanic white population is older than that of nonwhites, and white women are having fewer babies than nonwhite minority women. These fertility trends are partly irreversible, as a larger share of minority women will be in their childbearing years for many years to come (Dougherty 2010b). In addition, the growth of mixed marriages and multiracial births has further advanced the rise of what many are calling "the blended nation" (Tauber and Singh 2009).

Although minorities constituted 35 percent of the U.S. population between July 2008 and July 2009, the trend is predicted to be even higher in recent years, according to the U.S. Census. However, immigration, which is a politically fiery issue, is not the driving force behind the nation's growing diversity; it is gradual social and demographic change. The Hispanic population, which accounted for 54.7 percent of the total population increase in recent years, was mostly expanding because of an increase in the number of live births (Dougherty 2010b).

America is on the path toward transforming itself into a more diverse nation from within, not unlike where Hawai'i was when it became part of the United States. Moreover, during the past decade, with its strong undercurrents of assimilation on the one hand, and the housing boom on the other, diversity has advanced into the suburbs and across states that hadn't traditionally attracted immigrants (Dougherty 2010a).

Changes in the census collection categories instituted in 2000 have also been significantly responsible for identifying the multiracial population of the United States; racial demography is no longer mapped in terms of discrete, mutually exclusive categories, white, black, Hispanic, or other. Approximately 2 percent to 3 percent of the population now claims to be of more than one racial category. The multiracial category is likely to grow because of increased interracial and mixed marriages. In the near future, as Americans accept their destiny as a blended, mixed-race nation, many more of us will become part of each other's lives and selves.

This kind of mixing of races is not new, however; as many as 80 percent of African Americans may have at least some white blood, and almost 25 percent claim to have Native American ancestry. Mixed-race America might be as old as the founding of the nation itself, although clearly the big difference is that in the future the blending of ethnicities and races is likely to occur voluntarily. Thus, the process of defining one's hybrid identity, a fairly complex and highly individualized process, will be undertaken by millions of Americans in the near future.

Obama's Hybrid Identity

With respect to the idea of a mixed-race identity, Obama may be a change agent as well. He wrestled with how to define his mixed-race identity while living in Hawai'i. "It is in the blood," his father told him when the 10-year-old finally met him in 1971. The idea of fatherlessness had haunted him for as far back as he could remember. In fact, Obama does not consciously remember a time when he had a father, except through the second-hand stories told by others. His father's words gave language to his struggle to find himself, "to know where you belong" his father had told him (Obama 2004a, 114).

So where does Obama belong? Clearly, as an African American community organizer and young politician coming up the ranks his allegiances were racially aligned, but as president and a man of the world his reach must include all Americans and the larger humanity, an outlook rooted in his early upbringing. Does he even feel the burden of race anymore? asked Sugrue.

> Yet, Kansas or Kenyan, European or African American, Obama lives in an America where the principle of hypodescent—the one-drop rule—still shapes perceptions of those of African heritage, even if it scarcely corresponds to the polychromatic, multiethnic reality of the United States. For Obama, as for growing numbers of Americans of European, Latin American, and Asian descent, hybridity is a choice. But for most Americans of African descent adopting a hybrid identity is nearly impossible—and for many, indeed, undesirable. (Sugrue 2010, 123)

As the "post-soul president" who came of age after the civil rights struggles, is Obama pointing the way forward as a "cultural mulatto," reflexively playing with the century-old race categories that Shelby Steele (2007) has eloquently written about? Obama learned to slip back and forth between the white and black worlds with comfort and ease beginning in childhood; each world had its distinct slang, rules, customs, meanings, and subcultures, and he could decode them both. Even as Obama embraced the multifaceted cultural life of America, he claimed a bicultural status as a marker for his identity.

Novelist Zadie Smith claims that our president speaks in many tongues and many voices; he does not just represent the voice of black and white America. He can voice the concerns of "young Jewish male, black old lady from the South side, white woman from Kansas, Kenyan elders, white Harvard nerds, black Columbia nerds, activist women, churchmen, security guards, bank tellers and even a British man called Mr. Wilkerson, who on a starry night on safari says credibly British things like: 'I believe that's the Milky Way.'" Obama's story is about expanding the tent, not about shutting off the dialogue for the fear that it might spill into a noisy cacophony; he is "genuinely a many-voiced man" who wants to extend the conversation (Smith 2009, 24).

Obama's autobiography tells the story in fascinating details. However, as we dig a little deeper, Obama's story is a "postmodern bildungsroman," where the hero is driven to find out about his hybrid roots (Eijun 2008). As he journeys, his story becomes the search for his real father and what his father stood for, the meaning and the myth of a man he barely knew. The search for a hybrid self is transformed into a quintessentially masculine narrative as Obama identifies with and wants to become like his father and at least believes in the positive image of his father, even though the image shows some strains and blemishes with the passage of time.

When Obama's autobiography was first released in 1995, it garnered positive reviews but puzzled readers. Robert Detweiler (1996) of *Choice* wrote: "Obama writes well; his account is sensitive, probing and compelling." Hazel Rochman (1995) of *Booklist* reported feeling somewhat confused, "Will the truth set you free? Obama asks. Or will it disappoint? Both, it seems. His search for himself as a black American is rooted in the particulars of his daily life; it also reads like a wry commentary about all of us."

Paul Watkins, the reviewer for the *New York Times* grasped the message of the book but nevertheless found it hard to reconcile the apparent contradictions in the narrative:

> All men live in the shadow of their fathers—the more distant the father, the deeper the shadow. Barack Obama describes his confrontation with this shadow in his provocative autobiography, "Dreams From My Father," and he also persuasively describes the phenomenon of belonging to two different worlds, and thus belonging to neither. . . . At a young age and without much experience as a writer, Barack Obama has bravely tackled the complexities of his remarkable upbringing. But what would he have us learn? That people of mixed backgrounds must choose only one culture in which to make a spiritual home? That it is not possible to be both black and white, Old World and New? If this is indeed true, as Mr. Obama tells it, then the idea of America taking pride in itself as a nation derived of many different races seems strangely mocked. (Watkins 1995)

Indeed, Obama sees mixed-race individuals as tragic and does not find a forward-looking perspective on America's changing demographics.

Almost a decade later, Obama wrote in the new edition that the sales were "underwhelming," and after a few months he went on with his everyday life. In 1995, Obama's story was not fully understood, but when the new edition was printed in 2004 after his famous convention speech—"There is not a black America and a white America and Latino America and Asian America. There's the United States of America"—his stature was so overwhelming that some of the details of the book were not examined.

The book is an honest retelling of certain compartments of Obama's inner world. It is multifaceted and filled with textual nuances and illuminations. Similar to a growing number of biographies in American literature, according to Eijun (2008), an American studies expert, it fits the narrative styles of many different genres: genealogy, trauma narrative, ethnic identity narrative, memoir, and postmodern bildungsroman.

As a genealogy, the narrative is deeply compelling and shows his understanding of different cultures that are central to his life story as forming an authentic core rarely seen in a politician. Obama becomes a time traveler, retracing his roots back in time to Kenya and the Midwest. He validates his family history, retelling a story that is part fact and part narrative rendition; at times the story moves like a psychological case study, and at other moments he engages in oral history of his African roots. As an ethnic identity narrative, the book is a universalist history of the many branches of his family tree: African, Caucasian, Asian, and others. Given his mixed ancestry, Obama tries to create an overarching American narrative, while shunning his "mulatto" identity, finding in it a tragic outcome, becoming nobody yet representing everybody.

The book moves across time and geography with Obama as the narrator, observer, and participant, writing a reflective memoir about Hawai'i, Indonesia, Kenya, and Chicago. In openly revealing his self and personality development, he refers to his diaries, letters, and research notes to examine the public and personal lives of his family members. He concedes that his memory can at times be fallible, and as a literary self-invention, he may have been self-serving.

At the center of the narrative, Obama reveals a series of traumas that drive the story forward—trauma at the abandonment by his father, trauma from the dissolution of his mother's marriages and her itinerant lifestyle, and later trauma at the discovery of his racial identity. We discover that the "father wound" is central to Obama's story and is the underlying motivation for Obama's unrelenting drive. The search for his biological father in Africa deeply shapes the reconstruction of a racial identity in America.

Finally, according to Eijun (2008), Obama's narrative is a bildungsroman, or a journey of self-development, a story about the development and social formation of a young man, from Hawai'i and Indonesia to the mainland, from Punahou and Occidental to Columbia and Harvard, and from Honolulu to New York and Chicago. Obama's early socialization is as diverse as we have ever seen in the White House. Although he chooses to define himself as an African American for his census identity, the undeniable fact is that Obama is born of a multicultural America at the cusp of the age of globalization.

It is my conclusion that because Obama's core self was formed in Hawai'i and Indonesia, the crucible in the Pacific where East meets West, he is our first global president. The incredible pull that his father's image exercised on his identity is also undeniable. The lack of any potent hybrid alternatives as role models for an African American youth to aspire toward in the 1970s is also undeniable. Obama gravitated toward African American athletes, civil rights leaders, writers, and others. Although his political persona is clearly made in Chicago, his self is made up of identifications from Hawai'i, Indonesia, and his middle-class white upbringing in the Pacific. He is truly America's hybrid president, a man of many continents, races, cultures, and histories, who has defined himself as an African American politician.

However, one should not be mystified by Obama's global image and persona. Obama believes in the American creed as much as the other presidents who have claimed the state of Illinois as their home: Lincoln, Grant, and Reagan. Obama's globalism does not negate his Americanism. In fact, his globalism may have propagated even more forcefully a romantic and mythologized view of America to the rest of the world, where anything and everything is possible. Banita (2009) claims that at the core Obama believes in the Emersonian "self-reliance" and "reason" as his guiding principles. Although he may show a kind of transnational empathy for peoples around the world, he believes America is exceptional and is trying to renew the American agenda even while the future looks economically bleak. This is certainly the claim Kloppenberg (2010) makes in his intellectual biography of the president, discovering that Obama's legal philosophy is guided by American pragmatism.

Renewing American Identity

Every president tries to usher in a new era of American leadership. Reagan brought down the Iron Curtain by calling upon the Russians to "tear down this wall." After 9/11, Bush stood at Ground Zero with a megaphone and summoned the world to fight terrorism. Obama in turn lit up the crowd at Grant Park in Chicago by declaring that anyone who doubts American resolve, in a land where anything is still possible, is plainly wrong.

In recent times, no American leader has been more popular than Barack Obama with the world's masses, and at home Obama may have ushered in a new era of postethnic politics. As the Berkeley historian David Hollinger stated during the campaign, "The spectacle of John Lewis, Charles B. Rangel, and Andrew Young, among others, trying to persuade black Americans to vote for a white woman rather than the first black man with a real chance at the White House is a striking example of how the Obama campaign has become a postethnic phenomenon" (Hollinger 2008).

An education policy expert, Michael Peters (2009) claimed that Obama has tried to renew the American dream by proposing a more comprehensive vision of the American people, united as one nation, transcending all divisions. Highlighting the ethos of community service, Obama has reintroduced the idea of America as an organized collection of small to midsize local communities, calling for grassroots level action. As a legal pragmatist, he has put forth ideas with an evidence-based approach in educational and health care reform. As a progressive, he has attempted to give government more power to push through major reforms to renew the economy. Obama's cosmopolitanism should be seen as a complement to his deep roots in the pragmatic, progressive, and communitarian tradition within American culture.

At Obama's inaugural, the writer Naomi Wolf wondered aloud, "America certainly has its flaws and its struggles over race and national identity, but it also has much to be proud of in terms of how it assimilates those with foreign or minority backgrounds" (Wolf 2009). She drew inspiration from Obama's rise, an achievement that could not have been possible in Europe, even though many accomplished leaders from ethnic or racial "out-groups" are part of European cabinets.

Europeans went into a soul-searching of their own. Could the Obama phenomenon be replicated in Europe? many wondered aloud. Could a person of ethnicity and color get elected in Europe to a high office? After all, many European countries are considered more advanced when it comes to race. Why have we not seen more diversity among public leaders in the Old World? One of the reasons may be that the larger society and culture does not support it.

In other words, what should Americans be proud of? Wolf asked. What have they done right? She believes that, compared to other developed societies in the West, America's national identity is essentially about the social and cultural dynamics of immigration. It is different in essence from those of Western European stories. Unlike the French, the British, and the Germans, most Americans, except Native Americans, came from somewhere else. "All who are now part of the national elite have ancestors who came, often bedraggled and harassed, from somewhere else," declared Wolf (2009).

According to reporting done by NPR, approximately half a million Africans and 3 million Turks live and work in Germany. Many feel ignored or treated like foreigners, even though their families may have been there for generations. Germans do not have any kind of national debate on racial identity. Italians have about 7 percent of the immigrant population within their borders, but strict citizenship laws are evidence of the widespread suspicion toward immigrants. Likewise, despite long-standing notions of equality and fraternity, France has just started a national debate about racism and discrimination prompted by hard economic conditions and ethnic riots (NPR 2009).

On the other hand, America has for long excelled on the strength of new immigrants and the qualities they bring with them—"initiative, ambition, risk-taking"— who are constantly in the process of remaking themselves and thereby remaking America. They try to surpass their internalized expectations of the home country. Most immigrants in Western Europe, on the other hand, are invited to take jobs that no one else wants to perform, "creating a built-in incentive for natives to see them and their children as a servant class, incapable of entering, let alone leading, the larger society," claimed Wolf (2009).

In Europe immigrants are the constant reminder of the history of colonialism, but in America such an experience is rare. Newcomers to America do not feel the same pressures of defining their ethnicity or background in opposition to the larger sense of patriotism to the host country. Retaining an ethnic name and lineage and a hybrid identity is part and parcel of being American. Defining an identity in Europe may present stark choices, where people may not choose to identify with the host country, according to Wolf. Thus, many European nations contain zones of alienated Muslim youths living in their own isolated subcultures. Although there are many radical Muslims around the world who love to hate America, there are a growing number of Muslim immigrants in the United States who are rapidly assimilating and raising their children to love and respect their host country. Instead of listening to mullahs or radical clerics, they want to assimilate, have their children succeed in higher education, participate in

American sports, and celebrate secular or semireligious holidays, without diminishing their ties to a local religious community.

Which presidential candidate in 2008 best defined the American identity? Recent psychological evidence suggests that both implicit and explicit biases may have been operating in the selection of a candidate who best embodied the values of the American identity. On the face of it, Hillary Clinton and John McCain may have been seen as more American than Barack Obama, according to Devos et al. (2007). Obama might not have appeared American enough for the majority of the traditional voters, but all that changed on the day of the election.

Bobo and Charles (2009) similarly reviewed the history and sociology of "race in the American mind" from the Moynihan Report to the Obama candidacy and found a remarkable level of structural and individual level change since 1960, when the original report was written. They find that while the race "virus" has significantly retreated, especially given Obama's win, it has not been fully defeated.

According to filmmaker Ytasha Womack, a new era of black leadership has already taken shape, partly giving rise to the presidency of Barack Obama. Womack asserts that:

Post Black speaks to the new diversity and complex identity in African American culture. Whereas the social dynamics of decades before required a uniform black American identity to battle impending social injustice, the new opportunities afforded the generations of today as a result of victories won and fallen barriers have given rise to a growing diversity that some are enthused about and others are not. (Womack 2010)

University of Virginia law professor Guy-Uriel Charles has stated that Obama's election has serious implications for the emerging American identity. "Obama's presidency was not the result of the fact that a majority of whites voted for him, but the fact that a coalition of voters of color [cast their vote] in a lot of respects around this issue of racial consciousness," Charles said (2008). The ethnic mix of the votes for Obama clearly bears this out, something Obama would need in order to repeat his victory.

Long after Obama's policies are debated, his personal charisma will endure, very much like the Kennedy mystique, Reagan's morning in America, or the Clinton aura. People instinctively relate to Obama, not only in the United States but also in places like Kenya and Indonesia, because of his direct and immediate linkage with them. In an interview with James Traub of the *New York Times*, candidate Obama candidly revealed the basis of his hybrid identity as a way to open a new dialogue with the world: "If I am the face of American foreign policy and American power . . . if you can tell people 'We have a president in the White House who still has a grandmother living in a hut on the shores of Lake Victoria and has a sister who's half-Indonesian, married to a Chinese-Canadian,' then they're going to think that he may have a better sense of what's going on in our lives and in our country. And they'd be right" (Traub 2007).

However untested his vision may have been at the start of his term, Obama has charted a new course for America at the onset of the 21st century backed heavily by his own biography. As time cannot stand still, the post-9/11 world has marched ahead. America may have again seized the moment of global leadership, and the evidence from around the world bears this out.

Even as the global economy is being led out of the great recession by the growth in emerging economies, many nations remain deeply concerned (Pew Research 2010b). In addition, many believe their economies are still in bad shape; only one third or less of the people in most nations say they are satisfied with their local conditions. Governments may be seen as the main culprit in the current state of affairs.

President Obama, however, gets enthusiastic support from around the world for the way he handled the global financial crisis, though people in the United States continue to disapprove of his handling of the economy, especially the rescue of failing corporations and banks. The global opinion in 2010, according to the Pew Research Center's Global Attitudes Project (2010b), found that the president remained very popular everywhere else but at home. His job approval rating in the United States declined sharply during his second year in office. Overall, Americans are feeling a lot more downcast and economically depressed now than they were at the inspiring 2008 victory.

America's image in the world has remained fairly positive since Obama's election, far more positive than it was during George W. Bush's tenure. In Western Europe (e.g., France, Germany) and other allied countries (e.g., Japan, China, Russia, Poland, South Korea, Brazil), America is seen very favorably. The United States continues to receive a thumbs-up in South Asia and Southeast Asia—in India and in Indonesia, for example, which have the world's largest minority Muslim population and the world's largest predominantly Muslim population, respectively.

Closer to home, America's favorable rating dropped in Mexico because of "Arizona's enactment of a law aimed at dealing with illegal immigration by giving police increased powers to stop and detain people who are suspected of being in the country illegally" (Pew Research 2010b). Mexicans have given the United States a 44 percent favorable rating compared to 62 percent before the passage of the immigration bill.

In other Muslim countries, such as Turkey and Pakistan, the American image is having a much tougher time, despite signs of democratic uprising of early 2011 throughout the Arab world. These countries continue to hold negative views of the United States. Both Turkey and Pakistan give the United States a consistently low rating. Mainly because of the Afghanistan war, according to Pew, "The U.S. is slipping in some Muslim countries where opinion had edged up in 2009" (Pew Research 2010b).

The new survey also found that in most non-Muslim nations, opinions about Barack Obama remain fairly positive. In these countries, 71 percent of those surveyed believe he will do the right thing in global affairs, and 64 percent approve of his policies. Likewise, in several African nations, such as Kenya (89 percent) and Nigeria (74 percent), Obama received high approval for his policies.

Among Egyptians, the level of Muslim confidence in Obama has fallen from 41 percent to 31 percent; there is a slight uptick after the democratic revolution of 2011 but not a significant improvement. Similarly, in Turkey it has dropped from 33 percent to 23 percent. Thus, majority Muslim nations' initial thrill about Obama seems to have faded, except in Indonesia, where Obama lived for several years as a child. Because of the Afghan war, only 13 percent of Pakistani Muslims believe Obama would do the right thing, but this year that view has dropped to single digits (8 percent). Obama still arouses more positive opinions than President Bush did, however, a significant percentage of Muslims in these countries worry that the United States could turn into a military threat in their country.

What is the reason for this marked change compared with the previous administrations? Has Obama successfully projected a new American identity on the global stage? Based on the evidence, the answer to this question is clear and unequivocal. World opinion has changed significantly in favor of America since Obama took office, except in some nations with a Muslim majority. The new American identity that Obama has projected is one of a multicultural America which is open toward other nations and promises to innovate and change the world for the better, guided by the founding principles of this nation. However, in some Muslim nations where extremism has taken root, Americans are seen as threatening and capable of unilateral action. Obama has made a series of important speeches in the majority Muslim nations of Turkey, Egypt, and Indonesia, where perceptions have changed but the U.S. policies remain the same. According to observers who follow the opinion on the Islamic street (Zogby 2010), a renewal of American presence in the Arab world must include changes in its policies which will eventually lead to long-term changes in the American image abroad.

7

Obama's Mythic Dreams

Now and again, an individual is called upon (called upon by whom, only theologians claim to know, and by what only bad psychologists) to lift his personal conflicts to the level of cultural conflicts, and to try to solve for all what he could not solve for himself alone.

Erik Erikson (1958, 67)

From the standpoint of dream psychology the most extraordinary capacity of the human psyche is its genius for fabricating images.

Anthony Stevens (1997, 176)

Although Obama's outer life has been well chronicled, his inner world is less well understood. He has been portrayed as a superhero on comic books and compared to heroes from classical mythology. The public has been distracted from looking at the real person behind the political image. In this book, I have probed, interpreted, and analyzed Obama's early years with the goal of understanding Obama as a person, an individual in a particular time and place, and a president in the making, not simply as a political figure, the head of state, the representative of a race, or the leader of the democratic majority. Specifically, I have peered into the life of Barack Obama as he has lived it in different cultural contexts before he became a household name. Thus, I have attempted to present a cultural biography, not simply a psychological biography. Yet psyche and culture are forever intertwined, even though only a select group of psychologists and anthropologists would admit this (Shweder and LeVine 1994).

My goal has also been to understand the driving motivations underlying Obama's personality and meteoric rise in the preconditions and developmental constraints of his early upbringing. As Michiko Kakutani (2010) stated in a recent book review, the biographies of Barack Obama are multiplying, but very few have tried to explain and interpret his life trajectory from a psychological or a cultural standpoint; most biographies have attempted to view his life through a narrow prism of politics and race. Apparently, the real Obama, the human being or the person, still seems a bit aloof, remote, and hard to figure out. This book has attempted to fill in the gaps in Obama's public image by examining his early socialization and social personality in childhood and adolescence.

At the basic human level, Obama's developmental or psychological challenges are plain for everyone to see: his mother lived and worked mostly in Indonesia; after Obama was 10 years old his grandparents helped to raise him; he suffered father abandonment at the age of two years; and he finally contended with the issues related to his African American identity when he arrived on the mainland as a young man. However, a political man like Obama is not just the sum of his complexes. He is obviously larger than any of the developmental puzzles or psychological riddles life may have thrown at him. He has found a way to transcend the limits of his early social conditioning and island upbringing.

Obama's ability to weave a narrative identity is unique. It attests to his strong imagination, especially the power of his dreams or "private myths" (Stevens 1997). Private myths are the deepest realms of imagination, memories, and reflections. Obama has unearthed these private myths from time to time, excavating the deep recesses of his self; this has partly helped him to forge his unique path in life. As Joseph Campbell (1988, 48) has observed, "Myths are public dreams, dreams are private myths," and their power in structuring a life narrative cannot be underestimated, even in rapidly changing, modern, or postmodern times.

The scientific evidence on the power of dreams has been amassing; while it remains controversial, it is irrefutable that dreams from the deepest realms of our mind can shape our destiny. There are neurobiological, cognitive, and emotional theories of dreaming that highlight the value of dreams in everyday life (Stevens 1997; Tedlock 1987). There is evidence that lucid dreaming, a form of active dreaming, works to shape and alter our life's dreams and reshape our outer lives. Always pushing the individual toward individuation and self-actualization, dreams guide our outer life from the inside out. Many psychologists believe an action in the real world is not really worth pursuing if it does not have an antecedent or a correlate in the dream world.

I have followed the century-old debate within psychology and psychoanalysis for many years. The debate is still alive and kicking: Whether individual dreams are actually fragments of our individual self, our personal unconscious, or a representation of our larger collective dreams, collective unconscious, or a combination of both? However, in recent years the rise of neuroscience, brain research, and evolutionary psychology has led to a rapprochement or an integrative perspective on dreams and dreaming, which values the archaic and symbolic as well as the more intentional or creative dimensions of the human mind.

Thus, Obama's private myths, spanning continents, races, and generations, have helped him to confront several inherited developmental and psychological challenges. At the same time, his mythic dreams provided him with the bricks and mortar for constructing a larger-than-life narrative. While shaping his hopes and aspirations, including those directly passed on from his mother, grandparents, and biological father, Obama's dreams propelled him to seek a higher ground not only within himself but also within a social and cultural framework whose purview included America, Africa, Indonesia, and the emerging global civilization. Whereas a reductionist social, cultural, or psychological theory would reduce the man to his mere complexes, a positive or integrative psychology would accentuate the transcendental factor in Obama's life narrative. Without the transcendental factor, it is not possible to do justice to Obama's life or to offer a balanced interpretation of it.

Thus far in this book we have not directly focused on Obama's father as the source of his underlying drive and motivation in life. His father was not part of his everyday life except at certain key turning points: (1) at birth; (2) at the age of two years, when Obama's father left him to go to Harvard; (3) at the age of ten years, when Obama joined the Punahou School; and (4) at the age of 21 years, when Obama arrived in New York and learned that his father had died. Even in his absence, Obama Sr. left an indelible shadow on Barack Obama's psyche. Like Hamlet, Obama has wrestled with the ghost of his father, though in Obama's case it was a father he hardly knew. Over the years, Obama learned about his father primarily through soul-wrenching dreams and stories, some reliable and some only partially true.

Obama could only imagine what his father might have been like as a real-life, flesh-and-blood father who was present in his life. Likewise, we too can only imagine what Obama Sr.'s relationship with his son might have been. While Obama's internalized maternal image was formed by his mother's constant presence during the first 10 years of Obama's life, the internalized image of his father was formed by the shards of memories, whimsical stories, and anecdotes collected from an occasional letter or a distant phone call, and fleeting impressions gathered from his mother, his grandparents, and long-time friends who knew his father.

Obama's autobiography offers penetrating insights about his father's life (Obama 2004a). The book's emphasis on dreams highlights the importance of his father's dreams and how Obama inherited them. Yet the book also bares Obama's dreams about his father, indeed some revealing dreams and private myths he and his mother had imaginatively created about his father's life, character, and personality. Biologically, we are all driven to crave a father figure; we all have an underlying need for authority figures in our lives. Thus, we are compelled to create imaginary stories about our fathers, especially when they are not physically near us, when they do not live with us, and particularly when they may not measure up to our cultural ideals. The need for father figures in the family is as universal as the need for credible leaders in organizations, society, and politics. According to Howard Gardner (1996), an expert on leadership, this may be a biological drive.

Obama's speeches, especially on Father's Day and in open forums and town hall meetings, offer a glimpse of how he has tried to compensate for the lack of a biological father in his own life. When he preaches to an African American community about personal responsibility or to school-children about the importance of early education, he is simply voicing the inner dialogue he has had with himself on many occasions since he was young. Pulling himself up by the bootstraps is something Obama is very familiar with; it's a skill he acquired on the dusty streets of Jakarta and in the privacy of his grandparents' apartment on the island of Oahu.

As we have seen, Obama's mother was the immediate transmitter of cultural and social knowledge; she deeply shaped his self-development, including the idealistic image of his absent father. His biological father, although absent from his life, guided the son like an invisible hand shaping his destiny. However, his father's absence may have been what propelled Obama to reach even greater heights. Certainly, if he had had a live-in father, he might not have felt the intense need to create a larger-than-life image of a father figure, which is ultimately overthrown, yet whose image both in its negative and positive aspects guides him still. The reality of his father's presence might have been very different from what Obama imagined. According to Obama's Kenyan half-brother, Mark Obama Ndesandjo, Obama Sr.'s son with Ruth Ndesandjo, his third wife, a white

American woman, Obama Sr. was abusive toward his mother and a down-right "bad father" (Ndesandjo 2010).

In a candid interview with Tania Branigan of the *Guardian*, Ndesandjo revealed:

> My father beat my mother and my father beat me. . . . It's something which I think affected me for a long time, and it's something that I've just recently come to terms with. . . . I remember situations when I was growing up, and there would be a light coming from our living room, and I could hear thuds. I could hear thuds and screams, and my father's voice and my mother shouting. (Branigan 2009)

In other words, the real Obama Sr. was a markedly different man than the one Barack Obama had imagined growing up.

Etched deep into his soul, the idealized images of Obama's mother and father—the white woman from Kansas, and the black man from Kenya—provide a glimpse of Obama's subjective dynamics or narrative truth. His vision and outlook are partly based on a romanticized truth about his parents' short-lived union. Their doomed love affair and marriage reverberated throughout Obama's now well-known statements: "There are no red states or blue states, just the United States of America"; or when he echoes the preamble to the Constitution by saying, "We the people, in order to form a more perfect union"; or when he channels Abraham Lincoln, saying, "A house divided against itself cannot stand." In all of these public pronouncements and many others like it, Obama gives voice to the different parts of his self that were shaped by the experiences of a broken family, trying to repair and reunite at the national level what he could not repair for himself at the personal level.

The most powerful example of this underlying dynamic played out during the race speech in Philadelphia, when Obama juxtaposed his white grandmother with his black preacher. He could not disown his white grand-mother, who loved him more than anything she loved in the world, or his black preacher, whose church he had belonged to for more than 20 years. The grandmother represented the white Midwestern values that were responsible for his socialization in Hawai'i, and the black preacher and his church on the South Side of Chicago had made his political rise pos-sible; these two demographic and religious divisions of America are part of Obama's inner self. As Kruse (2009) has noted, black America and white

America represent two "racialized spaces" in Obama's geographical imagination, something he has been trying to unify in his mind for a long time.

The white grandmother who raised Obama had also raised Obama's mother. We can grasp his mother's vision and ideals from her main work, *Surviving Against the Odds* (Dunham 2009); her life is more or less an open book. Yet his father's image looms like a large shadow in Obama's mind. For this we must rely on the narrative provided by his half-brother in *Nairobi to Shenzhen* (Ndesandjo 2010) and other reports, including Obama Sr.'s own writings on economic development in East Africa (Obama 1965). Recently published biographies of the Obama family in Africa can also shed some much needed light on Barack Obama Sr. (Firstbrook 2010; Jacobs 2011).

Erik Erikson, the psychological historian and psychoanalyst, in his books analyzing the life of Indian pacifist Mahatma Gandhi (1969) and the Protestant reformer Martin Luther (1958), has stated that all charismatic leaders are guided by deeply cherished maternal and paternal images. These images resonate at a particular historical time and place with the masses or the general population. By invoking these images, all great leaders try to revive hope and a basic level of trust in our cultural institutions, trying to foster an existential faith in the species.

A charismatic leader has an unspoken bond with a population; thus, people listen to his every word, follow his every gesture, and take cues from his behavior. By projecting deeply held ideas and beliefs about life, meaning, purpose, and destiny, a charismatic leader can call millions to action, build solidarity in a community, and further its way of life; this is the essence of leadership. Thus, a good leader is able to move large groups of people to a desirable goal, even though the people themselves may not be aware of their ultimate destination and oftentimes may not be willing to follow a leader.

In the case of American presidents, however, several specific developmental factors seem to account for the rise of a history-making leader (Wead 2005; Gullan 2001). As suggested in the introduction to this book, the positive impact of a strong mother figure on the emergence of a presidential figure is clear. As we have seen through the preceding chapters, several presidents, including Washington, Lincoln, and Roosevelt, had a strong, controlling, somewhat eccentric, and domineering mother. Here, Obama stands in good company in having a mother who was idiosyncratic yet very strong-minded, and he was deeply attached to her. She was there to meet his needs during the first 10 years of his life, and he in turn tried to be there for her as a growing boy. Thus, Obama, not unlike many other presidents, experienced a strong separation-and-individuation process from his mother when he finally decided to separate from her at the age of 10. This developmental transition would have hearkened back to an earlier transition when as a young boy he would have explored the world for the first time using her as the secure base of psychological and emotional attachment.

The role of a powerful father in shaping the destiny of a future president is also evident. The fathers of presidents have included business magnates, clergymen, politicians, and even former presidents. Some presidents have had abusive and downright bad fathers, and others have had missing fathers, whether because the father abandoned the family or died young. Again, Obama is not unique in having effectively lost his father at an early age. Andrew Jackson, Rutherford Hayes, and Bill Clinton lost their fathers before they were born. James Garfield, Andrew Johnson, and Herbert Hoover lost their fathers in early childhood, and George Washington and Thomas Jefferson lost them in middle childhood.

The pattern of early parental loss in the lives of future presidents is remarkably common. In addition to father loss, several presidents have suffered the loss of their mother in childhood: John Tyler, Herbert Hoover, Abraham Lincoln, Calvin Coolidge, Andrew Jackson, and Benjamin Harrison all lost their biological mother before they entered adulthood. Some psychologists and presidential historians have argued that the loss of a parental figure in childhood is the factor behind revolutionary movements and world-changing ideologies (Wead 2005). They believe it forces a future leader to basically reconstruct his or her parent's image from the whole cloth or from the ground up and by extension they must discover a value system, worldview, and political ideology for themselves; in this life-altering and deeply psychological process, some of these boys who were earlier abandoned by their fathers or had lost their mother have gone on to become great leaders.

The void of a missing parental figure has to be filled by an imaginary authority figure, invariably a father figure, given our data by default is only about men. Thus, the men who have aspired to become president have either had powerful fathers or the reconstructed image of a missing or abusive father, both of which may predispose them to seek the highest office in the land. And some have had the political know-how, the intelligence or mental acumen, and the unrelenting drive to go all the way. Again we see that Obama matches the developmental profile of several previous presidents who had suffered an early loss or whose fathers were once powerful men but died young or suffered a fall from grace.

All of the key antecedents and psychological markers have predisposed Obama to seek the presidency, the highest office in the land. However, the specific historical circumstances surrounding his father complex also matter a great deal. Although the general loss of a parental figure, especially a father and in some cases a mother, in early childhood may drive certain people to become national leaders, the specificity of a historical time, place, and culture play an important role in the kind of leader a person might aspire to become. Obama's father was an African economist, who eventually returned to his home country, Kenya, after studying in America. This is a historical first and shaped Obama in manifestly different ways compared with other presidents, predisposing Obama to have a much wider and global perspective on the American civilization.

Obama's Symbols of Transformation

All successful presidential candidates have tried to infuse American democracy with mythology and folklore, going back to the founding of the nation. Whether it's the fable of Washington's refusal to lie when he cut down the cherry tree, the stories about honest Abe Lincoln, or the making of Kennedy Camelot myth, the right mixture of mythological imagery is almost necessary for a campaign to excite the general public.

In an article describing the mythic nature of the American presidency, Ted Anthony and Ron Fournier noted, "In a society that has mythologized itself from its earliest days, the president is the high priest of the national identity" (Anthony and Fournier 2008). During significant turning points in history a charismatic leader driven by his or her own motivation, private myths, and the collective dreams of a population can mobilize a generation of people into a transformational grassroots movement.

While Senator McCain during the campaign was mythologized as the maverick, the naval war hero with a Scots-Irish warrior lineage that could put Braveheart to shame, it is still unclear how Obama's overall mythic narrative resonates with the American people. According to Maureen Dowd, in a column written after she spoke with the candidate Obama, Obama does not think in terms of Greek mythology. Although he did tell a reporter that he knows, like the Greek myth of Icarus, the danger of "flying close to the sun" (Dowd 2008a).

Perhaps Obama's symbols of transformation, his campaign signs, posters, and Web site, suggest another mythic undercurrent, more archaic or Near Eastern in origin, due partly to his African background. His marketing materials, designed by the Chicago-based Sol Sender, present Obama as a modern-day sun god. "We were looking at the 'O' of his name and had the idea of a rising sun and a new day," Sender said. "The sun rising over the horizon evoked a new sense of hope" (Yue 2007). The color scheme of the Obama logo evoked the American flag, but the shape, design, and imagery were not typical of other campaign signs. "It begins to break with tradition while also rooting itself in tradition," said Peter Krivkovich, CEO of Cramer-Krassell advertising agency in Chicago. "Patriotism is the foundation, but above that is hope, opportunity, newness" (Yue 2007).

The letter *O* symbolically represents Obama as the white-hot sun, rising above the blue sky with the waves of red and white stripes representing the American flag over the plains. It is not that Obama does not know the dangers of flying too close to the sun but rather he has become the sun. The *O* then may symbolize Obama and the mythological figure of Osiris, the sun god personified in Near Eastern religions as life, death, and fertility; Apollo is the Greek equivalent of Osiris. The Obamas then metaphorically represent the Osiris-Isis pair, the power couple of Egyptian mythology. Osiris is the mythic king of Egyptian mythology with a fragmented core self, who is restored to life by his wife, Isis.

The ancient story tells of a great king, Osiris, who brought peace and prosperity to his people. He was a learned man, who traveled the world teaching his people about the right way of life and making laws for them to follow. After returning from a whirlwind tour, his brother Seth, who was jealous of him, trapped him in a beautiful coffin and sent him down the Nile river, killing him and scattering his body all across the delta. His wife, Isis, restored the body to life with the help of the gods. Osiris was eventually anointed king of the Egyptian people. Psychologists have interpreted this myth to be one of the earliest symbolic representations of the process of individuation and ego development.

Obama knows the basic sense of fragmentation that grips American society. Growing up without a father in a broken and scattered family, having to shuttle from one part of the world to another, Obama understands that the American experience in families can be highly diverse, at times fragmented, and sometimes broken from within. Obama is also aware that the American landscape is a collection of diverse states with different demographic stratifications that straddle the extremes of political, cultural, and ideological poles that are often sagging at the extremes. This landscape will become increasingly diverse and fractious in the coming years as more states become majority-minority states.

Obama understands that the challenges that can possibly disunite America along the lines of race, ethnicity, and religion can be transformed into its strengths; he has lived through it with his own family experience, pulling together the different strands of his genealogy and family background. The supposed disuniting of America represented by the increasing linguistic and cultural variation will be in demand in the 21st century. This is America's rich human capital cultivated by the open immigration policies of the past 30 years. Obama understands that the new face of America is not just white America, but it is also black, yellow, brown, and red America. America is increasingly transforming into a blended nation, as attested to by the latest U.S. Census figures.

The Islamist threat to America, which is often global and amorphous, is due to the regressive forces that fear and loathe the power of democratic institutions and the ideals of freedom, liberty, and equality, the same principles that have been at the root of Western civilization and governance. These ideals threaten monolithic societies that wish to retain politically subservient populations and that are tradition bound and backward looking. Most of these societies are closed to technological change and hold a purist or fundamentalist idea of the nation state, which is often static and resistant to any challenge to its authority. Obama has extended a hand of friendship to the Islamic nations, however, and will continue to do so in the future because as he said, "America is not and will never be at war with Islam" (Gardner 2009).

Obama's soaring rhetoric, while designed to be consistent with the progressive message of hope and change, represents a break with the hegemonic discourse of politics as usual. Israeli psychologist Erich Neumann (1954) wrote in *Origins and the History of Consciousness* that of the various kinds of heroes in world mythology, the extroverted type wants to change the world. The introverted hero is simply content to change his or her self and bring new insights into the cultural realm. In a chapter called,

"Transformation, or Osiris," he stated that "the aim of the extraverted type of hero is action: he is the founder, leader, and liberator whose deeds change the face of the world" (Neumann 1954).

Within this context, Osiris represents the original, albeit archaic, hero image in the history of Western consciousness, whose life cycle embodies the symbolic transformation through death, fertility, and rebirth. Like the sun god, he is the embodiment of peace and prosperity, who ushers in a new morning. Many other parallels can be found to the Osiris myth of transformation, especially in our contemporary media-driven culture. Hollywood is replete with mythic stories of superheroes returning from a near-death experience and wanting to change the world, whether it is *Superman Returns*, *Star Wars*, *The Mummy*, or the recent *Avatar*.

Although Obama's life story may represent the characteristics of the hero mythology, it is still important to explain why a political figure like Obama, who uses the rhetoric of changing the world emerged at this time. Was the Obama election simply a manifestation of the anti-Bush vote? Or did he represent a turning of the conservative political cycle in the United States? Is Obama the symbol of the post-American world or a sign of the revival of the new American century? All of these dynamics may have been the catalyst that provided the spark for the emergence of a political actor like Obama at this turning point in history.

As I have suggested throughout this book, Obama's narrative has striking parallels to the hero myth: the birth of the hero on an island under difficult circumstances, abandonment by the father, the search for an identity, and the discovery of a mythic father figure on the mainland. Thus, Obama's story is full of metaphor and meaning for our times and speaks to some of the challenges America faces today. All of these challenges in one form or another relate to America's shifting place within the emerging global civilization.

Obama's addresses to the Islamic world in Egypt, Turkey, and Indonesia have shown his change-making character, one that reached into the past—genealogically, historically, and culturally—to bridge a gulf with the Muslim populations. His attempts to make inroads into a part of the world where Western power is feared and detested are unprecedented on the part of an American president. Whether it will bear results remains to be seen, but it did break the ice in what has been dubbed by many as the clash of civilizations. As we continue to lose more lives in Afghanistan, we need leadership that can restore peace to the region and fundamentally transform it into an oasis of economic development.

The recent developments in Egypt provide the most compelling evidence that Obama's words had a ripple effect on the local populations and political institutions. The recent grassroots movements in North Africa, called the Arab Spring, have spread like wildfire and have toppled long-standing governments in Tunisia and Egypt and have spread to neighboring countries. Unlike the recent elections in Iran, where American influence was blocked, in Egypt the words Obama had spoken in an earlier Cairo speech seemed to have resonated:

> America does not presume to know what is best for everyone, just as we would not presume to pick the outcome of a peaceful election. But I do have an unyielding belief that all people yearn for certain things: the ability to speak your mind and have a say in how you are governed; confidence in the rule of law and the equal administration of justice; government that is transparent and doesn't steal from the people; the freedom to live as you choose. (Obama 2009)

When Egyptians took to the streets in large numbers and demanded their freedom and dignity in Tharir Square, Obama was in solidarity with them:

> There will be difficult days ahead. Many questions about Egypt's future remain unanswered. But I am confident that the people of Egypt will find those answers. That truth can be seen in the sense of community in the streets. It can be seen in the mothers and fathers embracing soldiers. And it can be seen in the Egyptians who linked arms to protect the national museum—a new generation protecting the treasures of antiquity; a human chain connecting a great and ancient civilization to the promise of a new day. (Obama 2011)

The underbelly of Obama's message may be that he identifies with the "victims of history" or those who have been left out of the great march of human progress. As the son of a progressive, white, American anthropologist mother and an African economist father, Obama was schooled in different cultures and on "other people's myths." His campaign built an antiwar movement and a coalition of diverse voices, such as African Americans, Native Americans, and Hispanic Americans.

Obama's inner hunger related to his father's absence and loss has been filled up by the larger-than-life reformers that were his role models, pictures of at least three of whom were prominently displayed on his Senate office walls: Abraham Lincoln, Martin Luther King Jr., and Mahatma Gandhi. Obama has incorporated and internalized their lessons and resolved his identity crisis by hitching his wagon to a humanitarian calling larger than himself, the key to the transcendental factor in his biography.

Comparisons between Obama and the 16th president, Abraham Lincoln, have been aptly drawn as Obama believes he is walking in the great man's footsteps. Obama's announcement to run for the presidency was made in Springfield, Illinois, in a place where Lincoln once stood: "And that is why, in the shadow of the Old State Capitol, where Lincoln once called on a house divided to stand together, where common hopes and common dreams still live, I stand before you today to announce my candidacy for President of the United States of America," declared Obama (2007).

Obama's acceptance speech for the democratic nomination was delivered from a miniaturized Greek temple, designed to evoke the Lincoln Memorial in Washington, D.C. During the Civil War, Lincoln carried the burden of a whole nation upon his shoulders. Like Lincoln, whom Walt Whitman eulogized as the "American Osiris," for he presided over the endless bloodshed of the Civil War, and whom Carl Sandburg later mythologized as the savior of the American union, Obama wishes to take on the challenge of Islamic threat abroad and politically uplift the disenfranchised groups at home. In taking on these causes, he may be destined to take on the mantle of the historic figures represented in ancient folklore and myths.

David C. Ward, a historian and curator at the Smithsonian Institution who has organized exhibitions on Abraham Lincoln, has claimed that genealogically, the symbol of Osiris as "the Green Man" has a long history in American culture stretching back to the Freemasons or perhaps even earlier (Ward 2006). Periodically these memories rise through the cultural crevices, for example, in the poetry of Walt Whitman and Carl Sandburg when they tried to capture Lincoln's image while presiding over the long, drawn-out Civil War. Sandburg's poem "Grass" (1950) recalled Whitman's "Leaves of Grass" (1883) in describing the cycles of birth, decay, and rebirth represented by the mythic Osiris, especially during times of war:

Grass
Pile the bodies high at Austerlitz and Waterloo.
Shovel them under and let me work—
I am the grass; I cover all.

And pile them high at Gettysburg
And pile them high at Ypres and Verdun.
Shovel them under and let me work.
Two years, ten years, and passengers ask the conductor:

What place is this?
Where are we now?

I am the grass.
Let me work.

The Obama campaign and messaging team has resurrected the specter of the Green Man by invoking a likeness to Abraham Lincoln. By taking on the war in Afghanistan, which is now the longest war in U.S. history, transitioning America toward a sustainable green economy, and trying to break the dependence on foreign oil, Barack Obama has repeatedly invoked the underlying symbols and myths of the great transformations in American history.

Obama as the Oedipal King

Symbols and myths represent universal and culture-specific themes in our dreams, which, according to Sigmund Freud, were "the royal road to the unconscious." Dreams can serve as a clearinghouse for daily activities, a tool for imaginative thinking, and a problem solver for our everyday challenges that the conscious mind cannot fully resolve or attend to. In his autobiography, Obama shares some private dreams in order for us to get to know him more intimately.

At the end of the first part of his autobiography, upon learning that his father has died in a car accident, Obama reveals a dream about his father. The timing of the dream is critical. The dream surfaces at a time when Obama has left the security of the Hawai'ian Islands, has been living on a very limited budget in New York City, and is about to move to Chicago for a job as a community organizer. Precipitated by the death of his father, the dream clearly marks a turning point in Obama's inner world, and it may represent the narrative truth about his father's challenging and complicated political career in the Kenyan government.

After his father's death, Obama felt no pain, only the vague sense of an opportunity lost. He was sorry that he never got to meet his father on the land of his forefathers. Yet, there was some grieving to be done. After he communicated the sad news to his mother, he mourned with her over the telephone. Hearing her cry he was flooded with sorrow. Listening to his mother's loud wailing and cries for his deceased father, he realized that she may have truly loved him even after all these years.

In one of the most critical passages in the book, Obama dreams that he is on a journey through green fields and tall grassy hills against the backdrop of a bright orange sky, a scene that seems right out of an African safari. He is traveling in a bus with a heavyset, older white man, who is sitting beside him reading a book; the person seems to represent his grandfather or Gramps, Stanley Dunham. Obama reads in Gramp's book that our souls are tested when we have to treat the old.

In the dream, Gramps tells him that he is a union man going to meet his daughter, which of course is Obama's mother. Ann Dunham, as we have seen, made no bones about being somewhat estranged from her father from childhood onward. Gramps is the one who gave her the masculine name Stanley because he had wanted a son rather than a daughter, and she had disliked the name because it was a source of teasing and pranks throughout her childhood. Now, in the dream, both Obama and Gramps together are trying to reach into their distant past to confront what is left unresolved and to revisit their old wounds. Next, Obama dives yet deeper into his dream. Traveling by himself on the bus now, he arrives at a courthouse or a jail, where his father is being held for a hearing. Inside, a lawyer is arguing with a judge against freeing his father who has been in the jail for a long time. The lawyer objects vigorously, but the judge shrugs off his protests and leaves the bench.

In one of the most poignant scenes in the book, Obama actually gets to have a meeting with his father in the dream. This is something he has wished for since he was a little boy. However, to his dismay Obama learns that his father is locked away in a small jail cell, near death, emaciated, and weak. This dream must have shocked his heart and mind at the time and may have begun to undercut the mythic image of his father that he had built over two decades.

Obama described the dream scene: "I stood before the cell, opened the padlock, and set it carefully on a window ledge. My father was before me, with only a cloth wrapped around his waist; he was very thin, with his large head and slender frame, his hairless arms and chest" (Obama 2004a, 128).

His father praises him: "'Look at you,' he said. 'So tall—and so thin. Gray hairs, even!' And I saw that it was true, and I walked up to him and we embraced" (Obama 2004a, 129). At the first sound of admiration and praise from his father, Obama is unable to contain himself and begins to weep profusely. He is ashamed at the sign of appearing weak, but cannot stop. How could he stop himself? This was the man he had heard so many great stories about. Obama had looked up to him all his life, but now here he was in the dream—in a jail, locked away, and dying.

His father tells him what every boy wants to hear from his long-lost father, "Barack, I always wanted to tell you how much I love you." Barack observes that his father has shrunk in size, "small in my arms now, the size of a boy" (Obama 2004a, 129). In a classic reversal of roles, in the inner world the father has become the boy and the boy his own father. The oedipal theme in the dream is undeniable: Obama appears responsible and father-like, and his father appears to be a criminal, behind bars and reduced in stature.

The developmental resolution of the Oedipus complex marks the establishment of moral authority in a child's mind, especially the authority of the father (Freud 1901). This authority could be represented as a moral code, a religious injunction, or some form of secular authority figure, such as an educator, a police officer, and a judge. In Obama's dream the authority of the father is suspect and under trial, and the son is represented as the responsible one who is trying to get the father released from the jail. This dream then shows that Obama may have resolved his Oedipus complex the only way he knew how, by becoming his own father; in his case, William Wordsworth's verse "the child is the father of the man" is not only figuratively true but rather literally true. The dream also shows that even in the absence of a biological father, the Oedipus complex is a universal milestone, something anthropologists have been arguing about since Sigmund Freud wrote *Totem and Taboo* (Freud 1919) and expounded on his controversial theory about the origins of Oedipal feelings of guilt.

It is plausible that some of the dream content, although definitely symbolic of Obama's inner world, is also based on some real-life events in Obama Sr.'s political life in Kenya. Barack Obama would have come across these facts while researching his father's life and career, and his Kenyan half-sister, Auma, who kept him informed about his father's political fall, would have shared these horrific details with her brother. Obama's father was caught in a messy political trial and provided testimony against the government in the assassination of 39-year-old Tom Mboya, a rising star in Kenyan politics and a potential rival to then prime minister Jomo Kenyatta. It was also suspected that Mboya had been gunned down by the "Big Man" among the tribal elites. Jomo Kenyatta was a member of the Kikuyu tribe, and Mboya and Obama were Lou. Obama Sr. had met Mboya shortly before his assassination. In late 1968, Obama Sr. had confided in Neil Abercrombie and a Hawai'ian friend, Pake Zane, that his career was going downhill and his life was going through a rather difficult patch. When I interviewed Abercrombie, he directed me to sources where this information could be confirmed (Jacobs 2008). Later, I made the psychological connection between Obama's prison dream about his father's trial and his father's testimony in a political trial surrounding Mboya's death.

In the remaining part of the dream, Obama describes his father sitting on a cot in his jail cell, staring away from him, adding, "He couldn't be budged, and when I whispered to him that we might leave together, he shook his head and told me it would be best if I left" (2004a, 129). Obama recalls that he woke up crying, "My first real tears for him—and for me, his jailer, his judge and his son. . . . And I realized, perhaps for the first time, how even in his absence his strong image had given me some bulwark on which to grow up" (Obama 2004a, 129).

My conclusions are further supported by another dream sequence, which leaves little doubt that one of the driving forces behind Obama's rise and what has been haunting him since early childhood is the oversized image of a paternal authority figure. The second dream occured during his journey through Kenya, when Obama and his half-sister, Auma, were making a pilgrimage to their family's village, the sacred land of their forefathers, which Obama had been daydreaming about for many years. Auma had told Obama that their grandfather was a cruelly exacting and self-righteous man, nicknamed "Terror" by his grandchildren. This seems to have prompted Obama's nightmarish dream in which, as he describes in *Dreams from My Father*, he is walking through a village, with Kenyan children and old men going about their daily business, when suddenly panic strikes and everybody runs from a ghostly visage standing behind Obama. As he hears the growl of a leopard, Obama runs for cover: "Panting for breath, I turned around to see the day turned night, and a giant figure looming as tall as the trees, wearing only a loincloth and a ghostly mask. The lifeless eyes bored into me, and I heard a thunderous voice saying that it was time, and my entire body began to shake violently with the sound, as if I were breaking apart" (Obama 2004, 372).

The loincloth as a detail recurs in this dream, suggesting the sheer physical and visceral nature of the dream. Without Obama's direct associations to the dream we can only surmise that Obama must have been affected by the traditional dress and costumes villagers were wearing. The giant figure reflects the doubling-down of the generational legacy, the cumulative effect of his father's and grandfather's ethical and moral standing in the village represented as a tree-like totemic figure. It is clear that Obama felt the awesome presence of his father and grandfather in the village.

Based on these dreams, it is plain to see that Obama's father wound was raw and palpable; its impact perhaps has not been fully understood, though it has reverberated throughout Obama's life and career. This conclusion is also suggested by another dream researcher. "His dreams reveal him to be acutely conscious of the ever-present power of family tradition in his life. He may feel deeply ambivalent toward his ancestors, but he has discovered he must find a way to accept their continuing influence over him. This suggests that Obama is perhaps more temperamentally conservative and respectful of paternal authority than most Americans assume" (Bulkeley 2008).

In his autobiography, it took him more than 450 pages to fully explore and work through the role his father played in his absence; the myth of the absent father touched Obama's body, mind, and soul. It is very telling that the opening pages of Obama's book reveal in touching detail how he learned about his father's death. In his speeches, in his daily routine, and with his own family, Obama has tried to play the role of a committed and responsible father, a role his own father did not play in his life.

Here, it is important to note that the psychological gap between the real father and the ideal father is of paramount importance. The gap that opened after Obama learned that his father was not what he imagined him to be left Obama vulnerable and looking for an explanation. It is my hypothesis that he dreamed the critical dream sometime after his father's demise, when he was about to move to Chicago or most likely after he learned the full truth about his father's career.

He would have learned the detailed truth about his father's political fate from his half-sister, Auma, who regularly called him from Heidelberg and London and visited him in Chicago when he was a community organizer. My hypothesis is further supported by Auma's admission that she first started corresponding with her younger brother after their father had died. "Barack's handwriting is exactly the same as my dad's. And he wrote to me on this large yellow foolscap paper that Americans use and that my dad used. It was weird," said Auma in a recent interview (Cohen 2008).

From Auma Obama learned that his father had many other children, mistreated his wives, could not fully look after his family, had become a drunkard, and most of all fell into disfavor with the Kenyan government, which led to his ultimate downfall. These facts are also confirmed by Obama's half-brother Mark Obama (Branigan 2009). After one such call from Auma, when she told him that one of his half-brothers, David Obama, had died in a motorcycle accident, Obama had decided to leave New York City to become a community organizer in Chicago. He had realized that a Wall Street job did not represent a path of success for his life. Instead, he decided on a path of community service, working with churches and organizing blacks and youth. This was in part a continuation of the kind of work his mother was already doing in Indonesia, but it also reflected a decision to follow his father's original calling, that is, to do something for his race and people. Driven by a sense of duty and higher purpose, Obama felt compelled to do right by the memory of his father. This life-altering decision came on the heels of approximately two years he had spent in isolation, studying and reflecting at Columbia University, during which time he decided to fully take on the name of his father. This time spent in hibernation allowed him time to mourn his father's passing, get in touch with his real values and authentic self, and claim his father's cause as his own.

This decision is very significant. Recall that Obama did not grow up in a traditional nuclear family and did not have a stable father figure. He felt uprooted by his mother's lifestyle. Although he may have felt loved and cared for, something still tugged at his heart and soul—a kind of restlessness about his fatherlessness had always stayed with him. This is a very normal process for adolescents, but in Obama's case the feelings were exacerbated by his broken family situation. He relied on authority figures, his maternal grandfather, his stepfather, Frank Marshall Davis, and other literary and political heroes. As mentioned previously, most of these surrogate father figures were tragic figures and could not measure up to the larger-than-life image of a paternal authority figure that his mother had helped to build up in his mind. Thus, the search for the ideal father figure was not complete, and it was marred by the developmental void during the early critical years.

Thus, Obama never came to terms with a live-in father, as most children are accustomed to during their early years. During the Indonesian years, he lived with his stepfather, as we have seen in the earlier chapters, but this family experience was also cut short. Obama left Jakarta when he was 10 years old, and his mother followed him a few years later.

The French psychoanalyst and linguist Jacques Lacan has claimed that the Oedipus complex is resolved when the name of the father has been fully internalized in the child's mind. It completes early self-development, separating the body of the mother from the emerging sense of self (Lacan 1968). The authority of the father enters the dyadic union of the mother and child, forever severing the dyadic bond and establishing the name of the father in the individual's psyche. Thus, the repeated attempts to challenge and question authority are fully resolved and internalized in most adults by the time they enter adolescence and are ready to move into young adulthood. In Obama's case, this was an open-ended and ongoing process, a psychosocial transition that had not been fully closed off. It began to come to an end with the death of his father; now he felt ready to take on his father's name and identify with his father's destiny. By the time he left New York City, Barry Obama had fully adopted his father's name, Barack Hussein Obama.

A visit from his half-sister, Auma, brought to the forefront the central issue of his life, namely, the larger-than-life mythic image of his father. When he had learned about his father's tragic fate, he realized that the king had been overthrown: "The king is overthrown, I thought. The emerald curtain is pulled aside. The rabble of my head is free to run riot; I can do what I damn well please," he exclaimed (Obama 2004, 221). Yet the legacy of his father had already been burned into his mind and soul. Try as he might he could not escape the complex fate handed down to him by his father's absence and the idealized image of a father passed on to him by his mother. When the teenage Obama looked in the mirror he saw a black man in Hawai'i. However, as a young adult when he struggled with his own fatherlessness, he looked around and saw the negative consequences of fatherlessness in the black community in New York City and Chicago. He at last found the reflection of his black soul in the community and felt the need to do something about this situation.

Thus, Obama decided to right the wrongs committed by his father who had abandoned him. In the aftermath of his father's death—upon learning the sad truth about his downfall in Kenya and finding out from his mother that his father had abandoned the family to go to Harvard—Obama decided to outdo the old man who had left him. The incremental effect of these small revelations added up to a big turning point. Whereas in his dreams he had become his father's jailer, judge, and son, in real life he decided to become a civil rights lawyer, a dutiful father, and a devoted husband with an eye toward a political career; his inner world deeply informed his outer decisions. Thus, as a counterpoint to his own father, Obama excelled as a community organizer, helped churches to organize their neighborhoods, and became a black man in Chicago. He would later go to Harvard and return as the model image of an authority figure that his father simply could not become.

The immediate contact Obama had with his father before he died was through his letters. Although we don't know the exact frequency and regularity of their correspondence, Obama's father would write to his son encouraging him to visit Kenya. His letters were filled with stories about Africa and the land of his forefathers. Obama Sr. was a literate man who had studied abroad, who often advised Barack Obama about how to excel in his studies. His letters were filled with African parables and stories. The father and son would share their intimate experiences with each other through letters. Obama endowed these stories with special meaning and power.

The impact of this long-distance correspondence fed into the construction of a fantastical image not only of his father but also of Africa, the magical land where his father's clan lived. On a trip to Kenya before starting Harvard Law School, Obama finally had a cathartic experience in the Luo village of Kisumu when he confronted the legacy of his father and grandfather. He had already dreamed about his grandfather's looming presence, but now, sitting amidst the graves of his ancestors, he simply broke down:

> For a long time I sat between the two graves and wept. When my tears were finally spent, I felt a calmness wash over me. I felt the circle finally close. I realized who I was, what I cared about, was no longer just a matter of intellect or obligation, no longer a construct of words. I saw my life in America—the black life, the white life, the sense of abandonment I'd felt as a boy, the frustration and hope I'd witnessed in Chicago—all of it was connected with this small plot of earth an ocean away, connected by more than the accident of a name or the color of my skin. The pain I felt was my father's pain. My questions were my brother's questions. Their struggle, my birthright. (Obama 2004a, 429–430)

Barack Obama Sr., along with many African writers, activists, and intellectuals, was a Pan-Africanist, members of a movement that emerged before and after colonialism. Like Jomo Kenyatta, Tom Mboya, and other Pan-African leaders of the newly founded nations on the African continent, Obama's father was struggling to find a way to advance Africa into the modern age. This worldview and value system was also passed on to the son through his father's letters. Barack Obama Sr. drilled into his son, through long letters written on yellow legal-size writing pads, that his identity first and foremost consisted of duty to his people. His admonitions were typically about making good for his people. Like the young cub Simba in the movie *The Lion King*, Obama could still hear the echo of his father's voice: "Like water finds its level, you will arrive at a career that suits you" (Obama 2004a, 76).

Like many of his contemporaries, Obama Sr. joined the struggle to develop an independent Kenya founded on a modern African identity. Armed with a Western education and a liberal worldview, yet concerned about putting Africa's past and future on the right path, Obama Sr., like the characters in modern African novels by Chinua Achebe, Ayi Kwei Armah, and Wole Soyinka, was experimenting with the emerging forms of African identity. Many of these individuals struggled with the forces of neocolonialism, ethnic rivalries, corruption in African states, and challenges of democracy in the tribal regions.

Interestingly, in Armah's fictional narratives, the modern-day version of Osiris and Isis, perhaps the oldest characters in Egyptian and African mythology have been struggling to find new ways to repair Africa's dismembered and broken destiny (Armah 1996; Agho 2002). Today, many Africans believe that, like the mythic Osiris, Africans should move from servitude to emancipation, from bondage to freedom, and from underdevelopment to development. The new African identity needs to rise despite the constraints of history, tribalism, and corruption (Adeoti 2005). However, as Obama Sr.'s life seemed to have fallen short of these ideals, the son needed to be cautious and avoid a similar fate. After all, he had the blood of Africa running through his veins and his family's history of tragedies and triumphs reflected through the larger African story. Obama knew full well that the tragic past that has haunted Africa also haunted his father's life and career (Pflanz 2009). Thus, Obama needed to be steadier, more measured, and more grounded; he needed to be part of a community. He needed other larger-than-life, mythic father figures to fill the gap left by the utter collapse of his father's mythic image. It is no coincidence that Obama gravitated toward Abraham Lincoln after he fully understood and felt the impact of his father's fall from grace. Over time and only gradually, after living and working in Chicago, through the extensive study of law, and after completing the long-awaited pilgrimage to Kenya, the larger-than-life image of his biological father was replaced by the father of the Emancipation Proclamation, Abraham Lincoln.

The biological father who was a mythic figure in his inner world was overthrown by the realization that he had met a less than perfect fate. However, Obama's mind needed to compensate for the profound loss and disillusionment that resulted from learning the truth about his father. The large gap left by his father had to be filled with an equally large if not larger mythic image; if Obama did not do this consciously, his mind did it unconsciously. His mind would have searched for a way to correct the irreversible loss. Identifying with the stoic, solitary, and totemic image of Abraham Lincoln, a perfect displacement for his own father figure, Obama could, in one fell swoop, not only make the world whole again but also fuel a lifelong ambition to become like the great emancipator of his people, completing the identification with the dreams from his father.

When Obama arrived in Chicago in 1983, he was carrying two guiding images as the moral yardsticks for his life: that of his mother, who had lived there for a short time after she was accepted to the University of Chicago, and that of his father, who had recently passed away. After being a community organizer for three years, Obama looked around and asked himself simply, "Whom can I trust?" He found no viable black leaders in the making as Obama decided to go away to law school. Harold Washington had just passed away and Jesse Jackson's power may have been waning. Obama eventually realized that the former Illinois state senator, Abraham Lincoln, was a more fitting image for his life's ambitions. Again, it is important to remember that Obama did not lack the power of imagination to recreate his life from the bottom up.

As his father's repeated messages still rang in his ears, he decided to reconstruct himself in the image of Abraham Lincoln. He realized that in identifying with the image of Abraham Lincoln he would remain true to the larger mission of his father's life, while exorcising the proverbial sins of the father. He also believed that through this process he might one day become a role model for his people. This is the most parsimonious and straightforward psychological explanation for Obama's towering ambition, a reconstructed identification with Abraham Lincoln, founded on the profound sense of loss of his own father.

Obama has spent many hours reading and studying at the feet of Lincoln. Lincoln's iconography as a stalwart figure, upholding America's moral ideals, reigns supreme in Obama's mind. At the altar of Lincoln, Obama resolved any residue of oedipal hostilities and washed away all the anger and pain that he may have harbored toward his own father, who had abandoned him; toward his mother, who had worked in Indonesia since he was 10 years old; and even toward his grandparents, who at times might have seemed like strangers or people from another distant era.

In Lincoln's life, Obama could find the mirror image of the self-made man he wanted to become, someone who succeeded where his father's life fell short. In Lincoln's life, Obama could find the deep pain and stoicism that he wanted to emulate. In Lincoln, Obama could also entertain the idea of being a martyr for his nation. How could anyone elevate himself and sacrifice his life for a cause and purpose larger than his own limited existence? Deep in his psyche, given his fatherlessness and his broken and biracial family background, Obama needed a figure like Lincoln to give unity, meaning, and purpose to his life and towering ambition. Monuments are built on a deep sense of loss and mourning (Freud 1939; Homans 1989), and so it is with Obama's idealization of Lincoln; it is founded on the deep and utter sense of loss of his own father.

In an essay, "What I See in Lincoln's Eyes," Obama (2005) described, with an artist's flair for detail, how much compassion he feels for the 16th president of the United States. Obama's idealization of Lincoln might be called a full-blown transference, in purely psychoanalytic terms, or love in everyday parlance, akin to Freud's description of his love for Michelangelo's Moses:

> My favorite portrait of Lincoln comes from the end of his life. In it, Lincoln's face is as finely lined as a pressed flower. He appears frail, almost broken; his eyes, averted from the camera's lens, seem to contain a heartbreaking melancholy, as if he sees before him what the nation had so recently endured. . . .
>
> So when I, a black man with a funny name, born in Hawai'i of a father from Kenya and a mother from Kansas, announced my candidacy for the U.S. Senate, it was hard to imagine a less likely scenario

than that I would win—except, perhaps, for the one that allowed a child born in the backwoods of Kentucky with less than a year of formal education to end up as Illinois' greatest citizen and our nation's greatest President.

In Lincoln's rise from poverty, his ultimate mastery of language and law, his capacity to overcome personal loss and remain determined in the face of repeated defeat—in all this, he reminded me not just of my own struggles. He also reminded me of a larger, fundamental element of American life—the enduring belief that we can constantly remake ourselves to fit our larger dreams. (Obama 2005)

When Obama moved to Chicago, however, he was simply searching for a community to belong to. Developmental research has shown that for highly gifted children and adolescents like Barack Obama, their identity crisis and conflict encompasses the entire world. They do not just want to change themselves. They want to change the entire world. Political figures mean the world to them as the leaders of social change and this was no different for Obama.

There is considerable developmental research on gifted children and youth (Frank and McBee 2003). The process of identity formation among gifted children and adolescents is not unlike the identity problems portrayed in the Harry Potter books. In *Harry Potter and the Sorcerer's Stone*, 11-year-old Harry is invited to attend the Hogwarts School, where he learns that he is a famous wizard. He looks in a magical mirror and sees his deceased parents and realizes that he survived the magical attack that killed them. His headmaster, Professor Dumbledore, explains to him, "The happiest man on earth would be able to use the Mirror of Erised like a normal mirror, that is, he would look into it and see himself exactly as he is. Does that help?" Harry did not understand at first, thinking that the mirror shows whatever we want. Professor Dumbledore explained again, "It shows us nothing more or less than the deepest, most desperate desires of our hearts." Gifted adolescents like the young Obama are able to look in the mirror, see their inner self, and grasp their destiny earlier than most people; they have a cognitively advanced understanding and a heightened emotional and moral sensitivity.

Following the path of his mother, who was a dreamer and a traveler all her life, Obama went to Chicago to serve as a community organizer.

Interestingly, his mother's friends who worked with her in Java describe her as community organizer in the guise of an anthropologist: "For me Ann is not the anthropologist doing research. . . . Ann is the community organizer in Central Java," said Jerry Silverman who worked with her on a United Nations project (Scott 2011, 207).

Both mother and son, however, were driven by the same progressive impulse to change the world. This is the spirit that sustains him despite setbacks and opposition. When they were growing up both Barack Obama and his mother were not content to leave the world as it is. They wanted to make a difference; they wanted to change the world and make it a better place for the future generations.

As Obama admitted to a reporter recently, his decision to go into public service, not necessarily politics, was deeply informed by his mother's life mission, "a sense that the greatest thing you can do in the world is to help somebody else, be kind, think about issues like poverty and how you give people greater opportunity. . . . So I have no doubt that a lot of my career choices are rooted in her and what she thought was important" (Scott 2011, 354).

Dreams from His Mother

On January 1, 1985, Ann opened up a spiral notebook and jotted down her long-range goals: "1. Finish Ph.D., 2. 60k, 3. In shape, 4. Remarry, 5. Another culture, 6. House + Land, 7. Pay-off debts (taxes), 8. Memoirs of Indon. 9. Spir. Develop (ilmu batin), 10. Raise Maya well, 11. Continuing constructive dialogue w/ Barry, 12. Relations w/ friends + family (corresp.)" (Scott 2011, 265). She did finish her PhD and raised her children well by all external measures, meeting some of her key objectives, but the rest of the goals may have remained elusive, with the lingering dreams unfinished or interrupted.

Obama has said that his mother "lived a classic expatriate life," which deeply shaped his own life; she gave him a childhood full of adventure. The flip side of that lifestyle was that she may have always felt like an outsider, like she belonged to the world but to no one particular culture exclusively. Although he understood the allure of his mother's globe-trotting professional life, he felt he needed to put down his roots in a specific place and history.

Almost 20 years after she completed her doctoral dissertation and 15 years after her premature death from cancer, Ann Dunham's life and work was finally celebrated at a panel at the American Anthropological Association. An esteemed group of economic and cultural anthropologists who had worked with Ann for more than 30 years, in no small measure due to the efforts of her daughter, Maya Soetoro-Ng, had gathered to give voice to her research in the Javanese villages.

Ann Dunham was a mixture of different worlds, reflecting the different interests and historical trends of her times. Like the Beat poets of the 1950s, she was not interested in materialism, took keen interest in different belief systems and religions, and was a romantic at heart. Just as the more expansive ideas of the beatniks were incorporated by the hippy movement, her interests evolved to encompass civil rights, eastern philosophies, and social reform on a global scale.

Ann raised her children with a radical sense of idealism and strict ethical values, recalled Alice Dewey, Obama's mother's mentor at the University of Hawai'i. When U.S. president Barack Obama accepted the Nobel Peace Prize, he fulfilled one of the cherished dreams of his mother for her son to be a peacemaker. "She would be so proud of him right now," said Alice Dewey as she became tearful.

In a candid interview, Obama told a reporter that his mother expected him to be "you know, sort of a cross between Einstein, Gandhi and Belafonte, right. . . . I think she wanted me to be the man that she probably would have liked my grandfather to be, that she would have liked my father to have turned out to be. . . . You know, somebody who was strong and honest and doing worthwhile things in the world" (Scott 2011, 194).

Ann Dunham was becoming well known in her own right and was recognized for her development work before she passed away. The book *Surviving against the Odds* is a testament to her lifelong passion for working for the development of rural populations around the world and presents an intensive review of the economic anthropology of rural Indonesia. Against the backdrop of the top-down Asian development programs of the 1970s and academic anthropology focused exclusively on low-wetland rice production, Dunham studied the scope of the nonagricultural sector, specifically blacksmithing, in six villages. Although she documented the rise of blacksmithing as a cottage industry, her focus was on the special craft of sword making, or *keris*, which carried great symbolic importance in Indonesian society.

Dunham studied the socioeconomic organization of metalworking industries, examining the clusters of enterprise units and how manufacturing, service, and repair are organized among them. She corrected the broad-based characterization of the Javanese economy as backward, tradition bound, irrational, and not driven by the basic principles of economics, a view propagated by leading academics. In a very detailed ethnography of a blacksmithing village, Kajar, in Yogyakarta, she showed that a large and well-stratified village, even in the rural hinterlands of Java, was driven by "capital as the engine of stratification" (Dunham 2009, 286).

Dunham spent almost 15 years intermittently collecting data in this village. She documented in painstaking detail some of the sociocultural and demographic changes that occurred there during the late 1970s to the early 1990s. The agricultural resource base continued to shrink due to population growth, which drove villagers to nonagricultural occupations. The subsistence economy shifted toward a mixed production mode because of endogenous and external government pressures. With increased support from financial and development agencies and the arrival of electricity and automobiles, blacksmithing continued to expand.

Dunham documented changes in the basic technology of blacksmithing as smiths acquired new machinery for metal blowing and finishing. Some of the villagers had become savvy about selling their products and learning how best to market their skills through local cooperatives. She made it clear that villagers were not passive participants in the development projects. They picked and chose development projects to suit their needs and goals based on cost-benefit analysis.

Like her mother, Madelyn Dunham, who was a vice president of escrow accounts at the Bank of Hawai'i, Ann Dunham also ended up working in the banking sector. She had developed a keen interest in tariffs, banking, and regulation policy while working at the Bank Rakyat Indonesia in Jakarta. Dunham challenged the notion of economic dualism then prevalent in academic anthropology, which suggested that the local villagers are somehow incapable of imagining their world in terms of the profit motive. Dunham took on the writings of J. H. Boeke and Clifford Geertz, along with the historical founders of economic anthropology, claiming that "the small and household metalworking industries coexist within the same villages and form a single socioeconomic and cultural complex" (Dunham 2009, 265).

Alice Dewey and Nancy Cooper, editors of Dunham's work, have placed her in the larger context of the economic anthropology of

Indonesia. Both believe Dunham was a humanist and not just an armchair theoretician or an academic. She deeply cared about local people and was driven to make a difference in the daily lives of populations around the world, a theme that consistently runs through Barack Obama's life as well. When I spoke with Kay Ikranagara at the Academy of Educational Development in Jakarta about Dunham's cultural and literary heroes, she said Dunham was a social activist who believed in the philosophies of Gandhi and Martin Luther King. Both Ann and Kay married Indonesian men and worked together in Jakarta in the early 1970s. Eventually, both became applied anthropologists for international development agencies and remained friends over three decades.

Fully acclimated to Indonesian society, both rejected traditional views of race as hypocritical. "We had all the same attitudes," Kay told a reporter. "When we met people who worked for the oil companies or the embassy, they belonged to a different culture than Ann and I. We felt they didn't mix with Indonesians, they were part of an insular American culture. Servants seemed to be the only Indonesians those Americans knew" (Scott 2011, 123).

The link between Gandhi and King is well known in the history of the civil rights movement, but the way it has played out in the life of the first black president through early socialization is not well understood. This unique mother-son relationship highlights how the revolutionary ideals of the 1960s were generationally transmitted by a Peace Corps–loving, liberal white woman from the Midwest, who came of age in Seattle and Hawai'i but spent most of her adult life in the villages of Indonesia. As she used to joke with her friends, a little girl from Kansas was not supposed to be such a path-breaker. In her own way, Dunham charted her own course.

Dunham's interest in small-scale local development projects was influenced by Gandhi's philosophy of supporting small-scale cottage industries against the onslaught of large-scale industrialization. The popular image of Gandhi spinning cotton was not just a photo opportunity for *Life* magazine; it was a lifestyle. Likewise, Dunham was a weaver and a collector of batik textiles who believed in supporting local artisans, craftspeople, and blacksmiths. E. F. Schumacher's Buddhist economic mantra, "Small is beautiful," describes her mission statement perfectly (Schumacher 1973).

When I asked Maya about her mother's interest in small-scale industry, she explained how her mother believed in the value of work that joined democracy and development at the root and the stem. Her work in anthropology was concerned with both democracy and development "in a populist sort of a way," she said. Thus, in the lives of King and Gandhi, "she found two heroes who were transformational and engaged in work that brought out the best in others. They revealed the great capacity of human beings to engage in selflessness," Maya said.

She added that her mother:

> Did believe, not in any new age way necessarily, but in a much more grounded way, in the capacity of people to express beauty and hero- ism. That was very much part of her work as an anthropologist and a development worker because she was an optimist at the end. She focused on minute relationships, hierarchies, and rituals; she was a weaver because she was fascinated by human creation. So she would take all of the details and then tie them up in this idea of human cre- ation. She was very curious. She would have us look under rocks and take a magnifying glass and look at what is underneath, embedded in the earth. She would also have us look through the telescope. . . . . The sadness of her passing is that she loved life so much with all its richness and really loved human beings. In spite of being faced with considerable disappointments, she never lost her sense of optimism; I think that has impacted me, her son, and many of her friends.

I asked, why would a woman born in the industrial Midwest be inter- ested in Gandhi's ideas of small-scale cottage industry? I wanted to know more about her interest in large- and small-scale economic development. Maya explained, "The idea of looking at crafts and creation, the work of the masses, the daily work to engage the multitude, and to then transform a nation; that was pretty powerful stuff. She loved the grassroots thinking; that's why there is a real connection in her work with Gandhi."

Robert Hefner, an anthropologist at Boston University who has written an afterword to Dunham's book, remembered her work fondly. At the book launch, he said, "She was documenting small facts to tell the larger truths" about the lives of Indonesian villagers (Hefner 2009). Her passion for work- ing with the rural poor in Indonesia was founded on her belief in equality, Martin Luther King, and the civil rights movement; her choices in life part- ners were a reflection of this commitment. Barack Obama grew up in the field—when Ann Dunham traveled around the islands of Indonesia and to other cultures both Barack and his sister, Maya, often accompanied her.

In a recent interview, Dewey bluntly told me that Barack Obama deserved the Nobel Peace Prize for ending policies that pitted America in a death match with other cultures. She said his mother above all was a humanist before she was an anthropologist—not a little Margaret Mead, but perhaps a junior Dorothy Day. "He learned from her that if you did the right things in the local cultures with everyday people that over time you could make a positive difference in people's lives," Dewey said.

"This was the reason she believed in microfinancing," Maya said. "She wanted to empower people economically by providing them more access and resources. If it was not for her early passing, she would have been doing micro-lending now in different countries and in different types of trades and crafts."

Dunham would often work on a dozen or more development projects at a time, ranging from helping women's literacy development to working with local artisans to secure microcredits or modest loans. This was long before microlending to the poor became the hot trend in global economics and probably shortly after Muhammad Yunus, the Noble laureate econo-mist, began his work in Bangladesh.

Bronwen Solyom, an Australian art historian and curator at the University of Hawai'i, who also worked in Indonesia with Dunham and provided most of the photographs displayed in the book, suggested that Dunham did not have any particular theory of social and economic justice. She was really interested in people and was a humanitarian. Although she wrote a 1,000-page dissertation on economic anthropology, it was reformers of nonviolent social change who inspired her.

On a more personal note, Maya offered some interesting insights about her mother's life and work. In the foreword to *Surviving Against the Odds*, she stated, "I had a marvelous time as a child, surrounded by pictures of anvils and forges, and stories about the magic of fire. My mother taught me to differentiate between a truly fine *keris* blade with its many layers subtly interwoven, and a sloppily crafted or unrefined blade" (Sotoero-Ng 2009, ix). The sense that Dunham truly respected and understood Javanese vil-lage communities came through her daughter's testimonials.

After reviewing Dunham's work and speaking with her circle of friends and colleagues, it dawned on me that the role of the social reformer, some-one with a heightened ability to deploy soft power as a political tool, is not just an abstract idea or a strategy for President Obama. It seems to be neither a clever gimmick nor a hopefully naive, idealistic, and doomed-to-fail policy designed by White House analysts. This runs deeper; it is in his DNA, part and parcel of an inheritance that hearkens back to his mother's early socialization. The role of the peacemaker is a product of a transmuted, intergenerational dream of changing the world one village at a time. His mother's dreams, albeit tenuously, still bind the elements of Obama's foreign and domestic policies with his political identity.

It was indeed a very humble statement when Obama addressed the Indian Parliament and summoned the memory of Martin Luther King, who had visited India some 50 years ago seeking inspiration for his way forward: "And I am mindful that I might not be standing before you today, as President of the United States, had it not been for Gandhi and the message he shared with America and the world" (Obama 2010c).

Obama added that throughout his life, including his work as a young man for the urban poor in Chicago, he has always found inspiration in Gandhi's simple life and message: "to be the change we seek in the world" (Obama 2010c). He recalled that after his sojourn to India, King had called Gandhi's philosophy of nonviolent resistance "the only logical and moral approach" in the struggle for justice and progress (Obama 2010c).

Thus, it is evident that for both mother and son the messages of King and Gandhi were important in their vision and in their professional careers. Obama's mother focused most of her energies on small-scale change, while for the son his mother's vision was the starting point for his own efforts. Ann Dunham's undeniable influence on Obama's political identity led me to pursue this connection further. I wanted to know how far his mother's driving passion and dreams shaped his political outlook. Thus, in an extensive interview with Obama's sister, as a follow-up to the launch of Dunham's book in Philadelphia, I discovered the underlying narrative that I believe completes the puzzle of Obama's soaring vision and rhetoric. Maya said:

> Our mother was the one who really raised us. My father was not there that much. She was adamant that we know the local culture as well as the universal in our thinking. So an example of that is in terms of faith; she had us read all of the good books of different faiths. The idea was that all of the books spoke to the human need to have meaning and a place in the world. There was something beautiful in everything; she was Jungian in that way, and we would watch Joseph Campbell and *The Power of Myth*, helping us to recognize points of commonality and the ways in which we are all fundamentally alike at the core. We need to therefore begin to

empathize more readily with one another and open our arms and hearts a bit more to others more readily. And I think that really impacted us as teachers, as community organizers, and as politicians.

When I asked her what types of stories or myths her mother loved to read to them as children, Maya replied:

Mom thought that storytelling and art were powerful representations of human desire, faith, strength, etc. And that the study of dreams, stories, myths around the world would help us understand overlapping humanity. We can see how alike we are and therefore how interconnected. She felt that we could use shared stories and the shared consciousness they illuminated to foster greater empathy and care. She loved the metaphorical implications of stories of growth and harvest in agricultural communities. She loved stories of transformation.

In other words, the stories of transformation Barack Obama tells in town hall meetings and in speeches to inspire and uplift the audience have a direct linkage with the transformational stories his mother used to read to him when he was a child. She did not necessarily discriminate between stories from different cultures. Of the countless stories that fill the pantheon of world mythology, ranging from Africa to Indonesia to the West, one of her favorite stories was the Arthurian legend. Passed down for centuries, the story of King Arthur and the Knights of the Round Table form the classic source of kingship in Western mythology, and it has been told and retold by people around the world. The Celtic-Irish-Scottish tale has many variations and permutations, but central to all of them is the theme of healing the land.

According to the tale, the king is ill and needs assistance from all of his knights; everybody must come forth and make a contribution. The search for the Holy Grail consists of finding out what ails the king and healing his wound. One of the key figures in the King Arthur legend is the Lady of the Lake, who, according to the legend, rises out of the deep waters and offers Arthur Excalibur, the sword of truth and justice, the mark of leadership. The Arthurian legend has been a regular staple of cultural literacy in American education and a point of fascination for Hollywood in many films and action thrillers, including, *Excalibur*, *Indiana Jones and the Last Crusade*, *The First Knight*, and *The Fisher King*.

Interestingly, the motif of swords or *keris* runs prominently through Ann Dunham's professional work in Indonesia; it was one of the main handicrafts she focused on, not only as a material, economic interest but more importantly for the symbolic significance it had for the Javanese villagers. In Indonesia, swords also represent kingship or a sign of a ruler among men; swords vary in terms of refinement and quality. The sultan, the head of the community, has the most refined sword, followed by the ministers, the generals, and so on.

Maya told me that her mother used to love a special place in Java, Sumber Kajar, which is fully detailed in her book:

> One reason why the springs of Kajar are considered sacred is their peculiar behavior. Once every few years they dry up and produce no water for a year or more. Then, about two weeks before the water returns to the springs, its arrival is heralded by a series of loud underground booming noises which sound like explosions. The villagers describe these booms as 'magic noises' or 'magic voices.'. . . Sumber Kajar is considered sacred for another reason. At the base of the spring is a wide, flat stone, worn smooth from water action. When the water level is low, one can look down and make out the clear shape of a keris in the stone. The keris is not carved into the stone but seems to be the result of a natural color variation in the stone itself. Villagers consider this image of a keris as proof that the men of Kajar are fated to be smiths and that men from neighboring villages do not share this fate. (Dunham 2009, 85)

Listening to these stories, I was immediately reminded of Neil Abercrombie's description of Ann Dunham, as he gently stroked his bushy white beard and spoke in a thoughtful and absorbing manner in his office in Washington, D.C.: "To get to know her you would have to look deep, for her the waters usually ran deep. You could not read her on the surface. She was almost passive on the surface. Barack Obama is more like his mother in this respect, and not at all like his father, who always dominated the conversation." Abercrombie was indeed very insightful in noting the same underlying emotional pattern and expressiveness in both the mother and son.

If Obama is Camelot's new knight, the Lancelot or the Parsifal, the inheritor of the Camelot legacy handed down by the Kennedy clan (Tucker

2008), then Ann Dunham was the lady of the lake, who gave the young Barack Obama the sword of true kingship. She taught him the real meaning of community service or how to try to heal the land and "whom does the Holy Grail serve." Presidential historian David Maraniss has said that Ann Dunham "was the real deal, devoting her career, unsung and underpaid, to helping poor women make their way in the modern world" (Maraniss 2008). This is not to suggest that other women in Obama's life have not supported his overall mission with a zeal and passion equal to his mother's, especially his wife, Michelle; his grandmother, Madelyn Dunham; or even his sisters, Maya Soetoro-Ng and Auma Obama. Instead, what I am suggesting is that his mother shaped his character, gave him the impetus that began his career in community service, and shaped his cherished values.

In the Arthurian legend, the healing of the land could only be achieved by an untainted young man who would merit the prize through his authenticity, hard work, and life experience. This is where Parsifal (piercer of the valley) enters the scene and aspires to become a knight. Parsifal was raised by his single mother and was on a journey to find his lost father. He came to the court and saw that the land was a wasteland because the king has been wounded and the kingdom is spiritually bankrupt. The wasteland story is about a society that is financially, morally, and intellectually barren by years of war. Traditionally, the myth concerned the struggle and the quest to restore fertility, livelihood, and peace to the land.

Enter the Obama world! Obama came to power as an antiwar candidate who promised to adjudicate two wars expeditiously, while restoring peace and prosperity to the land.

8

The Obama World

There is an African proverb that says, "If you want to go quickly, go alone. If you want to go far, go together." We need to go far, quickly.

Al Gore (2007)

"People are difficult to govern because they have too much knowledge."

Lao-Tzu (604 BC–531 BC)

We are living in a global age; the challenges America faces today are inherently global in nature. While in the previous century Americans confronted the Cold War, two world wars, and several fitful attempts at a better integration of global financial markets, these challenges were mostly concentrated in the developed economies. In the 21st century, the challenges America faces are in large part due to the rapid pace of globalization that encompasses the entire world. More than half of the world's population, left out of the march of human progress in the previous century, is now racing toward a globalized interconnected future.

Are Americans ready to lead this newly coalesced global world, a world that is partly a construction of the Western enlightenment and the liberal mind, sped up by the onset of jet travel and high-speed fiber-optic networks? As the global network continues to expand, several countries in Asia and Europe are chasing the American dream at hyper-speed while following their own economic pathway.

The process of globalization is a total phenomenon affecting every aspect of society, culture, and technology in the developed and the developing world. The old models for scaling and scoping the world are now limited. As a leader at the vanguard of change, America has anticipated and led such social change during two world wars and after the fall of communism.

It should not come as a surprise to observers of current affairs that a changemaker like Barack Obama, with a diverse lineage and background might be elected to the most powerful office in the country, which is also the seat of modern democratic institutions. There is an isomorphic connection between the times and the leader. Although Obama's rise can be accounted for by the multitudes of challenges internal to American society— post-9/11 security, economic decline, and demographic changes—there is no doubt that Obama is a reflection of the emerging narrative of the global age. During the campaign some began to jokingly refer to globalization as the "globamization" of the world, as practically the whole world was cheering America on (Tharoor 2008). Certainly, a convincing case can be made that a president who was elected on the back of the Internet and grassroots organization, and who continues to enjoy popular support around the world, might therefore be referred to as the first truly global president of our times. The forces that edged America toward selecting a global leader at this time were multifold and complex, and may be a blessing in disguise.

Pepe Escobar, the globe-trotting reporter for *Asia Times*, captures the narrative accurately when he locates Obama in the larger frame of what he calls *Obama Does Globalistan* (2009). As he notes, the year 2009 was the mother of all game changers. It marked 90 years since the Treaty of Versailles, 80 years since the Great Depression, 70 years since World War II, 60 years since NATO was formed, 50 years since the Cuban Revolution, 30 years since the Iranian Revolution, and 20 years since the fall of the Berlin Wall. "It's as if the world was turning on its gyre as in a psychedelic kaleidoscope reviving modern history in high-speed" (Escobar 2009, 1). Guess who comes out of the kaleidoscope at the dinner party, dressed like Sidney Poitier, in a cool and dapper manner—with the nuanced experience and intelligence about global diplomacy, perhaps marking the start of a multipolar world, Barack Hussein Obama!

What does the Obama presidency mean for America? We have already seen that Obama may be a sign of the demographic changes taking place within American society. Now, having examined his cultural biography in some depth, can we see the confluence between biography and history? Can Obama prepare America for a competitive multipolar world, reviving a sense of a new American century? Can Obama's outreach to the Muslim world put majority Islamic nations at ease in the Middle East and elsewhere? These are some of the key questions discussed at the beginning of this book. Now, we are in a much better position to answer them.

Fate of Empires

The summer of 1991 was a period of high drama in Moscow. The KGB's coup to take over the government had failed (Nenni 2005). Soviet monuments were under serious threat all over the city. At nightfall a rowdy crowd had gathered at the largest public squares in the city to protest the coup. The news about these events dominated the cable networks in America. I watched the events from a small Russian café located on Massachusetts Avenue in Cambridge, Massachusetts, with a Russian and an African American colleague.

I had arrived that summer to begin my doctoral studies in psychology and human development at Harvard University. Less than a decade earlier, Mikhail Gorbachev's policies of glasnost and perestroika had unleashed an independence movement within the Soviet Union. The leaders of the collection of states began to demand more control over their individual regions and, eventually, sovereignty from the Soviet Union. Gorbachev had anticipated a second revolution in Russia, but the coup attempt was the least expected outcome of the openness he had fostered. However, after his election as president in February 1990, many feared the onset of another dictatorship. When Boris Yeltsin leaped onto the turret of a tank and declared the coup unconstitutional, we thought we were witnessing history taking another unpredictable leap forward. I listened to the Russian experts at the Kennedy School of Government debate the fate of Russian democracy. Graham Allison and many others all seemed to agree that there was a power vacuum in Russia and the future looked bleak; the West should offer a grand bargain (Blackwill and Allison 1991).

Several polls showed that Russians had positive attitudes toward American democracy in 1991 (Pew 2006; Guriev 2008). The year had already seen a quick and decisive victory for Americans in the Gulf War in curtailing Saddam Hussein's aggression in Kuwait. American power was reaching new heights; both Ronald Reagan and George H. W. Bush were seen as elder statesmen around the world and national heroes at home, who had helped to bring down the Iron Curtain and bring about the collapse of the Soviet Empire.

Certainly, a new watershed moment was reached in the last decade of the 20th century, ringing in a resounding endorsement for Henry Luce's "American Century" (Brinkley 2010). American capitalism was moving ahead full throttle, and there was no looking back. Yet the summer of great progress and prosperity was not going to last forever. Within the span of a decade, America was confronting new challenges and threats at home and abroad that seemed much more menacing, veiled and amorphous.

External threats were emanating from terrorist groups making repeated attacks on Americans abroad, bombing the World Trade Center in 1993 and then driving planes into it on September 11, 2001. Domestically, the American economy, despite tremendous growth through the 1990s and the Dow Jones Index exceeding 10,000, had hit several major roadblocks with the dot.com boom-and-bust cycle and the great recession resulting from the housing and real estate bubble. With the increased outsourcing of manufacturing and service economy jobs, the American economy seemed to be sputtering to a halt, likely to produce erratic growth for 2010 and beyond.

At the onset of the 21st century, according to many observers, America seemed to be in the midst of a transformation of epochal proportions, a turn-of-the-century kind of shift that seemed to rattle its very foundation, and the echo chamber of talk radio, Fox News, and conservative political pundits seemed to give voice to the wary. Is the American experiment, the unique rendezvous with destiny at the dawn of the discovery of the New World, entering a phase of stagnation? Is the shining city on a hill losing its light and magical luster, no longer able to attract the tired and hungry masses to its shores? Have Americans lost their eternal optimism in the post-9/11 world, a spirit that had sustained the American people through turmoil for more than two centuries?

According to many political observers, the myth of American exceptionalism now seemed vulnerable to the logic of history and the rise and fall of great nations. Will America be resilient in the face of rising challenges from China, Russia, India, and Brazil, with their appetite for growth and an even deeper bench of human capital reserves? Will the civilization born of Ralph Waldo Emerson's dictum to "never imitate" be able to innovate in the face of challenges from emerging economies and an integrated European Union? At the start of the 21st century, Americans seemed to be playing catch-up on many social, educational, technological, and economic fronts.

Economically, no longer the trendsetters of a world on the horizon, Americans were struggling to find their place in the global world. The young and buoyant nation that had once taken the reins of power from its former colonizers, the British Empire, seemed now at the end of the 20th century to be running on empty. The nation that had given the world what Tom Brokaw (1998) called "the Greatest Generation" had indeed matured; saddled by debt, an anemic economy, and an aging population, Americans were struggling to find their competitive edge. Overburdened by the widening gap in income inequality over the past 30 years, America seemed to be less able to draw on the scientific work force from other parts of the world to keep ahead in innovative industries.

The accidental empire that had risen to supremacy after saving Europe from fascism had been spread thin around the world, receiving dwindling support and resources from its traditional allies. Will it go the way of a gentle giant like the British Empire, giving up control to emerging economies and the European Union? Many in the international community have begun thinking about these questions openly (Starobin 2009; Zakaria 2008).

Discussions about the fate of large empires are not new. They have been around as long as history books have been written. However, serious policy makers are now engaged in this type of active planning and strategizing within and outside the intelligence community. Around the world, America is seen as the global policeman. America did embrace this role, even though reluctantly, to the detriment of the nation's domestic agenda and often not without scorn from the rest of the world. Whereas the founders wanted no such dominion around the world, and instead believed in liberty, justice, and the pursuit of happiness for all, American policy makers today believe in some form of nation building, both through hard power and soft diplomacy, as part and parcel of their global purview.

In the coming decades, will America go into Islamic lands and try to wage war with those nations that harbor ill will against it and its allies? Although not a practical solution, this type of thinking is not uncommon among policy makers. They see no alternative to an all-out war, whether overt or covert, with the Islamists or the extreme elements in Islamic societies. Can we achieve a middle ground, a compromise solution, and a breakthrough between the more moderate elements in Islam and American civilization?

It will be a somber day when the American ideals of freedom, liberty, and equality are sacrificed at the altar of nation building in foreign lands. America's founding principles would need a thoroughgoing revision if America the majestic were to turn into a Roman fortress with security walls around its perimeter. America's ventures in Afghanistan are a perfect example of how attempts at nation building might over a longer duration drain the country of its precious resources in terms of human lives and capital as well as military reserves.

Afghanistan's history is littered with wounded warriors stretching back to Alexander the Great. Attempts by Western imperial powers to tame the tribal area between Afghanistan and Pakistan, now referred to as the "AfPak channel," have repeatedly failed. In *Gandhi and Churchill*, Herman described why the idealistic British goal of controlling the Khyber Pass "justified keeping a large native Indian army, 153,000 men in 1887 and all at the expense of Indian taxpayers, ostensibly to protect them from the Russian menace" (Herman 2008, 26). Change some words, and today's situation comes into focus.

Winston Churchill inherited his love for the Great Game from his father, Randolph Churchill, who came to prominence as a parliamentarian by successfully annexing Burma as an outpost of the empire. Herman outlines in painstaking detail how both father and son totally believed in the civilizing mission of the empire to salvage far-flung populations around the world, which would eventually run counter to Gandhi's mission and the global process of decolonization.

From an expedition in 1897, Winston Churchill wrote a telling description of the Pathan-speaking Afghan population as perpetually warring clans:

> Except at harvest time, when self-preservation enjoins a temporary truce, the Pathan tribes are always engaged in private or public war. Every man is a warrior, a politician, and a theologian. Every large house is a real feudal fortress made, it is true, only of sunbaked clay, but with battlements, turrets, loopholes, flanking towers, drawbridges, etc., complete. Every village has its defense. Every family cultivates its vendetta; every clan, its feud. The numerous tribes and combination of tribes all have their accounts to settle with one another. Nothing is ever forgotten and very few debts are left unpaid. (Churchill 1996, 134)

The American military may have ventured into a very difficult task. Its recent incursion into some of the world's toughest mountainous terrain may be more treacherous than the Vietnam War, and it is a task made even more politically unpalatable given President Obama's recent Nobel Peace Prize. Stephen Carter, a Yale law professor, while examining Obama's war policies suggests that just two years into the presidency it may have dawned on Obama that America confronts real enemies and in order to keep the peace America must go to battle (Carter 2011); there are just wars and unjust wars, as Obama said in his Nobel speech.

Obama now faces a challenge that has confronted other transformative leaders in previous generations. To paraphrase Robert Frost, is Obama going to take the path less traveled and bring peace to the Afghan valley? Or will he be mired in the same obstacles that blocked Alexander the Great, Queen Victoria's loyal soldiers, and Leonid Brezhnev's comrades? This conflict may cast a long shadow on Obama's leadership.

In an earlier era, Churchill believed with all of the might of the British Empire that it was the duty of the civilizing nations to govern the less fortunate populations around the world, but Gandhi squarely opposed this agenda. After World War II, as the British Empire began to crumble, history would prove Gandhi right in his principles of self-governance and Satyagraha. The epic battle between Gandhi and Churchill not only helped to shape the previous century, but it continues to affect fledgling democracies in the developing world. Can Obama afford to be on the wrong side of history? Given Obama's upbringing and diverse background, it can be argued that he finds himself in this position to bring lasting peace and security to Afghanistan and to avert the ongoing clash of civilizations. He certainly led his presidential campaign with a promise to adjudicate the war in Afghanistan with expediency.

The Rise of the Non-West

Experts in the fields of international relations are imagining several scenarios for a world in which America may not be the dominant force around the world, scenarios driven primarily by the economic "rise of the rest" the developing economies in Asia, Latin America, and Eastern Europe—especially China, India, Brazil, and Russia (Zakaria 2008). Who will replace America? Or, better yet, what will replace the infrastructure America and its NATO allies have kept in place to secure the peace (Starobin 2009)?

The most chaotic scenario suggests that disorder and anarchism will prevail as the American influence begins to wane. There will be a power vacuum in world leadership; world crises will simply drift along until someone assumes the role of a leader. Pepe Escobar may have it right again when he states that we are already looking at the beginning of the chaos that will follow from the end of the global American predominance: "Obama 'inherits' a globalistan where teeming masses have discovered, to their grief, that markets do not suppress poverty, unemployment and exploitation. The real globalistan is a Babel Tower where nations, mercenary peoples, terrorists, democracies, dictatorships, tribes, nomad mafias and religious outfits fight for wealth, faith, land and liberty" (Escobar 2009, 3).

This scenario assumes that earlier transitions followed the same pattern, for example, when the British Empire dissolved, when the Soviet Union collapsed, or when the Western Roman Empire fell in the fifth century AD. These were all times of transition, leaving disintegration in their wake. As a "universalist phase of the American mission" (Starobin 2009, 134) comes to an end, threats to American security will increase abroad and at home. A range of security threats, ranging from nuclear terrorism to biological warfare, could target America's financial and government infrastructure. According to most experts these threats have a significant probability of succeeding with irreversible damage to Americans, setting back the process of globalization by decades (Starobin 2009).

A period of chaos could also follow the end of the Pax Americana worldwide or on continents where American power is felt as a stabilizing force. The Middle East would feel the impact of the lack of American power most immediately. Sectarian violence could reignite in places like Iraq, Palestine, Lebanon, and the Israeli border, with spillover effects in Afghanistan, Pakistan, and states along the old Silk Route adjacent to Russia, China, and Turkey. Unless someone rises to assume power these regions could spin out of control.

Many analysts believe a multipolar world would be the ideal antidote to the splintering effects the world would experience without America as a global cop. As the power of America recedes, other emerging nations could assume a more active role in managing the world. When asked to vote at a General Assembly meeting which model would they prefer, a unipolar world with a single power center or a multipolar world where the power is balanced, most nations preferred a multipolar world (Starobin 2009). The closest the world has come to a multipolar world is the European Union (EU), where many nations act in accordance with the rules of global governance. Something like the EU model might be conceived on a global scale as a functional entity, where power-sharing arrangements might be reached between various factions and blocks of nation-states, including America, Russia, China, India, Brazil, the EU, Israel, and countries in the Middle East. Similar structural arrangements exist for nations that are part of the G8 and G20 networks. However, given the possibility of such a world is still far removed, it is highly likely that rival power centers like China might arise.

Are we biologically driven to prefer a leader of the pack or a top dog over a group of consensus-forming nations? Perhaps this is why the world has been turning to China as a potential global leader in the making. Recall that America's path to power was not through conquest; hence, China may follow America's lead in this respect and bide its time until the world community finds an opportune time to endow China with a leadership role. All reports indicate that China is on a march toward a huge transformation of its economy and society, which in a period of 10 to 20 years would secure its position as a fully developed nation alongside America, the EU nations, and Japan. Many analysts are betting that the 21st century might be a Chinese century, primarily because of China's growing manufacturing base, its large and relatively young population base, and its expanding military power.

The balance of a shift in power from the West to the East is simply a matter of time. It is bound to happen because of the networked world we live in today, even though the West may rule for now (Morris 2010). With the rise of the emerging economies, which is inevitable, the center of power may also shift from empires and nation-states to the city-states, such as Shanghai, Guangzhou, or Beijing, the most dynamically active and developing parts of modern China. Other new city-states may join the ranks of dynamic hubs of innovation and cosmopolitan values, where the national strategy may still be held down by the traditional economy and local culture; yet the city-states, as centers of capital flows, development, and global outlook, would welcome knowledge workers from around the world. This is a phenomenon already evident in the Arab world and the Middle East, where cities like Tel Aviv, Dubai, and Kuwait City have been leading centers for the knowledge economy while the region is still mired by political conflicts.

Thus, global city-states will help to define the future, connecting the old power hubs of the world, from New York and London, to the new markets in Singapore, Bangkok, and Bangalore. In this new world, city-states will emerge as hubs of global trade and cultural exchange, just as they did millennia ago when open trade routes linked the continents. Business executives, traders, and knowledge workers will travel to and from these city-states as the main nodes of global commerce. Local populations will remain relevant as far as each nation retains its local flavor, language, and culture. Each society will have its multinational class, whose members are truly global or internationalists. These people will work and mingle with other like-minded people. At the same time the local industries and economies will operate as they have always done within the framework of a local culture and governance.

What then might be the values that will define the new world order? Will it be the same set of values that led to the founding of the American civilization, such as open markets, capitalism, liberty, and equality? Or will the values vary based on the local history and culture, though still guided by the broad principles borrowed from the Western models of democracy? We don't have clear answers to these questions. Yet it is likely that the liberal values cherished by the likes of Henry Luce, who enunciated accurately the trends of the "American century," will in a significant way be the guiding principles of the emerging universal civilization (Starobin 2009).

All of these scenarios and their multifaceted outcomes have pushed the American century toward an eventual end run. The American mind in the coming decades will be fundamentally transformed as it must keep pace with the rapid changes around the world. Was Obama elected to preside over these landmark changes? Or is he a sign of the American revival, a new American century, perhaps? How these global developments will play out no one is quite sure, but one thing is certain: in order to adapt to these changing realities Americans must transform their lifestyles and reorient their minds toward the emerging global world.

Was the landmark Obama election possibly a reflection of these changing times, ushering in the kind of radical shift needed for America to get ahead of the curve in order to help manage the major changes taking place around the world? I believe that when we examine Obama's cultural biography, his socialization and education in Hawai'i, in Indonesia, and even on the mainland, the underlying message is very clear. Obama was elected to ease America's transition into the new global age. He is America's first global president. He was elected to attack the twofold challenge, first outlined by Samuel Huntington: a clash of civilizations between Islamists and America, on the one hand, and the clash between America and the rising economic and military powers like China in East Asia, on the other hand.

Averting the Clash of Civilizations

It is a historical truism that leaders can shape the course of history at decisive turning points. It is also the case that history seems to pick leaders suited for particular times, as if to turn a page in the history books or to start a new chapter in the life of a people. In 2008, when Americans, faced with the mounting challenges at home and abroad, went to the voting booths with the intent to elect their first black president, they were aware and mindful of the other key attributes needed in a leader of the free world at this critical point in history. In picking Obama, Americans found not only their first black president but also a multicultural president who was raised in Hawai'i and a global president who was raised in the largest secular Islamic democracy on the planet. Obama was a multicultural person before he became the first black president, and he was a biracial person before he went in search of his African American identity. To sum up, following are some of the features considered unique in Obama's biography from a cultural and psychological standpoint that have deeply informed his vision and leadership style.

Obama's father was an African economist, trained at the University of Hawai'i and Harvard University, and his mother was an American anthropologist, who worked in Indonesia and other developing countries. Obama had traveled extensively to Asia and Africa, which partly provided the necessary education for the making of a global president. His parents' brief union is reflected in his agenda for creating a more integrated America in terms of race and ethnicity and the coming demographic changes that will transform the American landscape.

Obama was raised in the last state to join the Union, Hawai'i, which is one of the most diverse states in the United States and the first majority-minority state, where no ethnic group has a political hold on the power structure. Hawai'i provided a formative experience for Obama with the rise of Asian economies in the 1970s and 1980s. Obama understands very clearly that remaining a Pacific power with an eye toward the East Asian economies is critical for America to succeed in the 21st century.

Obama was schooled and socialized in the largest Islamic constitutional democracy, Indonesia, which recognizes six other world religions as part of the state as outlined in the principle of Pancasila. Obama studied these founding principles in elementary school and learned to pray in both the Islamic and Christian ways. More than any other experience from his childhood, Indonesia provided Obama with the real life experiences of living on the Muslim street, side by side with Muslim friends and neighbors. This experience deeply informed his vision of creating a lasting peace with the Islamic world, which many conservatives believe is naive and excessively optimistic. Even though he was socialized in a secular Islamic democracy, Obama is not a Muslim, but the Islamic world may perceive him as one of their own primarily because of his genealogical roots and his Arabic-Swahili name. Based on the available evidence, Obama never converted to Islam or went through any ceremonial rites or rituals to become a Muslim while living in Jakarta. There is also no evidence to suggest that Obama was ever legally adopted by his stepfather, Lolo Soetoro, whom I have shown in this book was a secular Muslim in his ideas, beliefs, and practices.

Obama was educated at one of the elite private schools in Hawai'i, the Punahou School. This school has been practicing a missionary, Christian-based service ethic and a soft multiculturalism for more than a century. Contrary to popular belief, Obama did not become a community organizer overnight when he landed in Chicago. I have shown in this book that the seeds for a career in public service and as a community organizer may have been planted by his mother and later cultivated at the Punahou School.

Essentially, Obama grew up on two islands and moved to the mainland only when he started college. This was a somewhat traumatic transition as he had to reconstruct his racial identity on the mainland. In Hawai'i, Obama grew up with the aloha ethic, where everyone must get along with everyone else and be part of the one big family or *ohana*.

Obama began to come to grips with his racial identity when his father died shortly after he arrived in New York City. While living in New York City, he was exposed to a strong dose of African American religiosity and culture in the Baptist churches in Harlem, where he found solace and comfort for his loneliness and feelings of being cut off from his roots while also mourning his father's loss. At this turning point, he decided to fully take on his father's name, Barack Hussein Obama, thus beginning his journey on the mainland as a new kind of African American. He decided that he did not wish to be a tragic mulatto and that he wanted to be a transparently black person. However, in converting from Barry Obama to Barack Hussein Obama, he also marked a break with the prevailing racial dialogue in this country by subtly asserting that he was not descended from slaves.

After graduating from Columbia University, Obama briefly worked for a Wall Street firm but gave up this job to become a community organizer for black neighborhoods in Chicago. This decision was precipitated by the death of his father and later the death of one of his half-brothers in a motorcycle accident. Thus, his time in New York City was marked by several deaths in the African side of his family and an overwhelming mood of loss and melancholy.

In this book, I have tried to dig a bit deeper into Obama's background to show how Obama's genealogy was deeply rooted in the larger geopolitical and cultural forces of our times. His mother married men from underdeveloped countries of Kenya and Indonesia; both men were involved in national development projects for their respective nations. Both men were also secular Muslims or atheists in their religious orientation, and they had been schooled in Western liberal and democratic thought. This was one of the main reasons why these men were drawn to an American liberal woman like Ann Dunham as a life partner, because she represented the promise of liberalism and freedom in all its manifestations. She was not Lady Liberty, but these men valued what she symbolized. Thus, through his father and stepfather, secular Islam has been part of Obama's life from the very beginning and shaped his everyday life and destiny.

Obama's grandparents were a product of the Great Depression and World War II, in particular the history of the Pearl Harbor attacks on the Hawai'ian Islands. These events deeply shaped him because his grandparents were part of his daily life. They were his guardians, and they raised him and were responsible for his schooling. Thus, Obama gained a multigenerational perspective on American history and culture.

Obama grew up in highly diverse settings and was educated by teachers from different backgrounds. His mother, his first teacher, was an adventurer and a world traveler. His teachers in Indonesia were of diverse backgrounds—Catholic, Muslim, secularist, and humanist. Likewise, his education in Hawai'i was also diverse, where several of his teachers were Asian Americans and Pacific Islanders.

By the time Obama reached the mainland, he had been thoroughly socialized in the white middle-class Dunham household, which sheltered him from many of the negative stereotypes of his soon-to-be reconstructed African American identity on the mainland. His mother, who idealized African American artists, musicians, and writers, had passed on to him all of the positive images of African American culture.

His mother raised him to believe it was a moral privilege to be an African American in this country.

Thus, the driving force behind Obama's rise may have been his mother and grandparents' constancy, unconditional love, and support. Collectively, they all believed Barack was destined to do big things. Barack Obama took the best from each of the Dunham family members and made it his own. Yet the almost mythic image of his father also emerges as a significant driver in his life story. Although Obama Sr. contributed significantly to the Obama family's gene pool, he was, in the final analysis, primarily a sperm donor in his son's life. It is in Obama's reconstructed projection of his father's idealized image, fueled by the absence of a real flesh-and-blood father figure, that the boy who one day would become president of the United States had created his own idealized self-image. Obama's reconstructed image of his African father also drives his love and admiration of Abraham Lincoln.

It is his father's larger-than-life image that produces the highs and lows of his life. He is uplifted by his father's mythic image until he discovers that his father's feet were indeed made of clay; near the end of his life, the once gifted and driven man had taken to drinking and had lost both his legs in car accidents. The idealistic image of his father was part fantasy and part reality; his real father, he discovered, was a different man from what he had imagined.

The discovery of his father's real personality after his death shook Obama to the core of his being. The lengthy autobiography he wrote at the age of 33 years clearly suggests that Obama had a lot to work through and share with the world about his father. However, by the time Obama discovered his real father, he was a grown person, able to fully rationalize his father's failures and aberrant behavior. Because of the geographical and personal distance, his father's strengths and weaknesses did not carry the same emotional weight on his own psychological development. Remarkably, as a young adult, when Obama was trying to find his own way in the world, he was somewhat freed by the overbearing image of a distant but exacting father.

Obama felt vindicated, free to do what he wished with his life. Yet there is no doubt that from his father he inherited the soul of Africa and by extension an African American identity and an abiding concern for issues surrounding race in America. Thus, it is no coincidence that Obama replaced his father's reconstructed image with that of Abraham Lincoln, the great emancipator of the black people. Given his father's ambitious goals for Kenya, Obama's racial identity is also intertwined with hopes for Africa's development, something he might take up after he leaves the presidency, modeled after the Clinton Global Initiative or Jimmy Carter's Habitat for Humanity.

Obama has promised to transform America into a more competitive nation and an integrated nation. I have outlined how Obama's motivation to change America and the world is born of a heroic impulse rooted in his father's loss and his mother's trailblazing career. The Obama presidency represents a paradigmatic moment in the history of America and the world, where an African American politician has reached the highest office in the land and possibly the most powerful executive position in the world. There was an unprecedented level of excitement about the Obama election among the U.S. electorate and surprisingly among most of the populations surveyed around the world.

Although scores of opinion surveys have been conducted on the significance of this history-making event, a systematic analysis from the standpoint of behavioral and social sciences has not been undertaken. Can the Obama presidency change the American image around the globe in a significant manner? Is there indeed a change in world opinion about the United States because of the Obama election? The answers to these question may be an unequivocal yes, but the evidence is still amassing.

The effectiveness of Obama's policies will determine America's standing in the world both in the near term and in the distant future. At this momentous turning point in history, we need to fully understand the potential opportunities and limitations of the Obama presidency. Will the Obama presidency be able to prepare Americans for the upcoming challenges of the 21st century? How will the Obama agenda be implemented?

We have seen the enactment of the Obama agenda in terms of health care, financial reform, and international diplomacy. Although there is a robust debate about the merits of the Obama agenda (Ali 2010; Carter 2010; Hodge 2010; Kuttner 2010), there is no doubt that America is heading in a different direction. One of the central questions is this: Will the Obama presidency be a harbinger of the new American century or the beginning of the post-American world? On this score, the evidence is still forthcoming. But if Obama is able to enact his agenda, as his election foretold, America can reverse and recover from some of the negative historical trends signaling the rise and fall of nations.

A transformation of the American mind has already begun. Obama as a peacemaker is trying to avert the clash of civilizations between the West and the rest on multiple strategic fronts. Obama has altered America's relations with the Islamic world; his addresses in Turkey, Egypt, Ghana, and Indonesia directly spoke to his use of soft power, while he has forcefully applied America's military power in Afghanistan and Pakistan. The killing of Osama bin Laden has brought the war on terrorism to a turning point, but it remains to be seen whether Al Qaeda has been fully defeated in the longest war in American history (Bergen 2011; Escobar 2011).

Finally, with an increasingly cooperative yet competitive stance toward the emerging economies in the G20 nations, Obama seems to be preparing America for a transition toward the role of a global team player in a multipolar world, all the while trying to make significant investments in the America of the 21st century. However, it remains to be seen whether he can revive the American dream for the next generation.

9

Reimagining the American Dream

I join you, therefore, in branding as cowardly the idea that the human mind is incapable of further advances. This is precisely the doctrine which the present despots of the earth are inculcating and their friends here reechoing; and applying especially to religion and politics.... But thank heaven the American mind is already too much opened to listen to these impostures ... science can never be retrograde; what is once acquired of real knowledge can never be lost.

Thomas Jefferson (2004)

"Americans had dreamed since our national birth, and in the twenty-first century we were dreaming still."

(Brands 2010, 1)

In September 2010, on a balmy September in Philadelphia, just a few weeks before the winter of discontent called the midterm elections, Obama tried to re-create the magic of the historic 2008 victory at a rally with thousands of potential democratic voters. Lines stretched for miles, running through several blocks on each side of Germantown High School, where the rally was held. Though the tempo and pitch of the attendees seemed somewhat muted, the Obama devotees were still chanting the now famous slogan, "Yes we can. Yes we can."

Holding on to the faith in their political avatar, who had promised to change their world, the attendees represented people from all walks of life, racially and demographically mixed but with a strong contingency of the African American democratic voting base. Holding up political signs in their clutched fists, the poster board images of Obama swaying in the gentle autumn breeze—with a distant and dreamy look in his eyes as if to imagine a new world on the horizon—seemed to uplift many of the voters, but many more seemed to be moving sluggishly because of the hard economic realities.

Obama's campaign logo of the rising sun, once prominently displayed, seemed to be receding into the background as old T-shirts, buttons, and bumper stickers gave way to 2010 election souvenirs. Yet many families who had waited in lines for hours had positioned themselves near the stage to get a glimpse of the 44th president. Parents were waiting to lift their infants and young children onto their shoulders and even higher into the air to afford a glimpse of their political hero. Political rallies are multigenerational events, I realized, where everyone tries to catch a ray of hope and sunshine amid the flash of cameras and floodlights, hoping to alter their destinies in some unforeseeable fashion.

The psychology of a large crowd seemed to be in full force. Several thousand potential voters were packed into a high school yard, with a lineup of Democratic politicians ranging from Governor Ed Rendell to U.S. Representative Bob Casey, Mayor Michael Nutter, and Senate hopeful Joe Sestak encouraging people to get out and "vote, vote, and vote." A popular DJ and a rock band kept the enthusiasts interested, entertained, and bouncing on their happy feet. All of these factors were designed to motivate the audience for a late surge on the day of the election.

Despite the tough economy and the double-digit unemployment rate, the crowd exploded to a frenzied pitch when Vice President Joe Biden introduced President Obama to a thundering applause. His rock star–like reception, two years into the presidency, explained how he retained a moderately high rating, hovering around 48 percent, even in recessionary times; the audience seemed to be in rapture when they saw him walk onto the stage. Tall, tanned, and beaming with his infectious smile, Obama projected hope and strength that the future will turn out fine, no matter how challenging the times. This of course is the key to a charismatic leader's hold on a large group or a population. It is the unspoken bond with a people that a leader uses skillfully to mobilize them to political action; Obama displayed these skills in full measure, although with restraint. He reminded the voters about the financial mess he had inherited from the Republicans. Providing a strong dose of reality Obama repeated his pitch that change is never easy; change is hard. Sensing that the Obama agenda might be in jeopardy if the Democrats lost the majority in the House of Representatives, he exhorted the attendees to get out the vote.

Stimulating one of the largest economies in the world from the brink of major depression is like turning around a large ship, certainly not an easy task for any political leader to accomplish overnight. I could sense the weight of the job unfinished not only in what the president said but also on the faces in the crowd. The frenzied enthusiasm seen at earlier rallies had clearly died down. It seemed that economic realities had wakened the people from the perpetual American dream.

As we have seen throughout this book, the structural challenges America faces are multigenerational: the threat of Islamic terrorism, the rising economic challenges from China and the Asian economies, and the demographic changes that are altering the ethnic and electoral fabric of the society. All of these complex issues call for transformational leadership to keep America on the right track. Do Americans still have the willpower to take on big challenges? Is the country so fundamentally divided that it cannot form a consensus on how to move forward? Certainly, many Americans are asking these questions, wondering aloud whether the new normal means becoming the second- or the third-best nation in the world (Starobin 2009; Zakaria 2008). Has America lost its competitive edge in the world?

Trying to raise the crowd to action, Obama said that he wants the latest green economy jobs created here in this country, warning that China, India, or Korea are not cutting back on education. Obama pointed out that America now lags behind most of these countries in high school graduation rates and that America needs investments in science, technology, and education. Yet, at every turn the economy is constrained by the ballooning deficit, overspending, and the generational debt. At the midpoint of his first term, the Obama agenda for all its strength of vision seemed to be stalled by a determined opposition.

Obama claimed in a recent interview on the View that he takes a long view of history (ABC News 2010). He wants to do things that America has been putting off for a while—health care, education, energy, and financial reform—things that will prepare Americans for the 21st century. Yet the significant losses suffered at the midterm elections have put much of the Obama agenda in abeyance. The transformative nature of the presidency might have to take a backseat to incremental compromise on a whole host of issues. As the first two years of Obama's administration drew to a close, he was forced to compromise with the Republicans and even the moderate Democrats within his own party, which, according to many political observers, was a good strategy.

Obama Goes East

After the midterm, Obama traveled East on a jaunt through Asia—India, Indonesia, South Korea, and Japan—to confront head-on the economic challenges America is now facing. Accompanied by a large group of American CEOs and business executives, he wanted to do some hard selling and soft diplomacy with the leaders of various emerging economies. Hoping to revive job growth at home, his trip seemed to be flying high in India, where he not only paid homage to the Gandhi/Martin Luther King legacy (Obama 2010c), while mingling with people at various universities and schools, but also managed to convince Indian high-tech firms to adopt a whole host of technology transfers from the United States, totaling about $10 billion.

The strategic interest in India at this time serves two functions: (1) India's relative growth is keeping pace with China's; and (2) India, like the United States, is a thriving democracy. Both of these factors provide a rationale for an alliance with India as a counterbalance to China (Phillipp 2010). Aroon Purie (2010), a senior editor of *India Today,* recalled telling Obama, "I hope you get more credit for this trip than you get for all the good work you have done in America." To which Obama replied, "You know, you can never be a prophet in your own land" (Purie 2010). The Indian media seemed to have fallen in love with Michelle and Barack Obama, with his witty responses to college students in town hall meetings and with her extemporaneous dance moves with school children. Their story of triumph resonated with the students in Mumbai and Delhi, many of whom still aspire to go abroad for work or study.

In Indonesia, Obama's childhood home, he stayed just long enough not to be stranded by the volcanic ash from Mount Merapi. He excited the local population and whetted his appetite for a later visit. In a speech at the University of Indonesia (Obama 2010b), he managed to push all of the right buttons while reminiscing poetically in the Indonesian Bahasha language, suggesting that Indonesia is an important part of him, which is of course one of the central claims of this book.

He also praised Indonesia's long-standing support for democratic institutions and secular values, reached out to Muslims by visiting the Istiqlal Mosque, and exhorted young Indonesians not to succumb to extremism and Islamic fundamentalism and not to cave in to Al Qaeda or other extremist groups, such as Jamaat-e-Islamia. He said his administration had made modest diplomatic progress with Islamic nations to avert the clash of civilizations, but that more work needed to be done (Obama 2010b). This is one of the other claims of this book given Obama's upbringing in a secular Islamic democracy. America needs to engage Islamic democracies beyond just the basic security concerns, Obama said, something his administration is actively pursuing as part of the new "Comprehensive Partnership."

On the next leg of his journey, in Seoul, South Korea, Obama seemed to hit a roadblock. At the G20 summit, America was criticized for starting a trade war by implementing quantitative easing. The United States became the target for China and the other South East Asian economies, who were upset that America is going further into debt and appeared to be becoming protectionist. The same tone continued at the Asia-Pacific Economic Cooperation summit in Yokohama, Japan.

Yet from a distance it seemed as if the Obama administration was engaging in the central concerns of his administration, namely, economic recovery and partnership with the emerging economies in Asia. Some of the Asian press gave voice to the Chinese concerns, predicted the start of currency wars over the next few years, and the economic clash over currencies was now in full force between America and China. Some of the leading foreign affairs journalists took a decidedly mixed view on the results the Asian trip had produced. Frank Rich of the *New York Times* wrote, "Barack Obama, Phone Home," given the President's political woes in the newly elected Republican Congress were about to heat up (Rich 2010). However, as China is moving fast, the entire Southeast Asian region is on a competitive run. America has to step up its game to remain economically competitive and a military presence in the region. Upon returning to the United States Obama said: "Everything I hear from leaders and people is that we are central and they still want us there" (Feller and Werner 2010). The Asian economies are investing in their people, providing education and training their labor force, rebuilding and redesigning their infrastructure, and looking to open new markets. As a Pacific power, America cannot lag behind, and must stay engaged and take a leadership role, said Obama (Feller and Werner 2010). In fact, the whole Asian trip, with its focus on strong emerging democracies, was designed to counterbalance the growing economic influence and military presence of China in the region.

The issue raised in Asia has become the campaign theme: Americans must innovate out of this economic slump as they have done previously.

Innovators at a recent summit on technology believe the best thing America has going for it is openness and a spirit of entrepreneurship compared with other global economies. We don't know where the next big idea or invention is going to come from, but if we back enough bold and creative ventures, one or two of them will deliver the results that will be scalable in the entire market. In an interview with Elizabeth Corcoran of *Forbes*, Vinod Khosla, an energy investor and a cofounder of Sun Microsystems, said he believes in the "black swan theory of innovation," where improbably rare events can change the marketplace, such as the creation and commercialization of the Internet or search engines like Google (Rapier 2010).

Progressive Tools

Princeton physicist Freeman Dyson (1999), in a pithy meditation on the nature of scientific, technological, and social progress, suggested that the nature of scientific revolutions is not, as Thomas Kuhn had predicted, driven by large, cohesive paradigms that are overtaken by more precise, inclusive, and expansive paradigms. Rather progress is driven by tools and sudden, haphazard discoveries of new technologies that push human knowledge and social structures toward radical social change. In his book of the same title, Dyson has argued that "The Internet, the Genome, and the Sun" have spurred ground-breaking technologies that have the potential of changing scientific paradigms (Dyson 1999). Khosla as a venture capitalist has certainly applied this principle to innovating green technologies.

I have tried to argue, while applying Kuhn's ideas of scientific and technological progress to the societal realm, that the Obama presidency represents a paradigmatic shift in politics. There are stable long-term trends that enable the rise of a political figure like Obama. These trends, as I have pointed out, relate directly to the post–World War II demographic changes in the United States, the rise of radical Islam abroad and at home, and the forces of economic and cultural globalization. I have shown in the preceding chapters that these larger trends have a specific cultural and historical resonance with Obama's own biography and life history, which in part have led to the making of a global president.

From an alternative viewpoint, where scientific progress is more random, driven by chance discoveries and technological convergences, it is the tools of scientific discovery that drive progress and change. Progress is halting and moves in fits and starts; it is not primarily driven by large ideological pendulum swings. In this visionary outlook, Dyson (1999) argues that technology can fundamentally alter our ethical and social arrangements.

Dyson (1999) identifies three profound, rapidly developing technologies—solar energy, genetic engineering, and worldwide communication systems—that have the potential to create a more equal distribution of the world's wealth. He demonstrates that new tools are often the spark that ignites scientific discovery and leads to social change. Consequently, such tool-driven revolutions have profound social implications.

Dyson, who voted for Obama and supports his increased investments in basic science, research, and development, believes a politician like Obama is a reflection of the times (Dawidoff 2009), showing how far scientific progress and societal progress have traveled together. Certainly, it is difficult to imagine how a politician like Obama could have been elected without the Internet, a tool that made organizing online possible. It is even more enlightening to see in parallel how the understanding of our biological origins has evolved through genomic technologies, leading to a deconstruction of our ideas about race or ethnicity in politics. It is precisely the post-genomic consciousness that allows candidates like Obama to enter the public discourse in the first place and makes it possible for him to win.

By this logic, even if Obama is a once-in-a-lifetime politician, a "black swan," rare mutation of some future on the horizon, his politics nonetheless are a reflection of human progress. As a counterargument to my thesis, if his election does not represent a paradigm shift, but rather a meteoric flash in the pan, Obama will remain a marker of what can be actualized by the next generations. In other words, if Obama is simply an early prototype of the change we have envisioned, or an avatar-like figure from the future, and not a stable paradigm shift with linear coattails, then we better anticipate a dramatic pushback from the opposition, which looking at the current field of candidates in 2011 does seem likely.

The opposing view on President Obama has latched on to "the paranoid style of American politics" (Hofstadter 1996). Obama is often portrayed as a machine politician and an extreme left-leaning progressive. As the first black president, one with a mixed-race genealogy, he has been subjected to some wild and weird interpretations. Talk radio and conservative blogs are filled with rants that Obama is not a real American, theories that question the validity of his birth certificate, and doubts about his patriotism. He is portrayed as the other, the foreigner, the socialist, the Marxist, the Muslim, the Manchurian candidate, the post-American president, the anticolonial president, and so on.

Behind these smokescreens, misplaced labels, and the political rhetoric, I have shown empirically with newly gathered evidence and new interviews that Obama is a product of America's adventures in globalization in the Pacific region and Southeast Asia. First and foremost, he is a globalist because his parents were practicing a kind of global thinking at the edge of the world in the early 1960s; he is a direct reflection of their trailblazing and somewhat chaotic lives that touched all major continents. They raised him to feel and think globally, beyond one's borders, while acting locally as a community activist and lawyer, making a difference in the lives of everyday people.

Second, he is a globalist by virtue of where he was born and raised. He is a product of the global education and multicultural sensibility he acquired in places like Hawai'i and Indonesia. Hawai'i was the first majority-minority state of the United States, and Indonesia has the largest secular Muslim population in the world. I have presented evidence from Hawai'i and Indonesia, distilling the impact of his global schooling in Jakarta and the internationalist approach to global affairs he acquired growing up in Hawai'i, not too far from the East-West Center where his mother, father, and stepfather met and studied.

Finally, he is a globalist because we are living in the post-9/11 world. The events of 9/11, whereby America was drawn into long conflicts in Iraq and Afghanistan, were the historic precursors for Obama's U.S. Senate race. More than ever before, America needs to be engaged with the rest of the world. Obama cannot help being pushed and pulled by the unprecedented historical circumstances that American power has created in the world.

Obama is a harbinger of the social and demographic changes that will reshape the American landscape and what it means to be an American in the 21st century. As a changemaker, he has lived through some of the very changes Americans confront today in their own lives, changes brought on by the shifting demographics and the emerging global marketplace. Nowhere is this fact more evident than in his use of the social media to gather support and raise funds for his historic campaign. He is by all accounts an Internet president, who may become a genomic and solar president to follow Dyson's analogy, but only if his forward-looking science and technology policies are fully implemented.

An Internet President

Nowadays a social revolution needs a human technology nexus, a language or a code for communication and a virtual meeting place. The digital world in the postindustrial information economy has made it easier to bring people together electronically and to mobilize them for political action (Sharma 2004; Brown and Duguid 2000). However, at the outset of the 2008 elections, it was not guaranteed that a grassroots movement of diverse interest groups could be cobbled together using new media technologies to form a majority democratic coalition. Furthermore, in response to the Obama presidency, very few people anticipated that another grassroots movement, the Tea Party, would spring up within a year and would also rely heavily on the new social media tools.

In the 2008 election, many Democrats were still reeling from the sting of defeat of the two previous general elections, and the Republicans were lumbering under the burden of fatigue from eight years of George W. Bush. Political pundits were attempting to divine the future; the same cast of talking heads from the 2000 and 2004 elections was evangelizing on cable T.V. and news networks. Yet few paid attention to the digital tidal waves that lay dormant in the Obama camp. None could have predicted that Obama's digital tidal wave would eventually deluge all of the democratic candidates, including favored Hillary Clinton, and overtake all of the Republican candidates too. After all, only white southern governors from large states had managed to win the general election on the Democratic ticket over the past 40 years.

Going back to Franklin Roosevelt's fireside chats, Marshall McLuhan, the seer of the information age, introduced the idea of the "global village" (McLuhan and Powers 1992). However, it was to Howard Rheingold's credit that we have learned about the recent phenomenon of the "smart mobs" (Rheingold 2002). According to the original definition, "a smart mob is a form of self-structuring social organization through technology-mediated, intelligent emergent behavior" (Rheingold 2002, 23). Simply stated, smart mobs are the newly emerging masses of humanity seen in major cities or metro areas that are on their blackberries and cell phones, seamlessly connected to the Web; they are perpetually logged on to the digital information network at home, at work, and while in transit.

The evidence is overwhelming that the Obama team transformed these emerging smart mobs into even smarter mobs and online political activists. On the closing day of the 2008 campaign, it was Obama's intelligent mobs who truly deserved a victory lap around Chicago's Grant Park when Obama declared, "If there is anyone out there who still doubts that America is a place where all things are possible, who still wonders if the dream of our founders is alive in our time, who still questions the power of our democracy, tonight is your answer" (Obama 2008).

Now the Tea Party candidates have taken a page from the Obama playbook. Building on the original complaints of the Boston colonists who dumped tea into the harbor in protest over high taxation by the British, Tea Party followers want to reduce the size of the government. Why the Tea Party never formed when the Republicans were in power for eight years is not clear. Yet the Tea Partiers have now used the language of a grassroots organization to build an online movement against the Obama administration.

The Obama team may have to rely on the intelligent mobs to mobilize social media networks again in the next national election. Deloitte Consulting (2008) analyzed the new media production and consumption in the 2008 election and concluded that this was a turning point for Internet-based electoral technologies. Since the election of President Kennedy, network T.V. has been a significant force in electoral politics. The 24/7 cable news networks have also shaped the public opinion for almost 25 years, while the Internet news and information portals began changing the political landscape almost a decade ago. Yet, the combined potential of cable television news cycles and Internet technologies to usher in a paradigmatic change had not been fully realized until the 2008 campaign cycle.

The convergence of three specific digital capabilities produced the Obama victory: social networking Web sites, video sharing Web sites, and more portable communications tools. This digital convergence had been anticipated by the new media companies and the business community since the heyday of the dot-com economy, which seems to have finally arrived after a boom-and-bust cycle (Silverthrone 2006). The election cycle of 2008, however, provided a real-world test case for the intensification of the digital convergence.

More than any other national campaign in the past four decades, Obama tapped into the voice of the masses. While Hillary Clinton's campaign managers were deriding Obama's campaign as one that looks like Facebook, Chris Hughes, the 24-year-old cofounder of the social networking Web site was brewing up an online storm. Hughes befriended Obama and helped him organize his Web strategy. A history and literature major at Harvard,

Hughes had an in-depth understanding of the human dimension of social networking; as many marketers know, new social media approaches are as much about sociology as they are about technology (Solis and Breakenridge 2009). Before the Iowa primaries Obama was trailing in the polls, not anywhere near the top of the Democratic heap of candidates. "We were completely focused on making sure that people knew on a very basic level how, where, and why to caucus in Iowa. And a local network, like Facebook, was ideal for that," Hughes told a reporter from *Fast Company* (McGirt 2008). Online technologies were an easy, reliable, and cost-effective way to connect with people at the human level. On the day after the election, *Fast Company* reported that "during the long and winding road to the White House, there was an interesting side story that played out about which candidate really "got" technology, particularly IT. Obama was portrayed as web-savvy, carrying a blackberry and regularly using the Internet. In contrast, the much older McCain was seen as out of touch, even personally admitting that he didn't use a computer or email" (Atkinson 2008).

As we have seen, the use of the digital technologies was not just an interesting side story. It was one of the main drivers of the election, emblematic of Obama's bottoms-up candidacy and changemaking personality. The Obama candidacy brought the first online grassroots movement to the White House, a movement created by the people, for the people, and of the people. A large share of Obama's success had to be credited to the online networking and new media technologies, which were important causal links in the chain of events that led to his success. As Obama said repeatedly: "One of my fundamental beliefs from my days as a community organizer is that real change comes from the bottom up. . . . And there's no more powerful tool for grass-roots organizing than the Internet" (Stelter 2008).

As Morley Winograd and Michael Hais, former consultants to the Clinton and Gore team, have observed, the combination of the generational and technological factors led to "new winners with new ideas and new ways of winning" in the 2006 election (Winograd and Hais 2006, 140). They observed that in the 2008 election there was a new wave of change taking over America, "threatening to sweep away business, power structures, and institutions that were built on the beliefs and technologies of a previous era" (Winograd and Hais 2006, 140). To win elections in the coming decades, parties, candidates, and campaigns must find innovative ways to communicate with the voters if they want to remain relevant for the 21st century.

Given the generational political realignment and the technological shift under way in American society, Obama's continued success depends on staying on top of this demographic, cultural, and social change by enlisting more converts and newcomers; hence, he must continue to perfect his message and the medium. Will the new administration carry forward the objectives enunciated during the 2008 campaign and fully transform America into a digital nation? Will that naturally make Obama our first digital president?

The Obama team has established an office of information technology which plans to lead open governance, spread broadband widely and into rural areas, and transform health care by setting up electronic health records. However, will the Obama administration use information technology to accomplish targeted and narrow goals or aim for large system-wide initiatives? Many have suggested that information and communication technologies are now at a level where they can be applied more broadly to solve large challenges that the nation faces, such as "growing the economy in the short term and the long term, addressing climate change, reforming health care, improving education, and making government work" (Atkinson 2008). This may truly be the first digital presidency if the Obama team is able to deploy the full range of digital technologies and prepare the country for competition in the 21st century.

Will Obama's intelligent mobs complete the digital revolution begun during the campaign by providing access to the information economy to all segments of the American society? The vision of an egalitarian and interconnected world guided the American baby boomers, the hippies, and the counterculture movement in the 1960s and 1970s, which gave rise to the digital world at the end of the previous century (Sharma 2004; Turner 2006). Transformation of human societies from nomadic hunter-gatherers to sedentary agriculturalists to industrialists brought us to the information age, which has accelerated the pace of globalization. As the children of the information age are coming into their own, there is a real danger that certain segments of the American population might be left behind in the global economy.

The Obama team was on message during the campaign while displaying their commitment to science and innovation, and they released a sweeping statement on technology:

Revolutionary advances in information technology, biotechnology, nanotechnology and other fields are reshaping the global economy. Without renewed efforts the United States risks losing leadership in

science, technology and innovation. As a share of the Gross Domestic Product, American federal investment in the physical sciences and
engineering research has dropped by half since 1970. . . .

   Too many Americans are not prepared to participate in a 21st century
economy: A recent international study found that U.S. students perform
lower on scientific assessments than students in 16 other economically
developed nations, and lower than 20 economically developed nations
in math performance. Only one-third of middle class physical science
teachers are qualified to teach in that subject, and only one-half of middle school math sciences have an educational background in that subject
area. (Obama and Biden 2008, 1)

   Under an Obama administration, will America catch up with the world
in broadband penetration as it has done in the commercialization of Internet? Americans will need to compete with countries that have leapfrogged
ahead and have nearly 100 percent broadband. This of course calls for
heavy investment in and incentives for development. The Obama team
believes "we can get true broadband to every community in America
through a combination of reform of the Universal Service Fund, better use
of the nation's wireless spectrum, promotion of next-generation facilities,
technologies and applications, and new tax and loan incentives" (Obama
and Biden 2008, 2).

   Progress in the Obama world will be measured on multiple fronts,
including the areas of technology, science, and innovation. How quickly
we move ahead on these ambitious goals will determine the shape of
things to come. If the Obama presidency truly represents a generational
change and a major political realignment, then we are likely to see a level
of social and cultural change that prepares this country for the next American century.

Obama's Genomics

It is "in my DNA, trying to promote mutual understanding to insist that
we all share common hopes and common dreams as Americans and as
human beings," Barack Obama said repeatedly during the 2008 presidential campaign, especially during the Reverend Wright controversy (Obama
2008b). In the bicentennial year of the birth of both Lincoln and Darwin

(both were born February 12, 1809), it is interesting that Americans inaugurated the first African American and the first global president. We all know that race is not so much a biological category but above all a political and social one, especially in a nation of immigrants. We owe this insight to the scientific work of biologists, who are all Darwinians now, and to the long march of civil rights leaders, who are all Lincoln's descendants.

Highlighting the remarkable confluence of these two parallel lives, Malcolm Jones, in a recent article in *Newsweek*, noted that, "Lincoln and Darwin were both revolutionaries, in the sense that both men upended realities that prevailed when they were born. They seem—and sound—modern to us, because the world they left behind them is more or less the one we still live in" (Jones 2008).

People around the world know the definition of democracy as a form of governance "of the people, for the people and by the people," although they may not be familiar with its source, the Gettysburg Address, which Lincoln thought "the world will little note" (Lincoln 1863).

Likewise, many have heard about the Darwinian theory of evolution, and may know about the DNA or the genome. However, they may be bored by the complex history of human origins, population genetics, and applications to pharmaceuticals and modern medicine. In an editorial in the *New York Times*, Olivia Judson revealed yet another significant parallel between Lincoln and Darwin: They both disapproved of slavery. Darwin "came from a family of ardent abolitionists, and he was revolted by what he saw in slave countries" (Judson 2009).

The idea that there are hard-wired, essential differences between populations will be further repudiated with the rise of the Obama Democrats. When human populations lived in geographically isolated societies, race, language, culture, and borders were tightly nested. Rapid travel, the information revolution, and globalization all helped to obliterate these 20th-century ideas while paving the way for an American brand of multiculturalism.

As Craig Venter (2008) has said, we need medicine tailored to your genome, not your race. In a history-making event, when President Clinton announced the completion of the first survey of the book of human life or the genome on June 26, 2000, he pointed to the vast scientific landscape that has been opened by these discoveries:

Today, we are learning the language in which God created life. We are gaining ever more awe for the complex'ity, the beauty, the wonder of

God's most divine and sacred gift. With this profound new knowledge, humankind is on the verge of gaining immense new power to heal. Genome science will have a real impact on all our lives—and even more, on the lives of our children. It will revolutionize the diagnosis, prevention, and treatment of most, if not all, human diseases. (Collins 2009, 304)

Francis Fukuyama, in *Our Posthuman Future*, has claimed that the new forms of genomics and reproductive technologies are steadily ushering in Aldous Huxley's "brave new world," in need of new social and cultural policies (Fukuyama 2002). Ninety-nine percent of the human genome is shared by most people. The remaining 1 percent accounts for individual variation in phenotypic differences, such as eye and skin color or hard-wired pharmacoethnic outcomes, like the clinical response to a pharmaceutical drug.

As a senator, Obama introduced the Genomics and Personalized Medicine Act of 2006 to advance medical research and innovation, and, as president, he is likely to sponsor similar legislation in the near future. By setting aside funding for genomics research, providing tax incentives, modernizing the Food and Drug Administration and the Centers for Medicare and Medicaid Services, and offering greater consumer protections, this legislation will lead to the development of new therapies and diagnostic tests. Obama is already moving forward on his stem-cell policy. Bioethicist Arthur Caplan commented that:

Obama's decision to permit federal funding of embryonic stem cell research is—finally—the correct policy for the United States to follow. We have the scientific expertise and infrastructure to establish whether embryonic stem cell research can deliver cures. And we have sufficient moral consensus that it is the right thing to do. Obama's decision puts the sick and severely disabled at the center of federal research efforts— right where they should be. (Caplan 2009)

As Obama's election has shown, it is the natural genius of the American experiment that new-blooded Americans renew the nation's promise in successive generations. Standing on the shoulders of giants like Lincoln and Darwin, the mounting evidence from genomics in the coming decades, fortified by the greater support from governmental and private funds, will relegate the concept of race to a vestige of humanity's past.

Here Come the Solar Panels

In his campaign platform, Obama identified the 21st-century energy policy as one of the grand issues of our times. The dependence on foreign
oil is not only an economic but also a national security threat. Although
Al Gore may have popularized global warming and the need for clean
energy, anathema of many conservative-minded policy makers, today
almost everyone accepts that something has to be done about America's
dependence on foreign oil. Perhaps more than any other social policy,
transforming America's energy consumption from dependence to independence from foreign oil is central to America's growth as a leader on
multiple fronts.

It is central to the transformation that the Obama administration hoped
to achieve when he was elected under the campaign banner of the rising sun across the American prairie. Based on the turnout and results of
the 2010 midterm elections, this policy may be in jeopardy and may take
a long time to accomplish, especially with the cap-and-trade component
central to Obama's energy plans.

Jimmy Carter had hoped to reduce America's dependence on oil, and
in 1979 he sought to set an example by installing the first solar panels on
the White House roof. In 1986, however, Reagan took down the solar panels to repair the roof, and he also discontinued the solar tax benefits, which
short-circuited the budding solar industry. The panels were shipped to a
small university in Maine, where they still heat the water in the cafeteria.
After more than 30 years, solar panels have returned to the White House
as a source of real energy, but it is unclear whether a substantive policy
change will follow soon, though China is rapidly expanding its subsidized
solar power industry. Overall, the solar-panel industry has changed for
the better. The White House panels are now lighter, stronger, and more
efficient than those manufactured 30 years ago, but they must still be supported by governmental rebates and tax breaks to be economically viable.

Solar-industry advocates hope to turn the country around with the
White House example. As the costs of photovoltaic panels decline and the
solar industry scales up the use of solar energy, it will become more competitive with coal and natural gas. Solar industry will not only deploy new
technologies nationwide, but will also help America regain its leadership
in a sector it invented. It will not only create new jobs but will also, as a
source of clean energy, help reduce global warming.

Conservatives chided Obama for "channeling his inner Jimmy Carter again," which is perhaps not a good sign (Loris 2010). However, clean energy advocates are not considered oddballs or freaks any longer, and this is another trend that has changed in the past 30 years. It wouldn't be surprising at all if solar panels begin to appear on less prestigious buildings around the nation, and Obama, who hails from the sunny tropics of Hawai'i and Indonesia, is dubbed as the solar president.

As we approach another general election in 2012, it will be worth reminding ourselves based on the cultural biography of Barack Obama that he is the most diverse president we have elected in 232-year history of this country. His inauguration may have been the most globalized event watched by people around the world on television, the Internet, cell phones, Blackberries, and other high-speed devices.

As an editorial writer from the *Jakarta Post* noted about his inauguration, "Get this. He is a Chicago man, born in Hawai'i, with an African father, an Indonesian stepfather and a mother from English-Irish stock with Native American elements. His first name is Swahili for 'blessed one', his second is Arabic for 'good-looking' and his third is a town in Japan. His family members speak French, Cantonese, Bahasa Indonesia and German" (Vittachi 2009).

As a sign of the new world on the horizon, Obama's election suggested that America still has the competitive edge. If Obama succeeds in reorienting the country, specifically in terms of innovation and global security, along the axis that Huntington identified as forming the clash of civilization on both economic and cultural fronts, then Luce's American century can be a model for greater transformations in the future. There is no valid reason why, notwithstanding the emergence of other powers in the world, the American dream cannot be reimagined or has to be interrupted.

List of References

ABC News. 2010. "Obama on 'The View': Ticks Off Highs and Lows of Presidency," July 29. Accessed May 24, 2011. http://abcnews.go.com/GMA/Politics/obama-ticks-off-highs-lows-presidency-view/story?id=11276835.

Adeoti, G. 2005. "The Remaking of Africa." *African Media Review* 13, no. 2: 1–15. Accessed December 15, 2010. https://www.codesria.org/IMG/pdf/01_adeoti.pdf.

Agho, J. 2002. "Armah's Osiris Rising." *Ariel: A Review of International English Literature* 33, no. 2: 57–69. Accessed December 15, 2010. http://ariel.synergiesprairies.ca/ariel/index.php/ariel/article/view/3942/3877.

Akande, Benjamin. 2008. "The Obama Generation." Reuters News, July 7. Accessed December 3, 2010. http://www.reuters.com/article/pressRelease/idUS189202+07-Jul-2008+PRN20080707.

Ali, Tariq. 2010. *The Obama Syndrome: Surrender at Home, War Abroad*. New York: Verso Books.

Alter, Jonathan. 2010. *The Promise: President Obama, Year One*. New York: Simon and Schuster.

American Enterprise Institute for Public Policy Research (AEI). 2009. Rendezvous with Destiny: A Panel on Ronald Reagan. February 6. Accessed May 25, 2011. http://www.aei.org/event/1883.

Anthony, Ted, and Ron Fournier. 2008. "The Mythic Presidency." *The Post and Courier*, February 3. Accessed December 15, 2010. http://www.postandcourier.com/news/2008/feb/03/mythic_presidency/.

Arakawa, Lynda. 2004. "Convention Speaker Says Hawai'i Shaped His Life." *Honolulu Advertiser*, July 24. Accessed December 1, 2010. http://the.honoluluadvertiser.com/article/2004/Jul/27/ln/ln03a.html.

Armah, Ayi Kwei. 1996. *Osiris Rising*. Popenguine, Senegal: Per Ankh Press.

Asad, Talal. 1995. *Anthropology and the Colonial Encounter*. New York: Prometheus Books.

Asim, Jabri. 2009. *What Obama Means*. New York: William Morrow.

Atkinson, R. 2008. "First Digital President?" *Fast Company*, November 5. Accessed December 15, 2010. http://www.fastcompany.com/blog/robert-atkinson/washington-watch/first-digital-president.

Aubert, Jean-Eric, and Derek H. C. Chen. 2008. "The Island Factor as a Growth Booster for Nations: A Mental Advantage Econometrically Revealed." *Journal of Intellectual Capital* 9, no. 2: 178–205.

Audi, Tamara. "How Barack Obama Became the Accidental Occidental President." *Wall Street Journal*, October 9. Accessed December 2, 2010. http://online.wsj.com/article/SB125504077432074491.html.

Ausdale, Debra. 2001. *The First R*. New York: Rowman and Littlefield Publishers.

Barnes, Robert. 2008. "Obama Visits Ill 'Rock of the Family.'" *Los Angeles Times*, October 25. Accessed November 30, 2010. http://articles.latimes.com/2008/oct/25/nation/na-obama25.

Baumrind, Diane. 1966. "Effects of Authoritative Parenting Control on Child Behavior." *Child Development* 37 (4): 887–907.

Baumrind, Diane. 1967. "Child Care Practices Anteceding Three Patterns of Preschool Behavior." *Genetic Psychology Monographs* 75, no. 1: 43–88.

Bayuni, Endy M. 2009. "Obama's Indonesian Classroom." *New York Times*, January 17. Accessed November 30, 2010. http://www.nytimes.com/2009/01/18/opinion/18bayuni.html.

BBC News. 2008a. "Celebrity Reaction to Obama Win." Video, November 5. Accessed November 29, 2010. http://news.bbc.co.uk/2/hi/americas/us_elections_2008/7710681.stm.

BBC News. 2008b. "Obama Win Preferred in World Poll." September 10. Accessed November 30, 2010. http://news.bbc.co.uk/2/hi/americas/7606100.stm.

Beech, Hannah. 2010. "Why Obama Is Disappointing Asia." *Time*, March 29. Accessed December 1, 2010. http://www.time.com/time/magazine/article/0,9171,1973182,00.html.

Beinart, Peter. 2010. *The Icarus Syndrome: A History of American Hubris*. New York: Harper.

Bennetts, Leslie. 2007. "First Lady in Waiting." *Vanity Fair*, December 27. Accessed December 3, 2010. http://www.vanityfair.com/politics/features/2007/12/michelle_obama200712.

Bergen, Peter L. 2011. *The Longest War: The Enduring Conflict Between America and Al-Qaeda*. New York: Free Press.

Berry, Mary Frances, and Josh Gottheimer. 2010. *Power in Words: The Stories Behind Barack Obama's Speeches, from the State House to the White House*. Boston, MA: Beacon Press.

Blackwill, Robert, and Graham Allison. 1991. "On with the Grand Bargain." *Washington Post*, August 27. Accessed December 2, 2010. http://belfercenter.ksg.harvard.edu/publication/1301/on_with_the_grand_bargain.html.

Bloom, Alan. 1987. *The Closing of the American Mind*. New York: Simon and Schuster.

Boas, Franz. 1940. *Race, Language and Culture*. Chicago: University of Chicago Press.

Bobo, Lawrence D., and Camille Z. Charles. "Race in the American Mind: From the Moynihan Report to the Obama Presidency." *Annals of the American Academy of Political and Social Science* 621, no. 1: 243–259. Accessed May 20, 2011. http://ann.sagepub.com/content/621/1/243.abstract.

Brands, H. W. 2011. *American Dreams: The United States Since 1945*. New York: Penguin.

Branigan, Tania. 2009. "Barack Obama's Half-Brother Writes Book." *The Guardian*, November 4. Accessed December 3, 2010. http://www.guardian.co.uk/world/2009/nov/04/barack-obama-father-abuse.

Breed, Allen. 2008. "Toot: Obama Grandmother a Force that Shaped Him." *Real Clear Politics*, August 23. Accessed May 20, 2011. http://www.realclearpolitics.com/news/ap/politics/2008/Aug/23/_toot_obama_grandmother_a_force_that_shaped_him.html.

Brinkley, Alan. 2010. *The Publisher: Henry Luce and His American Century*. New York: Knopf.

Brokaw, Tom. 1998. *The Greatest Generation*. New York: Random House.

Brown, John, and Paul Duguid. 2000. *The Social Life of Information*. Boston: Harvard Business Press.

Bulkeley, Kelly. 2008. "Dreams Shed Light on Obama's Values." *San Francisco Chronicle*, August 17. Accessed May 23, 2011. http://www.sfgate.com/cgi-bin/article.cgi?file=/c/a/2008/08/17/INCU12BG4G.DTL.

Burns, James MacGregor. 1978. *Leadership*. New York: Harper & Row.

Burns, James MacGregor. 2004. *Transforming Leadership*. New York: Grove Press.

Calmes, Jackie. 2009. "On Campus, Obama and Memories." *New York Times*, January 3. Accessed December 1, 2010. http://www.nytimes.com/2009/01/03/us/politics/03Reunion.html.

Campbell, Joseph. 1949. *The Hero with a Thousand Faces*. Princeton, NJ: Princeton University Press.

Campbell, Joseph. 1988. *The Power of Myth*. New York: Anchor Books.

Caplan, Arthur. 2009. "Finally, a Coherent Stem-cell Policy." MSNBC, March 9. Accessed November 28, 2010. http://www.msnbc.msn.com/id/29588190/ns/health-health_care/.

Carter, Stephen. 2011. *The Violence of Peace: America's Wars in the Age of Obama*. New York: Daily Beast Books.

Charles, Guy-Uriel. 2008. "Election May Affect African-American Identity." The University of Virginia School of Law Web site, November 25. Accessed December 3, 2010. http://www.law.virginia.edu/html/news/2008_fall/charles.htm.

Chodorow, Nancy. 1999. *The Reproduction of Mothering*. Berkeley: University of California Press.

Churchill, Winston. 1996. *My Early Life, 1874–1904*. New York: Touchstone.

Clinton, Hillary Rodham. 1996. *It Takes a Village*. New York: Simon and Schuster.

CNN/Opinion Research. 2011. Opinion research poll, May 6, 2011. Accessed May 24, 2011. http://i2.cdn.turner.com/cnn/2011/images/05/06/rel7d.pdf.

Coffman, Tom. 1973. *Catch a Wave: A Case Study of Hawai'i's New Politics*. Honolulu: University of Hawai'i Press.

Cohen, Roger. 2008. "The Obamas of the World." *New York Times*, March 6. Accessed December 12, 2010. http://www.nytimes.com/2008/03/06/opinion/06cohen.html?_r=1.

Collins, Francis. 2009. *The Language of Life*. New York: Harper Collins.

Collins, Gail. 2009. *When Everything Changed*. New York: Little Brown.

Cooper, Frank. 2009. "Our First Unisex President?" *Denver University Law Review* 86: 633.

Corsi, Jerome R. 2008. *Obama Nation: Leftist Politics and the Cult of Personality*. New York: Simon and Schuster.

Corsi, Jerome R. 2009. "Obama Mama: 15 Days from Birth to Seattle Class." *World Net Daily*, August 4. Accessed November 30, 2010. http://www.wnd.com/index.php?pageId=106018.

Corsi, Jerome R. 2011. *Where Is the Birth Certificate? The Case that Barack Obama Is Not Eligible to Be President*. New York: WND Books.

Dawidoff, Nicholas. 2010. "The Civil Heretic." *New York Times*, March 25. Accessed November 29, 2010. http://www.nytimes.com /2009/03/29/magazine/29Dyson-t.html.

De Beauvoir, Simone. 1989. *The Second Sex*. New York: Vintage.

Deloitte Consulting, LLP. 2008. "New Media and the 2008 Election Campaign Season." Accessed December 15, 2010. http://www.deloitte .com/dtt/article/0,1002,cid%253D195149,00.html.

Democracy Now. 2007. "Studs Terkel at 95: 'Ordinary People Are Capable of Doing Extraordinary Things, and That's What It's All About. They Must Count!'" Democracy Now Web site, May 16. Accessed December 1, 2010. http://www.democracynow.org/2007/5/16/studs_terkel_at_95 _ordinary_people.

Detweiler, Robert. 1996. "Dreams from My Father (Book Review)." *Choice* 33: 1012.

Devos, Thiery, Debbie Ma, and Travis Gaffud. 2008. "Is Barack Obama American Enough to Be the Next President?" Poster presentation. San Diego State University Web site, Accessed December 2, 2010. http:// www-rohan.sdsu.edu/~tdevos/thd/Devos_spsp2008.pdf.

Dewey, John. 2006. "Quotations on Education." In *Classic Wisdom for a Good Life*, edited by Bryan Curtis, 16. Nashville, TN: Rutledge Hill Press.

Donne, John. 1962. *Sermons of John Donne: Meditations 17, 1623*. Berkeley: University of California Press.

Dougherty, Conor. 2010a. "Some States Already Have 'Majority-Minority' of Kids." *Wall Street Journal* blogs, June 11. Accessed December 1, 2010. http://blogs.wsj.com/economics/2010/06/11/some-states -already-have-majority-minority-of-kids/?mod=e2tw.

Dougherty, Conor. 2010b. "U.S. Nears a Racial Milestone." *Wall Street Journal*, June 11. Accessed December 2, 2010. http://online.wsj .com/article/SB10001424052748704312104575298512006681060.html.

Dowd, Maureen. 2008a. "Cyclops and Cunning." *New York Times*, July 30. Accessed December 15, 2010. http://www.nytimes.com/2008 /07/30/opinion/30dowd.html?scp=1&sq=cyclops&st=cse.

Dowd, Maureen. 2008b. "More Phony Myths." *New York Times*, June 25. Accessed December 2, 2010. http://www.nytimes.com/2008/06/25/opinion/25dowd.html.

Du Bois, W.E.B. 1903. *The Souls of Black Folk*. New York: Dodd, Mead.

Dunham, Ann. 1992. "Peasant Blacksmithing in Indonesia: Surviving and Thriving Against All Odds." PhD diss., University of Hawai'i.

Dunham, Stanley Ann. 2009. *Surviving Against the Odds*. Edited and with a preface by Alice G. Dewey and Nancy I. Cooper. Durham, NC: Duke University Press.

Dyson, Freeman. 1999. *The Sun, the Genome and the Internet*. New York: Oxford University Press.

East-West Center. 2010. "EWC 50 Spotlight, July 2-5." Accessed November 30, 2010. http://www.eastwestcenter.org/index.php?id=5590&print=1.

Economist. "Democracy in America, Vote 2008." Accessed November 30, 2010. http://www.economist.com/Vote2008/.

Edwards, Joella. 2008. "Buff'n Blue and Black." In *Obamaland*, edited by Ron Jacobs, 60–63. Honolulu: Trade Publishing.

Eijun, Senaha. 2008. "Barack Obama and His Story." *Nanzan Review of American Studies* 30: 211–221. Accessed December 15, 2010. http://www.ic.nanzan-u.ac.jp/AMERICA/kanko/documents/32Senaha.pdf.

Elaide, Mircea. 1954. *Cosmos and History: Myth of the Eternal Return*. Chicago: University of Chicago Press.

Emerson, Ralph Waldo. 2003. *Selected Writings of Ralph Waldo Emerson*. New York: Penguin.

Erikson, Erik. 1958. *Young Man Luther*. New York: W. W. Norton.

Erikson, Erik. 1963. *Childhood and Society*. New York: W. W. Norton.

Erikson, Erik. 1969. *Gandhi's Truth: On the Origins of Militant Non-violence*. New York: W. W. Norton.

Erikson, Erik. 1972. *Insight and Responsibility*. New York: W. W. Norton.

Escobar, Pepe. 2009. *Obama Does Globalistan*. Ann Arbor, MI: Nimble Books.

Escobar, Pepe. 2011. "Welcome to the Post-Osama World." *Asia Times Online*, May 5. Accessed May 25, 2011. http://www.atimes.com/atimes/Middle_East/ME06Ak01.html.

Essoyan, Susan. 2008. "A Woman of the People." *Star Bulletin* 13:257, September 13. Accessed December 3, 2010. http://archives.starbulletin.com/2008/09/13/news/story09.html.

Falk, Avner. 2010. *The Riddle of Barack Obama: A Psychobiogarphy*. Westport, CT: Praeger.

Fanon, Franz. 1967. *Black Skin, White Masks*. New York: Grove.

Feller, Ben, and Erica Werner. 2010. "Obama's Asia Trip Shows America's Limits." *Times Herald*. Accessed November 28, 2010. http://www.timesherald.com/articles/2010/11/14/business/doc4ce0a37762e48440466435.txt.

Firstbrook, Peter. 2010. *The Obamas: The Untold Story of an African Family*. New York: Preface Publishing.

Foner, Eric. 2004. "Rethinking American History in the Post-9/11 World." *History News Network*, Spetember 6. Accessed December 3, 2010. http://hnn.us/articles/6961.html.

Foster, Richard. and Sarah Kaplan. 2001. *Creative Destruction*. New York: Random House.

Frank, Andrew, and Matthew McBee. 2003. "The Use of Harry Potter and the Sorcerer's Stone to Discuss Identity Development with Gifted Adolescents." *Journal of Secondary Gifted Education* 15: 33–39.

Freddoso, David. 2008. *The Case Against Barack Obama: The Unlikely Rise and Unexamined Agenda of the Media's Favorite Candidate*. Washington, D.C.: Regnery Publishers.

Freud, Sigmund. 1901. *The Interpretation of Dreams*. London: Hogarth Press.

Freud, Sigmund. 1919. *Totem and Taboo*. London: Hogarth Press.

Freud, Sigmund. 1939. *Moses and Monotheism*. New York: Basic Books.

Freud, Sigmund. 1957. *The Life and Work of Sigmund Freud*. 3 vols. New York: Basic Books.

Friedman, Thomas. 2010. "What 7 Republicans Could Do." *New York Times*, July 7. Accessed November 26, 2010. http://www.nytimes.com/2010/07/21/opinion/21friedman.html.

Fukuyama, Francis. 2002. *Our Posthuman Future*. New York: Farrar, Strauss and Giroux.

Gammell, Caroline. 2009. "Academic Prowess of Obama's Mother Revealed." *The Telegraph*, September 16. Accessed December 3, 2010. http://www.telegraph.co.uk/news/worldnews/northamerica/usa/barackobama/6196237/Academic-prowess-of-Barack-Obamas-mother-disclosed.html.

Gardner, David. 2009. "America Is Not—and Never Will Be—at War with Islam." *The Daily Mail*, June 5. Accessed December 5, 2010. http://

www.dailymail.co.uk/news/worldnews/article-1190726/America—war -Islam-Barack-Hussein-Obama-courts-billion-Muslims.html.

Gardner, Howard. 1983. *Frames of Mind: A Theory of Multiple Intelligences*. New York: Basic Books.

Gardner, Howard, and Emma Laskins. 1996. *Leading Minds*. New York: Basic Books.

Geertz, Clifford. 1977. *Interpretation of Cultures*. New York: Basic Books.

Gilligan, Carol. 1993. *In a Different Voice*. Cambridge, MA: Harvard University Press.

Glauberman, Stu, and Jerry Burris. 2008. *The Dream Begins: How Hawai'i Shaped Barack Obama*. Honolulu: Watermark.

Glazer, Nathan. 1996. *We Are All Multiculturalists Now*. Cambridge, MA: Harvard University Press.

Goldenberg, Suzzane. 2008. "U.S. Election 2008." *The Guardian*, July 11. Accessed December 2, 2010. http://www.guardian.co.uk/world/2008/jul/11/barackobama.uselections2008.

Goleman, Daniel. 1997. *Emotional Intelligence*. New York: Basic Books.

Gordon, Larry. 2007. "Occidental Recalls Barry Obama." *Los Angeles Times*, January 29. Accessed December 2, 2010. http://articles.latimes .com/2007/jan/29/local/me-oxy29.

Gore, Albert. 2007. "Nobel lecture, December 10." Oslo, Norway. Nobel Prize Web site. Accessed December 3, 2010. http://nobelprize.org /mediaplayer/index.php?id=796.

Gullan, Harold. 2001. *Faith of Our Mothers*. Grand Rapids, MI: Eerdmans Publishing.

Guriev, Sergie, Maxim Trudolyubov, and Aleh Tsyvinski. 2008. "Russian Attitudes Towards the West." Working Paper 135, Center for Economic and Financial Research at New Economic School. Accessed May 25, 2011. http://www.econ.yale.edu/faculty1/tsyvinski/WP135.pdf.

Hachigian, Nina, and Mona Sutphen. 2008. *The Next American Century*. New York: Simon and Schuster.

Hart, Keith. 2000. *The Memory Bank*. London: Profile Books. Accessed December 10, 2010. http://www.thememorybank.co.uk/book/.

Hefner, R. 2009. Afterword. In *Surviving Against the Odds* by Ann S. Dunham. Durham, NC: Duke University Press.

Hendrowinoto, Nurinwa. 2009. *Obama Party in Bali*. Bali, Indonesia: Udayana University Press.

Henri-Levy, Bernard. 2007. *American Vertigo*. New York: Random House.

Herman, Arthur. 2008. *Gandhi and Churchill: The Epic Rivalry that Destroyed an Empire and Forged Our Age.* New York: Bantam Books.

Hoare, Carol. 2002. *Erikson on Development in Adulthood.* New York: Oxford University Press.

Hodge, Roger D. 2010. *The Mendacity of Hope: Barack Obama and the Betrayal of American Liberalism.* New York: Harper Collins.

Hofstadter, Richard. 1966. *Anti-Intellectualism in American Life.* New York: Penguin Press.

Hofstadter, Richard. 1996. *The Paranoid Style in American Politics and Other Essays.* Cambridge, MA: Harvard University Press.

Hollinger, David. 2008. "Obama, Blackness and Postethnic America." *The Chronicle of Higher Education* 54, no. 25 (February 29): B7.

Homans, Peter. 1989. *The Ability to Mourn: Disillusionment and the Social Origins of Psychoanalysis.* Chicago: University of Chicago Press.

Huntington, Samuel P. 1998. *The Clash of Civilizations and the Remaking of World Order.* New York: Simon and Schuster.

Huntington, Samuel P. 2004. *Who Are We?: The Challenges to America's National Identity.* New York: Simon and Schuster.

Ifill, Gwen. 2008. *Breakthrough.* New York: Doubleday.

Iyer, Pico. 2009. "Outsourcing American Dreams and Hollywood Endings." *Los Angeles Times*, May 17. Accessed May 25, 2011. http://articles.latimes.com/2009/may/17/opinion/oe-iyer17/2.

Jacobs, Sally. 2008. "A Father's Charmed Absence." *Boston Globe*, September 21. Accessed December 3, 2010. http://www.boston.com/news/politics/2008/articles/2008/09/21/a_fathers_charm_absence/.

Jacobs, Sally. 2011. *The Other Obama: The Bold and Reckless Life of President Obama's Father.* New York: Public Affairs.

Jacoby, T. 2004. *Reinventing the Melting Pot.* New York: Basic Books.

James, William. 1909. *Pluralistic Universe.* Lincoln, NE: University of Nebraska Press.

Jefferson, Thomas. 2004. *The Papers of Thomas Jefferson, Volume 31: 1 February 1799 to 31 May 1800*, 126–130. Princeton, NJ: Princeton University Press. Accessed November 28, 2010. http://www.princeton.edu/~tjpapers/munford/munford.html.

Jones, Malcolm. 2008. "Who Was More Important: Darwin or Lincoln?" *Newsweek*, June 28. Accessed November 27, 2010. http://www.newsweek.com/2008/06/28/who-was-more-important-lincoln-or-darwin.html.

Jones, Tim. 2007. "Barack Obama: Mother Not Just a Girl from Kansas." *Chicago Tribune*, March 27. Accessed November 28, 2010. http://www.chicagotribune.com/news/politics/obama/chi-0703270151mar27-archive,0,2623808.story.

Judson, Olivia. 2009. "The Origin of Darwin." *New York Times*, February 11. Accessed December 15, 2010. http://www.nytimes.com/2009/02/12/opinion/12judson.html.

Jung, Carl. 1956. *Symbols of Transformation*. Princeton, NJ: Princeton University Press.

Jung, Carl. 1973. *Mandala Symbolism: A Collection of Three Works*. Translated by R.F.C. Hull. Princeton, NJ: Princeton University Press.

Kakar, Sudhir. 1981. *The Inner World: A Psychoanalytic Study of Childhood and Society in India*. New Delhi, India: Oxford University Press.

Kakutani, Michiko. 2010. "Seeking Identity, Shaping a Nation's." Review of *The Bridge*, by David Remnick. *New York Times*, April 5. Accessed December 3, 2010. http://www.nytimes.com/2010/04/06/books/06book.html.

Kantor, Jodi. 2009a. "Nation's Many Faces in Extended First Family." *New York Times*, January 20. Accessed December 2, 2010. http://www.nytimes.com/learning/teachers/featured_articles/20090126monday.html.

Kantor, Jodi. 2009b. "Obama Supporters Take His Middle Name as Their Own." *New York Times*, June 28. Accessed December 2, 2010. http://www.nytimes.com/2008/06/29/world/americas/29iht-29hussein.14068007.html.

Kay, Rob. "Obama's Hawai'i Neighborhood." Obama's Neighborhood Web site. Accessed December 1, 2010. http://obamasneighborhood.com/makiki.html.

Kendall, Diane. 2007. *Sociology in Our Times*. Belmont, CA: Wadsworth Books.

Klein, Aaron, and Brenda Elliott. 2010. *The Manchurian President: Barack Obama's Ties to Communists, Socialists, and Other Anti-American Extremists*. New York: WND Books.

Kristoff, Nicholas. 2007. "Obama: Man of the World." *New York Times*, March 6. Accessed November 30, 2010. http://select.nytimes.com/2007/03/06/opinion/06kristof.html.

Kruse, Robert. 2009. "The Geographical Imagination of Barack Obama: Representing Race and Space in America." *Southeastern Geographer* 49, no. 3: 221–239.

Kuhn, Thomas. 1962. *Structure of Scientific Revolution*. Chicago: University of Chicago Press.

Kuroda, Yasumasa. 2009. "*Ha* Model of Multi-Ethnic-Culture in a City Without Majority." *Behaviormetrika* 36, no. 2:181–203. Accessed May 25, 2011. http://www.jstage.jst.go.jp/browse/bhmk/36/2/_contents.

Kuttner, Robert. 2008. *Obama's Challenge: America's Economic Crisis and the Power of a Transformative Presidency*. White River Junction, VT: Chelsea Green Publishing.

Kuttner, Robert. 2010. *The Presidency in Peril: The Inside Story of Obama's Promise, Wall Street's Power, and the Struggle to Control Our Economic Future*. White River Junction, VT: Chelsea Green Publishing.

Lacan, Jacques. 1968. *The Language of the Self*. Baltimore: Johns Hopkins Press.

Landler, Mark. 2009. "In Obama's Boyhood Home, Clinton Hails Indonesian Politics." *New York Times*, February 19. Accessed December 3, 2010. http://www.nytimes.com/2009/02/19/washington/19diplo.html.

Lao-Tzu. 1992. *Tao Te Ching*. Translated by Stephen Mitchell. New York: Harper Perennial.

Lee, Jennifer. 2008. "Like the Dwights and Lyndons of Old, Baby Baracks All Over." *New York Times*, November 8. Accessed December 3, 2010. http://www.nytimes.com/2008/11/10/us/politics/10babies.html?_r=1.

Levine, Lawrence. 1997. *The Opening of the American Mind*. New York: Beacon Press.

Levinson, Daniel J. 1984. *The Seasons of a Man's Life*. New York: Ballantine Books.

Lewin, Ellen. 2006. *Feminist Anthropology: A Reader*. New York: Wiley-Blackwell.

Lin, Sara. 2008. "Obama Slept Here." *Wall Street Journal*, November 7. Accessed November 29, 2010. http://online.wsj.com/article/SB122600398764506079.html.

Lincoln, Abraham. 1863. "The Gettysburg Address." Accessed May 24, 2011. http://www.ourdocuments.gov/doc.php?flash=true&doc=36.

Lincoln, Abraham. 1953. "Annual Message to Congress, December 1, 1862." In *The Collected Works of Abraham Lincoln*, edited by Roy Basler. New Brunswick, NJ: Rutgers University Press. Accessed November 26, 2010. http://showcase.netins.net/web/creative/lincoln/speeches/congress.htm.

Litwak, Robert. 2002. "The Imperial Republic After 9/11." *The Wilson Quarterly* 26 (June): 76–82. Accessed December 3, 2010. http://www.wilson center.org/topics/pubs/imperial.pdf.

Loris, Nicholas. 2010. "White House Solar Installation Symbolic of Solar Energy Push." *The Foundry*, October 5. Accessed December 15, 2010. http://blog.heritage.org/2010/10/05/white-house-solar-installation -symbolic-of-solar-energy-push/.

Mansfield, Stephen. 2008. *The Faith of Barack Obama*. Nashville, TN: Thomas Nelson.

Maraniss, D. 2008. "Though Obama Had to Leave to Find Himself, It Is Hawai'i that Made His Rise Possible." *Washington Post*, August 22. Accessed December 15, 2010. http://www.washingtonpost.com/wp-dyn /content/article/2008/08/22/AR2008082201679.html.

Marzui, Ali. 1987. *Africa: A Triple Heritage*. New York: Little Brown.

McAdam, Thomas. 2009. "Teacher Claims to Remember Obama's Birth." *Louisville City Hall Examiner*, July 15. Accessed November 30, 2010. http:// www.examiner.com/city-hall-in-louisville/teacher-claims-to-remember -obama-s-birth.

McAdams, Dan P. 2011. *George W. Bush and the Redemptive Dream: A Psychological Portrait*. New York: Oxford University Press.

McClelland, Edward. 2010. *Young Mr. Obama: Chicago and the Making of a Black President*. New York: Bloomsbury Press.

McGinley, Ann. 2009. "Hillary Clinton, Sarah Palin, and Michelle Obama: Performing Gender, Race, and Class on the Campaign Trail." *University of Denver Law Review*, March 6. Accessed December 3, 2010. http://law.du.edu/documents/denver-university-law-review/mcginley.pdf.

McGirt, Ellen. 2009. "How Chris Hughes Helped Launch Facebook and the Barack Obama Campaign," *Fast Company*, April 1. Accessed December 2, 2010, http://www.fastcompany.com/magazine/134/boy wonder .html.

McLuhan, Marshall, and Bruce Powers. 1992. *The Global Village*. New York: Oxford University Press.

Meacham, John. 2008. "On His Own." *Newsweek*, August 22. Accessed December 15, 2010. http://www.newsweek.com/2008/08/22 /on-his-own.html.

Media Matters. 2010. "Newsweek's Alter Slams Fox-promoted Obama Myths." *Media Matters*, August 30. Accessed December 3, 2010. http://mediamatters.org/blog/201008300028.

Megawangi, Ratna. 1997. "Gender Perspectives in Early Childhood Care and Development in Indonesia." *Coordinator's Notebook*, No. 20. Accessed December 4, 2010. http://www.ecdgroup.com/download/ca120fgs.pdf.

Melville, Herman. 1849. *Redburn: His First Voyage.* New York: Harper & Brothers.

Mendell, David. 2007. *Obama, from Promise to Power.* New York: Harper Collins.

Merton, Thomas. 1955. *No Man Is an Island.* Boston: Shambhala Books.

Mishan, Ligaya. 2008. "Election 2008." *New Yorker*, November 3. Accessed December 3, 2010. http://www.newyorker.com/online/blogs/books/2008/11/election-2008-n.html.

Moore, Elizabeth. 2009. "Obama's Mother, Hillary Clinton." *Seattle Times*, December 28. Accessed November 28, 2010. http://seattle-times.nwsource.com/html/nationworld/2008568642_oblinton29.html?syndication=rss.

Moore, Sarah, and Aubrey Immelman. 2008. "Obama's Conciliatory Tendency Could Be Cause for Concern." Unit for the Study of Personality in Politics, St. John's University, Minnesota. Accessed December 4, 2010. http://www1.csbsju.edu/uspp/Obama/Obama_Moore_10-15-2008.html.

Morris, Ian. 2010. *Why the West Rules—For Now: The Patterns of History, and What They Reveal About the Future.* New York: Farrar Straus Geroux.

Naipaul, V. S. 1984. *Finding the Center.* New York: Knopf.

Ndesandjo, Mark Obama. 2010. *Nairobi to Shenzhen.* San Diego, CA: Aventine Press.

Nenni, Scott. 2005. "The Russian Coup of 1991." UCLA International Institute, December 9. Accessed December 3, 2010. http://www.international.ucla.edu/article.asp?parentid=35414.

Neumann, Erich. 1954. *Origins and the History of Consciousness.* Princeton, NJ: Princeton University Press.

Neumann, Erich. 1972. *The Great Mother*, translated by Ralph Manheim. Princeton, NJ: Princeton University Press.

Nishimura, Shigeo. 1995. "The Development of Pancasila Moral Education in Indonesia." *Southeast Asian Studies* 333: 303–316.

Nordhal, Rolf. 2008. "Gramp's Dream." In *Obamaland*, edited by Ron Jacobs. Honolulu: Trade Publishing.

Norgren, Jill, and Sarena Nanada. 2006. *American Cultural Pluralism and Law.* Westport, CT: Praeger Publishers.

Nurbaiti, Ati. 2010. "Cheer Amid the Gloom." *Jakarta Post*, December 8. Accessed November 30, 2010. http://www.thejakartapost .com/news/2010/11/14/cheer-amid-gloom.html.

Obama, Barack. 1965. "Problems Facing Our Socialism." *East African Journal* 2–3 (July): 26–36.

Obama, Barack. 2004a. *Dreams from My Father: A Story of Race and Inheritance.* Rev. ed. New York: Three Rivers Press.

Obama, Barack. 2004b. "Keynote Speech to the DNC 2004 on C-Span." YouTube. Accessed November 28, 2010. http://www.youtube .com/watch?v=eWynt87PaJ0.

Obama, Barack. 2005. "What I See in Lincoln's Eyes." *Time*, June 26. Accessed December 2, 2010. http://www.time.com/time/magazine/ article/0,9171,1077287,00.html.

Obama, Barack. 2006. *The Audacity of Hope: Thoughts on Reclaiming the American Dream.* New York: Vintage.

Obama, Barack. 2007. "Illinois Senator Barack Obama's Announce-ment Speech." *Washington Post*, February 10. Accessed December 5, 2010. http://www.washingtonpost.com/wp-dyn/content/article/2007/02/10/ AR2007021000879.html.

Obama, Barack. 2008a. "Obama's Race Speech." Huffington Post. Accessed May 11, 2011. http://www.huffingtonpost.com/2008/03/18/ obama-race-speech-read-th_n_92077.html.

Obama, Barack. 2008. "This Is Your Victory." Speech presented at Grant Park, Chicago, IL. CNNPolitics. Accessed November 28, 2010. http://edition.cnn.com/2008/POLITICS/11/04/obama.transcript/.

Obama, Barack. 2008b. "Transcript: Obama's Speech on Rev. Wright." April 29, 2008. Accessed May 24, 2011. http://www.npr.org/templates/ story/story.php?storyId=90040477.

Obama, Barack. 2010a. "Obama Holds a Town Hall Meeting; the First Lady Also Attends." Transcript of a speech presented at St. Xavier College, Mumbai, India, November 7. "In Obama's Words," *Washington Post*. Accessed December 4, 2010. http://projects.washingtonpost.com/ obama-speeches/speech/481/.

Obama, Barack. 2010. Obama's Prepared Remarks in Indonesia. *Wall Street Journal*, November 9. Accessed May 12, 2011. http://blogs.wsj.com/ washwire/2010/11/09/full-text-obamas-prepared-remarks-in-indonesia/.

Obama, Barack. 2010b. "President Obama's Speech in Jakarta, Indonesia." November 9. Accessed May 25, 2011. http://www.america.gov /st/texttrans-english/2010/November/20101109213225su0.4249035.html.

Obama, Barack. 2010c. "President Barack Obama's remarks to the Indian Parliament." *Wall Street Journal*, November 8. Accessed December 4, 2010. http://blogs.wsj.com/indiarealtime/2010/11/08/president-barack-obamas-remarks-to-indias-parliament/.

Obama, Barack. 2011. "Obama's Mideast Speech." *New York Times*, May 19. Accessed on May 25, 2011. http://www.nytimes.com/2011/05/20/world/middleeast/20prexy-text.html.

Obama, Barack, and Joseph Biden. 2008. "Science, Technology and Innovation for a New Generation." Accessed May 25, 2011. http://www.moveleft.org/obamas_promises/www_barackobama_com_issues_technology.pdf.

Ogbu, John. 1978. *Minority Education and Caste: The American System in Cross-Cultural Perspective*. San Diego, CA: Academic Press.

Onishi, Norimitsu. 2010. "Obama Visits a Nation that Knew Him as Barry." *New York Times*, November 8. Accessed December 3, 2010. http://www.nytimes.com/2010/11/09/world/asia/09indo.html?pagewanted=all.

Onofre, Clara. 2008. "The Lusosphere for Obama." Global Voices Web site, November 5. Accessed November 27. 2010. http://global-voicesonline.org/2008/11/05/the-lusosphere-for-obama/.

O'Toole, James. 2008. "Obama vs. Clinton: Leadership Styles." *Business Week*, February 8. Accessed December 5, 2010. http://www.businessweek.com/managing/content/feb2008/ca2008028_331189.htm.

Oxford Analytica. "Europe Breaks Away from Multiculturalism." *Forbes*, November 20. Accessed November 26, 2010. http://www.forbes.com/2006/11/17/multiculturalism-assimilation-europe-biz-cx_1120oxford.html.

Pang, George. 2004. "Democrats Call Obama Hawai'i's Third Senator." *Honolulu Advertiser*, December 17. Accessed December 1, 2010. http://the.honoluluadvertiser.com/article/2004/Dec/17/ln/ln20p.html.

Pew Research. 2006. "Russia's Weakened Democratic Embrace: Prosperity Tops Political Reform." Accessed May 24, 2011. http://pewglobal.org/2006/01/05/russias-weakened-democratic-embrace/.

Pew Research. 2010a. "Growing Number of Americans Believe Obama Is Muslim." August 19. Accessed December 3, 2010. http://pewresearch.org/pubs/1701/poll-obama-muslim-christian-church-out-of-politics-political-leaders-religious.

Pew Research. 2010b. "Obama More Popular Abroad than at Home, Global image of U.S. Continues to Benefit." June 17. Accessed December 3, 2010. http://pewglobal.org/2010/06/17/obama-more-popular-abroad-than-at-home/.

Pew Research. 2010c. "Public Divided Over Tone of Mosque Fight." September 1. Accessed December 3, 2010. http://pewresearch.org/pubs /1715/tone-of-debate-over-new-york-mosque-debate.

Pflanz, Mike. 2009. "Obama Tells Africa to Stop Blaming the West for its Woes." *The Telegraph*, July 11. Accessed December 2, 2010. http://www.telegraph.co.uk/news/worldnews/northamerica/usa/baracko bama/5804828/Barack-Obama-tells-Africa-to-stop-blaming-the-West -for-its-woes-on-historic-Ghana-visit.html.

Phillipp, Joshua. 2010. "Obama's Asia Trip Has China Tensions as Underlying Theme." *Epoch Times*, November 25. Accessed November 28, 2010. http://www.theepochtimes.com/n2/content/view/45844/.

Pickler, Nedra. 2008. "Obama Visits Grandfather's Kansas Town." *USA Today*, January 29. Accessed November 30, 2010. http://www .usatoday.com/news/politics/2008-01-29-2873054939_x.htm.

Pipes, Daniel. 2008. "Barack Obama's Muslim Childhood." *History News Network*, April 29. Accessed December 15, 2010. http://hnn.us /roundup/entries/50148.html.

Powell, Colin. Goldman Sachs Foundation for International Educa- tion. Accessed December 3, 2010. http://sites.asiasociety.org/education /prizes/2003.htm.

Powell, Michael. 2008. "The American Wanderer, in All His Stripes." *New York Times*, August 4. Accessed December 2, 2010. http://www .nytimes.com/2008/08/24/weekinreview/24powe.html?ref=michaelpowell.

Punahou School. Campus. September 21, 2010. Accessed December 1, 2010. http://www.punahou.edu/page.cfm?p=1539.

Purdum, Todd. 2008. "Raising Obama." *Vanity Fair*, March. Accessed December 7, 2010. http://www.vanityfair.com/politics/features/2008/03/ obama200803.

Purie, Arun. 2010. "India Today Editor-In-Chief Aroon Purie on Gains from the Obama Visit." *India Today*, November 11. Accessed November 27, 2010. http://indiatoday.intoday.in/site/Story/119521/Editors.

Putri, Nadhifa. 2008. "Jejak Barack Obama: Dari menteng dalam ke dempo." April 2. Accessed November 30, 2010. http://laotze.blogspot.com/ 2008/02/obama-on-indonesian-television-part-1.html.

Raasch, Chuck. 2009."Obama is America's First Global President." *USA Today*, April 7. Accessed June 6, 2011. http://www.usatoday.com/ news/opinion/columnist/raasch/2009-04-07-newpolitics_N.htm.

Rank, Otto. 1914. *The Myth of the Birth of the Hero*. New York: Journal of the Nervous and Mental Disease Publications.

Rapier, Robert. 2009. "Vinod Khosla at Milken Institute: Part III." *Consumer Energy Report*, May 4. Accessed November 28, 2010. http://www.consumerenergyreport.com/2009/05/04/vinod-khosla-at-milken-institute-part-iii/.

Remnick, David. 2010. *The Bridge: The Life and Rise of Barack Obama*. New York: Random House.

Renshon, Stanley. 2004. *In His Father's Shadow: The Transformations of George W. Bush*. New York: Macmillan.

Reppen, Joseph. 1985. *Beyond Freud*. Mahwah, NJ: Analytic Press.

Rheingold, Howard. 2002. *Smart Mobs: The Next Social Revolution*. New York: Basic Books.

Rich, Frank. 2010. "Barack Obama Phone Home." *New York Times*, November 6. Accessed November 26, 2010. http://www.nytimes.com/2010/11/07/opinion/07rich.html.

Richter, Stephen. 2008. "Obama's Secret: The Son Bill and Hillary Never Had." *The Globalist*, February 20. Accessed December 15, 2010. http://www.theglobalist.com/storyid.aspx?storyid=6096.

Ripley, A. 2008. "The Story of Barack Obama's Mother." *Time*, April 9. Accessed December 15, 2010. http://www.time.com/time/nation/article/0,8599,1729524,00.html.

Rochman, Hazel. 1995. "Dreams from My Father: A Story of Race and Inheritance." *Booklist* 91, no. 21 (July), 1844.

Rogers, Everett. 1995. *Diffusion of Innovations*. New York: Simon and Schuster.

Sachs, Jeffery. 1998. "Globalization and the Rule of Law." Paper presented at Yale Law School Lillian Goldman Law Library, New Haven, CT. Accessed May 3, 2011. http://www.earth.columbia.edu/sitefiles/file/about/director/pubs/YaleLawSchool1098.pdf.

Sandburg, Carl. 1950. *The Complete Poems of Carl Sandburg*. New York: Harcourt.

Schachtman, Thomas. 2009. *Airlift to America*. New York: St. Martin's Press.

Schumacher, E. F. 1973. *Small Is Beautiful*. New York: Blond and Briggs.

Schumpeter, Joseph. 1974. *Capitalism, Socialism and Democracy*. New York: Routledge.

Scott, Janny. 2011. *A Singular Woman: The Untold Story of Barack Obama's Mother*. New York: Riverhead Books.

Sharma, Dinesh. 2004. *Human Technogenesis: Cultural Pathways through the Information Age*. New York: John Wiley.

Sharma, Dinesh. 2008a. "Obama's Satyagraha: Or, Did Obama Swallow the Mahatma?" *OpEdNews*, June 27. Accessed December 3, 2010. http://www.opednews.com/articles/Obama-s-Satyagraha—Or—Di -by-Dinesh-Sharma-080626-187.html.

Sharma, Dinesh. 2008b. "New-blooded Americans: Obamagenomics and the End of Race." *Media Monitors Network*, September 8. Accessed December 3, 2010. http://world.mediamonitors.net/content/view/full/54568/.

Sharma, Dinesh. 2008c. "Post-Obama World: Can America Close the Achievement Gap?" *OpEdNews*, September 27. Accessed November 28, 2010. http://www.opednews.com/articles/Post-Obama-World-Can-Amer- by-Dinesh-Sharma-080926-733.html.

Sharma, Dinesh. 2008d. "What's in a Name Anyway?" *Middle East Online*, July 17. Accessed December 3, 2010. http://www.middle-east -online.com/english/?id=26965.

Sharma, Dinesh. and Kurt W. Fischer. 1989. *Socioemotional Development Across Cultures*. New Directions for Child and Adolescent Development, No. 81. New York: John Wiley.

Sheehy, Gail. 1996. *New Passages: Mapping Your Life Across Time*. New York: Ballantine Books.

Shweder, Richard. 2007. "A True Culture War." *New York Times*, October 27. Accessed December 15, 2010. http://www.nytimes.com/2007/ 10/27/opinion/27shweder.html.

Shweder, Richard, and Robert Levine. 1984. *Culture Theory: Essays on Mind, Self, and Emotion*. New York: Cambridge University Press.

Siddiqui, Haroon. 2007. "Obama's Muslim Heritage." *Toronto Star*, June 14. Accessed November 30, 2010. http://www.thestar.com/comment/ article/225233.

Silverthorne, S. 2006. "Developing Strategy for Digital Convergence." HBS Working Knowledge, July 17. Accessed May 25, 2011. http://hbswk .hbs.edu/item/5445.html.

Soetoro-Ng, Maya. 2009. Foreword. In *Surviving Against the Odds* by Ann Dunham Soetoro. 2008. Durham, NC: Duke University Press.

Solis, Brian, and Diedre Breakenridge. *Putting the Public Back in Public Relations*. Saddle River, NJ: Pearson Education Press.

Spengler. 2008. "Obama's Women Reveal His Secret." *Asia Times Online*, February 26. Accessed December 5, 2010. http://www.atimes .com/atimes/Front_Page/JB26Aa01.html.

Starobin, Paul. 2009. *After-America: Narratives of the Next Global Age*. New York: Viking.

Steele, Shelby. 2007. *A Bound Man: Why We Are Excited About Obama and Why He Can't Win*. New York: Free Press.

Steinhauer, Jennifer. 2007. "Charisma and a Search for Self in Obama's Hawai'i an Childhood." *New York Times*, March 17. Accessed December 15, 2010. http://www.nytimes.com/2007/03/17/us/politics/17hawai'i.html.

Stelter, Brian. 2008. "The Facebooker Who Friended Obama." *New York Times*, July 7. Accsessed May 25, 2011. http://www.nytimes.com/2008/07/07/technology/07hughes.html.

Sternberg, Robert. 2008. "The WICS Approach to Leadership." *Leadership Quarterly* 19, no. 3: 360–371.

Stevens, Anthony. 1997. *Private Myths: Dreams and Dreaming*. Cambridge, MA: Harvard University Press.

Strupp, Joe. 2011. "Corsi: We Are Still Asking 'Where Is the Birth Certificate?'" *Media Matters*, May 19. Accessed May 28, 2011. http://mediamatters.org/blog/201105190033.

Suryakusuma, Julia. 2004. *Sex, Power and Nation*. Jakarta, Indonesia: Metafor Books.

Takaki, Ronald. 1993. *A Different Mirror: A History of Multicultural America*. Boston: Little Brown.

Takaki, Ronald. 2008. "Barack Obama: A Candidate Whose Time Has Come." Asian Americans for Progress Web site, March 1. Accessed December 1, 2010. http://www.apaforprogress.org/takakis-op-ed-on-obama.

Tani, Carlyn. 2007. "A Kid Called Barry." Punahou School, Spring. Accessed December 1, 2010. http://www.punahou.edu/page.cfm?p=1715.

Tauber, Mike, and Pamela Singh. 2009. *Blended Nation: Portraits and Interviews of Mixed-Race America*. New York: Channel Photographics.

Tedlock, Barbara. 1987. *Dreaming: Anthropological and Psychological Interpretations*. New York: Cambridge University Press.

Tharoor, Shashi. 2008. "Barack Obama and the American Global Image." FORATV, July 21. Accessed December 3, 2010. http://www.omniveda.com/bing/barack-obama-in-india-barack-obama-and-the-american-global-image-shashi-tharoor.html.

Todd, Chuck. 2008. *How Barack Obama Won*. New York: Alfred Knopf.

Traub, James. 2007. "Is (His) Biography (Our) Destiny?" *New York Times*, November 4. Accessed December 3, 2010. http://www.nytimes.com/2007/11/04/magazine/04obama-t.html.

Tucker, N. 2008. "Barack Obama, Camelot's New Knight." *Washington Post*, January 29. Accessed December 15, 2010. http://www.washingtonpost.com/wp-dyn/content/article/2008/01/28/AR2008012802730.html.

Turner, Frank. 2006. *From Counterculture to Cyberculture*. Chicago: University of Chicago Press.

U.S. Census Bureau. 2008. "U.S. Minorities Will Be the Majority by 2042, Census Bureau Says." America.gov Web site. Accessed May 15, 2011. http://www.america.gov/st/diversity-english/2008/August/2008081 5140005xlrennef0.1078106.html#ixzz1MdJfMwdT.

U.S. Census Bureau. 2010a. "Grandparents Day 2010: Sept. 12." July 12. Accessed on December 1, 2010. http://www.census.gov/newsroom/releases/ archives/facts_for_features_special_editions/cb10-ff16.html.

U.S. Census Bureau. 2010b. "Hawai'i County, Hawai'i—ACS Demographic and Housing Estimates: 2006–2008." Accessed December 1, 2010. http://www.factfinder.census.gov/servlet/ADPTable?-geo_id=05000 US15001&-qr_name=ACS_2008_3YR_G00_DP3YR5&-ds_ name=ACS_2008_3YR_G00_.

Usborne, David. 2008. "Obama's Beloved Grandmother Dies." *The Independent*, November 4. Accessed November 30, 2010. http://www .independent.co.uk/news/world/americas/obamas-beloved-grandmother -dies-989946.html.

Valsiner, Jaan. 2006. "Father in the White House: American Children and the Remaking of Political Order." In *The Development of Political Attitude in Children*, edited by Robert D. Hess, Judith V. Torney, and Judith Torney-Purta, xv–xxii. Piscataway, NJ: Transactions Publishers.

Venter, Craig. 2008. *My Life Decoded*. New York: Penguin Books.

Vittachi, Nury. 2009. "Obama Is the Key Example of Globalization." *Jakarta Post*, January 25. Accessed May 24, 2011. http://www.thejakartapost .com/news/2009/01/25/obama-key-example-globalization.html.

WABC Radio. 2009. "Warner Wolf on Imus in the Morning Discussing 9/11/01." September 11. Accessed November 28, 2010. http://www .wabcradio.com/Article.asp?id=1495424&spid=22807.

Wade, Nicholas. 2007. "Cheney and Obama: It's Not Genetic." *New York Times*, October 21. Accessed November 30, 2010. http://www .nytimes.com/2007/10/21/weekinreview/21basic.html.

Ward, David. 2006. "The Green Man: Walt Whitman and the Civil War." *PN Review*. Accessed May 25, 2011. http://www.pnreview .co.uk/cgi-bin/scribe?item_id=2717.

Watkins, Boyce. 2008. "Barack Obama: Kunta Kinte of 2008?" *USLaw*, April 30. Accessed December 2, 2010. http://www.uslaw.com/library/ Academic/Barack_Obama_Kunta_Kinte_2008.php?item=128285.

Watkins, Paul. 1995. "A Promise of Redemption." *New York Times*, August 6. Accessed December 3, 2010. http://www.nytimes.com/1995/08/06/books/review/06obama-dreams.html.

Watson, Paul. 2007. "Islam an Unknown Factor in Obama Bid." *Baltimore Sun*, March 16. Accessed December 15, 2010. http://articles.baltimoresun.com/2007-03-16/news/0703160141_1_barack-obama-mosque.

Wead, Douglas. 2005. *The Raising of a President*. New York: Atria Books.

Weber, Max, and S. N. Eisenstadt. 1968. *On Charisma and Institution Building*. Chicago: University of Chicago Press.

White, Jack. 2008. "Digging Kunta Kinte: Does it Matter if Alex Haley's Character Really Existed?" *The Root*, February 28. Accessed December 2, 2010. http://www.theroot.com/views/digging-kunta-kinte.

Whitman, Walt. 1883. *Leaves of Grass*. Philadelphia: David McKay.

Will, George. 2009. "Obama: The First 'Pacific President'?" *Newsweek*, November 20. Accessed November 26, 2010. http://www.newsweek.com/2009/11/20/the-first-pacific-president.html.

Winograd, Morley, and Michael Hais. 2008. *Millennial Makeover: MySpace, YouTube and the Future of American Politics*. Newark, NJ: Rutgers University Press.

Wolf, Naomi. 2009. "Learning from America." *The Washington Examiner*, January 2. Accessed December 3, 2010. http://washingtonexaminer.com/opinion/learning-america?quicktabs_1=0.

Wolffe, Richard. 2008. "When Barry Became Barack." *Newsweek*, March 22. Accessed December 2, 2010. http://www.newsweek.com/2008/03/22/when-barry-became-barack.html.

Wolffe, Richard. 2009. *Renegade: The Making of a President*. New York: Random House.

Wolfowitz, Paul. 2009. "Indonesia Is a Model Muslim Democracy." *Wall Street Journal*, Eastern edition, July 17, A13.

Womack, Ytasha. 2010. "Post-Black: How a New Generation Is Redefining African American Identity." *Huffington Post*, March 18. Accessed December 3, 2010. http://www.huffingtonpost.com/ytasha-l-womack/post-black-how-a-new-gene_b_504590.html.

Yoffe, Emily. 2008. "The Supervisor, the Champion and the Promoter." *Slate*, February 20. Accessed December 3, 2010. http://www.slate.com/id/2184696/pagenum/2.

Yue, Lorene. 2007. "Chicago Designers Create Obama's Logo." *Chicago Business*, February 22. Accessed December 15, 2010. http://

www.chicagobusiness.com/article/20070222/NEWS/200023974/
chicago-designers-create-obamas-logo.

Yunus, Muhammad. 2007. *Creating a World Without Poverty*. New York: Public Affairs.

Zakaria, Fareed. 2008. *The Post-American World*. New York: W. W. Norton.

Zakaria, Fareed. 2009. "Huntington, Prescient and Principled." *Washington Post*, January 4. Accessed November 26, 2010. http://newsweek .washingtonpost.com/postglobal/fareed_zakaria/2009/01/huntington _prescient_and_princ.html.

Zogby, James. 2010. *Arab Voices: What They Are Saying to Us and Why It Matters*. New York: Palgrave Macmillan.

Zogby, John. 2008. *The Way We'll Be: The Zogby Report on the Transformation of the American Dream*. New York: Random House.

Index

About the Author

Dinesh Sharma, PhD, is a cultural psychologist and marketing consultant with a doctorate from Harvard University. He has consulted for Fortune 500 clients for almost ten years across different industries, including healthcare, pharmaceuticals, biotech, technology, media, publishing, and consumer products. He is currently a senior fellow at the Institute for International and Cross-Cultural Research at St. Francis College, New York. He is the author/editor of three books and many peer-reviewed articles. Sharma is a regular contributor to *Asia Times Online,* where he writes about globalization, politics, terrorism, AfPak region, and India-US relations. His writings have appeared in a range of other newspapers and journals, including the *Wall Street Journal Online, Far Eastern Economic Review, Middle East Times, Health Affairs, Biotech Law Review, Genomics, Society and Policy, International Psychology Bulletin* and other scientific periodicals. He lives in the Princeton, New Jersey area with his wife and two children.